ALSO BY ED SLOTT

The Retirement Savings Time Bomb . . . and How to Defuse It

Parlay Your IRA into a Family Fortune

YOUR COMPLETE RETIREMENT PLANNING ROAD MAP

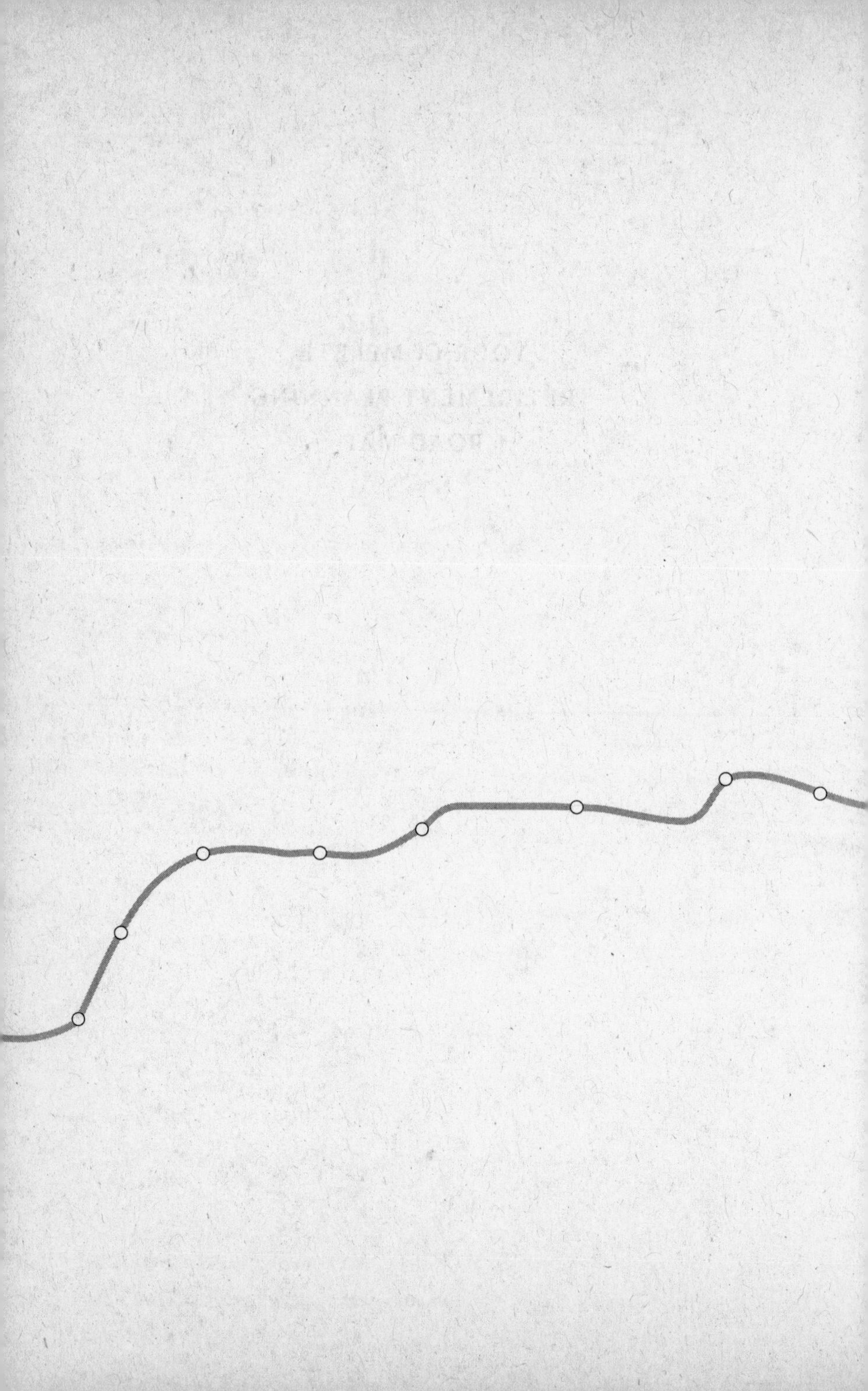

YOUR COMPLETE RETIREMENT PLANNING ROAD MAP

A Comprehensive Action Plan for Securing IRAs, 401(k)s, and Other Retirement Plans for Yourself and Your Family

ED SLOTT

BALLANTINE BOOKS NEW YORK

Your Complete Retirement Planning Road Map is a commonsense guide to personal finance. In practical advice books, as in life, there are no guarantees, and readers are cautioned to rely on their own judgment about their individual circumstances and to act accordingly. Readers are also reminded that this book is intended for informational purposes only and is not meant to take the place of professional advice. The laws in this area are complex and constantly changing. You should consult with an experienced professional to apply the relevant laws in your state to your unique situation.

2008 Ballantine Books Trade Paperback Edition

Published in the United States by Ballantine Books,
an imprint of The Random House Publishing Group,
a division of Random House, Inc., New York.

BALLANTINE and colophon are registered trademarks of Random House, Inc.

Originally published in hardcover in the United States by
Ballantine Books, an imprint of The Random House Publishing Group,
a division of Random House, Inc., in 2007.

LIBRARY OF CONGRESS CATALOGING-IN-PUBLICATION DATA

Slott, Ed.
Your complete retirement planning road map : a comprehensive action plan for securing IRAs, 401(k)s, and other retirement plans for yourself and your family / [Ed Slott].
p. cm.
Includes index.
ISBN: 978-0-345-49456-6
1. Retirement income—United States—Planning. 2. Finance, Personal. I. Title.
HG179.S534 2007
332.024'014—dc22 2006051037

Printed in the United States of America

www.ballantinebooks.com

6 8 9 7 5

Book design by Mary A. Wirth

To my wife, Linda, and our children,
Ilana, Rachel, and Jennifer

Author's Note

Legislatively speaking, 2006 turned out to be a banner year for retirement savers. As I write these words, three new tax laws have been enacted by Congress and signed into law by the president. They offer many new, more flexible opportunities for you to sock more of your money away for your retirement and to keep it growing tax deferred for you and your family. I have filtered this latest retirement-planning information throughout this book in the appropriate sections and checklists. And I am alerting you to that important fact here so you will know, as you go through this book creating your road map, that you are working with the most timely, up-to-the-minute data available.

—ED SLOTT

Contents

Introduction

THE LONG, HAPPY LIFE OF YOUR RETIREMENT SAVINGS

"Lou was a daredevil. His last words were, 'Watch this!' "

—Obituary featured in *USA Today* (June 22, 2006)

Planning for retirement is no place to be a daredevil, and yet most people are just that, even though they may not think of themselves as one. But anyone who spends a lifetime building up a retirement nest egg and does not take the time to check up on it once in a while to make sure all systems are go is indeed flying without a net and tempting fate.

Imagine getting in your car day after day without ever giving a thought to whether it's got oil in the crankcase or needs a tune-up, without ever having a mechanic take a look under the hood or kick the tires—just to trust that it will always start, always get you where you want to go. You wouldn't think of treating your car that way, and yet if a car breaks down, it can be fixed or replaced. You can call AAA and get it towed, or just leave it by the side of the road and walk away—as I once did years ago when my 1966 Mustang suddenly died on me at the Southern State Parkway tollbooth on Long Island. My dad had to come and pick me up, shaking his head at me in disbelief as my brother gave me his "what a moron" laugh. But, hey, what was the big deal? It was just a car.

The same cannot be said of your life savings. If that breaks down due to lack of proper care and maintenance, it would take another lifetime to replace—and nobody gets a second chance!

So, this book is for all you daredevils out there who seldom if ever look under the hood of your retirement savings, wherever your account (or accounts) may be housed: a 401(k) plan; a 403(b) plan (also known as a Tax Sheltered Annuity Plan) for employees of schools, hospitals, and tax-exempt organizations; a 457 plan (for governmental employees) or any other company-sponsored retirement plan; an Individual Retirement Account (IRA); a Roth IRA; or a self-employed retirement plan like a Keogh, SEP IRA (Simplified Employee Pension) or SIMPLE IRA (Savings Incentive Match Plan for Employees).

What Can Possibly Go Wrong?

Now that I am older and wiser, I do bring my car in for servicing, where the service department manager tells me that he gives it a proper checkup by putting it through a rigorous fifty-eight-point diagnostic using the latest computer technology. If pressed, I probably couldn't come up with more than five things to look at under the hood of my car that might conceivably break down—and he listed fifty-eight!

It suddenly hit me that the same is true for retirement accounts, where many things can go *kaput* without careful monitoring. Most people just open an account, make contributions, maybe make some investment choices, and that's about it until they retire and start collecting. But by then it's too late to fix what may have gone wrong along the way—and believe me, bad, bad things can happen. For example, you could go broke and end up giving most of your retirement funds back to the government. Of course, going broke is not the end of the world. Lots of people go broke. That's why it's important to know how the prospect of having to declare bankruptcy will affect your retirement savings, tax-wise and otherwise. Remember, unless you're in a Roth IRA, where you pay the tax on your contributions up front, your retirement account has yet to be taxed, so not all of the money you have saved all these years is really yours.

A healthy retirement account is always a function of a long period of disciplined saving and investing (unless you inherited it, which is an even better plan and a great shortcut!). You would hate to think that after twenty, thirty, or even forty years or more of diligent saving that you slipped up in the end by passing most of it on to Uncle Sam rather than your family. And that's just one of the things that can go wrong!

So, I decided that a process for giving retirement accounts a regular, thorough look under the hood and kick of the tires, a checkup with the same rigorous precision of an automotive diagnostic, was needed. A system that would ensure no moving parts were overlooked—and thus keep retirement account owners, their beneficiaries and families from being financial daredevils.

Your Complete Retirement Planning Road Map is that system. There are many, many things relating to retirement accounts that demand regular attention and monitoring in order to make sure nothing goes off track. How many can you come up with—without looking at the Contents page, that is? This book looks at more than 250 of them—and,

Ask Ed . . .

Q: Does your system also tell me how to invest for retirement?

A: No, this book is not about which stocks or funds to buy. I assume you are already doing that on your own or with professional help, and that you have accumulated some level of retirement savings, large or small, that you will want to protect and preserve, which is where my system steps in. I will say this, however: The best strategy for building retirement savings, one that works all the time, and no one can deny this, is to contribute the maximum you can each year to your retirement account, and to start as early as possible by making saving for retirement a priority from your first day on the job. In other words, pay yourself first, as the saying goes.

most important, shows you how to keep proper tabs on those potential problem areas and tune things up BEFORE they become an issue!

Customized Care for Your Retirement Savings

So, this book is for anyone who is serious about protecting, preserving, and passing the balance (if any) in their retirement account to their heirs *no matter where they are in the planning process.*

For example, you might just be starting to save for retirement in a 401(k) plan at work—in which case, this system of looking under the hood is the perfect way to develop good habits early, from the time you put your first dollar into that 401(k). On the other hand, perhaps you have just retired and moved your retirement savings to an IRA. Or, you might be anywhere in between those two points. Wherever you are in the process of saving for your retirement years, you'll be able to use this system to make sure your money is well protected against *the most common and costly retirement planning mistakes,* and that you won't miss out on any of the many tax breaks you can capitalize on to increase your savings for yourself and your loved ones.

For the first time, you will be assured that you will have done all you can to make the most of your retirement earnings or inherited account, using every possible tax benefit available to leverage exponentially that nest egg into a lifetime of financial peace of mind.

You will then be able to share this information with your family, and boastfully say, "Watch this," with the confidence of knowing that you're not going to go *splat.*

How to Use This Book

My care solution for looking under the hood of your retirement savings consists of five conveniently organized, easy-to-use sections, each made up of a series of checklists relevant to the issues covered in that section. Together, these five sections will address all of the most common retirement savings issues, including many special issues, that most of you will face at some point either as a retirement account owner, account beneficiary, or both. I have purposely excluded, however, some of the more obscure tax issues because this book is intended to be a user-friendly guide for most Americans to keeping their retirement accounts healthy, not an overwhelming and intimidating exploration of the tax code. If you believe you have a complex tax situation it is always a good idea to have a conversation with an experienced tax professional, and I would urge you to do so. The sections are as follows:

- **SECTION I: My Account Inventory**
  As I noted earlier, it is not uncommon these days for people to own and pass on multiple retirement accounts of different types—401(k), 403(b), IRA, and so on—to multiple beneficiaries. So, proper care of a retirement account or accounts begins here with knowing all there is to know about every account you've got and where that information is. Therefore, this section *applies to every one of you using this book.* It shows you how to survey and keep track of each originally owned account or inherited account now owned by you, then summarize that information for fast, easy reference as you move to the subsequent checklists pertinent to you.

- **SECTION II: The Account Owner's Care Solution**
  This section addresses the key ownership issues specifically affecting all holders of an IRA, 401(k) or any other type of retirement account. Failure to address even one of these ownership issues all but guarantees that your account(s) will lose money at some point, either when you start taking distributions or when the money passes to your beneficiaries. Completing this section will give you what you need to avoid these ownership pitfalls. *Keep your beneficiaries in the loop as you plan your decisions in this section. Remember, your beneficiaries will be stuck with those decisions. Inviting their input now will help to ensure a smooth transition down the road and a nest egg that can keep growing instead of losing substantial amounts to taxes.*

- **SECTION III: The Account Beneficiary's Care Solution**
  This section addresses the key issues affecting all inheritors of a retirement account or accounts. It is for any type of beneficiary—spouse,

child, grandchild, other family member, friend, favorite charity, or a family trust. Here you or the inheriting entity will be given the tools to map out what you need to be attending to—and when—in order to take advantage of every available tax opportunity if the person you are inheriting from has not kept you in the loop. *This section will also tip you off to key opportunities and pitfalls to avoid that you should make the account owner aware of (if not too late) in his or her planning because they will affect you. Once you have inherited and transferred title and ownership to inherited account(s), thereafter* ***you*** *are the account owner and will use Section II in planning opportunities for your own beneficiaries.*

- **SECTION IV: The Special Issues Care Solution**
  This section shows how to address those unique issues that do not apply across the board to every retirement account owner or beneficiary, *but may apply to one and/or the other of you (each checklist will tell you who) at some time.* Here, you will see how to handle these stray issues, such as: accessing retirement funds early without incurring a tax penalty; taking advantage of company stock tax breaks; proper Roth IRA planning; making decisions in the event you or your beneficiary becomes incapacitated. This section is the most complete coverage of these special issues ever compiled for retirement account owners and beneficiaries. If you have a special issue that is *not* covered here, this means yours is a really, *really* special situation that you should address with a professional financial advisor right away.

- **SECTION V: The Follow-Up Care Solution**
  Whether you are the account owner or beneficiary of an inherited account, this section serves as your safety net, providing you with all the reminders each of you will need to check up and follow through on during the year (and by year-end) to keep your respective road maps current and your planning on track. This final section also shows how to make sure either *as an owner or a beneficiary of the account*(s) that your respective financial advisor or fund manager attends to every detail you have covered so that nothing goes

awry on the management end in the implementation and maintenance phase of your planning. The checklists here will give you the peace of mind of knowing that your financial advisor has the proper expertise, as well as everything he or she needs from you, to do what you want done correctly—and if not, what to look for in finding one who does.

Structured for Practical Use

I have put this book together in a way that allows you to go straight to the section covering the issues specific to you as the original owner or the beneficiary of one or more retirement accounts, and start working on those issues; then move to the section addressing the *special issues* you may face as either an account owner or a beneficiary.

Furthermore, if, for example, you are the beneficiary of an account, whatever you may need to know as an owner-to-be about issues facing original owners will be cross-referenced to that section, providing you with an extra check so that no important detail gets overlooked or neglected in customizing your retirement plan care solution.

This is the same diagnostic system I use with my own clients and with the financial advisors I train. So, going through it will be like having me sitting beside you, whispering in your ear, guiding you every step of the way.

An Ongoing Process

Once you have addressed the areas in this book relevant to you, be sure to revisit them as events occur in your life—a birth, a death, a marriage, a divorce, ill health, or new financial responsibilities. This means going beyond your year-end checkup. Anytime there is a change in any of the factors that go into your planning, you can use and reuse this book to make sure your overall plan is always up-to-date and in line with those changes—that your plan will always reflect your *current* situation, including any special circumstances.

How to Use the Checklists

Each checklist is divided into two columns. On the left are all the items you will need to address on the particular issue or subject at hand, and on the right is ample space for including your response to each item. Depending upon the item, your response may just be a simple check mark to indicate that you have attended to the item; writing in a brief "Yes" or "No" to a specific question about the item; or providing more detailed remarks should more information or explanation on your part be required. Unless you can do the *New York Times* crossword in pen without making a mistake (but even then), I urge you to use a pencil since you may want or need to make changes later on.

In fact, the more changes you go through in your life, the more valuable this book becomes as a diagnostic. A 30-year-old person, for example, will experience many more changes in his or her lifetime than a 65-year-old person—i.e., marriage, having kids, financing the purchase of a first home, additional schooling for themselves or college for their kids. Each of these changes can affect how you should set up your retirement account. My system gives you the flexibility to monitor this and make the adjustments necessary to respond to each new life challenge and issue you face.

As a result, you can use this book as a resource for the life of your retirement accounts. That is why I say you should start addressing the issue of retirement distribution planning NOW, and make a lifelong commitment to revisit it.

In the end, the reason you are doing this is for complete financial security, not only for you but also for everyone you care about and have saved for as well. Saving means sacrifice. Somewhere, in order to get something, you had to give something up. *Your Complete Retirement Planning Road Map* ensures that these sacrifices will not have been in vain.

Section I

MY ACCOUNT INVENTORY

for everybody

What It Does

We start here because this section applies to ALL of you who are the proud owner (original holder or inheritor-owner) of an IRA or any other type of retirement account, or multiple accounts (as many people are nowadays). You will use this section to inventory each of your accounts in detail—because you will need to know this information in order to facilitate use of the checklists in the sections of the book that follow.

Your objective here is to gather as much information as possible about your accounts so that nothing escapes your attention. For example, many people who have several retirement accounts sometimes forget about one (don't laugh; it happens!). *This information will be used by your financial advisor, your family lawyer and accountant, your spouse and your kids (if they are your beneficiaries) to determine and carry out your wishes for each account after you are gone.* If your spouse or domestic partner has an IRA and/or other retirement account, he or she will want to complete this part for each of their originally owned and/or inherited accounts as well.

- **General Information—Original Owner Accounts.** This checklist surveys each retirement account you own or have rolled over to your own name from a spouse (it does not include accounts you have inherited from someone else including your spouse if you remain a beneficiary on the account): 401(k), 403(b), Roth IRA, traditional IRA, SEP IRA, and SIMPLE IRA just to name a few of the most common. The rules surrounding these accounts can be vastly different (and complicated); and if you are not in full command of the law, you or your heirs could encounter penalties when the time comes to withdraw funds from them.

- **General Information—Inherited Accounts.** This checklist surveys each account you now own because you inherited it from someone upon his or her death. This is an important distinction because even though the beneficiary of a retirement account does, in effect, become the owner of that account once he or she inherits it, the documentation requirements, planning opportunities, and especially the tax rules can be and often are stricter for inheritors of an account than for the original owners. This checklist will enable you to stay out of trouble.

- **Summary Information—All Accounts.** This checklist summarizes the information you have collected on each of your originally held or inherited accounts for quick referral as you move through the other sections of this book. This summary of basic data from your general information checklists is what you will probably refer to most often while monitoring your retirement savings (and seeing how much it grows!). It gives you a total picture of all your retirement money without having to go back and dig into the details of each account. This summary also will be extremely valuable to your financial advisor (Section V) who will surely have many questions about your

Ask Ed . . .

Q: How long will it take?

A: Everyone's portfolio is different. The more accounts you have, the more spadework you will have to do by phone and in person to pull together information on each one. But once this is done, the process of continuously updating your account information should take you no time at all—and you will always have that sense of being well organized and in total control.

account(s), and you can now provide answers quickly in a well-organized, easy-to-read, easy-to-access form.

In order to avoid any confusion, here are explanations of some of the key items you will be covering in this and subsequent sections:

- **Type of Account:** The kind of retirement plan that the funds are in—e.g., IRA, Roth IRA, 401(k).
- **Account ____ of ____:** If you are the original owner or inheritor-owner of several accounts, the one you are describing—e.g., Account 1 of 3.
- **Institution or Company:** The name of the custodian (such as a bank or brokerage firm) or the employer holding the account.
- **Account #:** The identifying number the custodian has assigned to the account.
- **Balance:** The total amount in the account as of your last statement.
- **Basis:** The amount of after-tax funds in the retirement account according to your company plan statement or the Form 8606 filed with your tax return.
- **Primary Beneficiary:** The name of the *key* beneficiary—e.g., a spouse—listed on your beneficiary form for this account (see Section II).
- **Contingent Beneficiary:** The name(s) of your second, third, fourth or however many secondary beneficiaries as listed on your beneficiary form (see Section II) for this account.
- **Date:** When you filled out the information sheet.

What's In It for Me?

Your objective in gathering this information is to find out what you have in retirement holdings, where you have it, and what you need to do to make sure you address all the key planning and distribution issues central to the growth and security of each account. I suggest making photocopies of these and, perhaps, other checklist pages throughout the book should you need more copies. As noted in the introduction, I strongly recommend you fill these pages out in pencil so that you can make changes later on since the process of updating information on your IRA(s) and other accounts is an ongoing one. You might even want to have several copies of the book on hand for that purpose.

What If I Don't?

Overlooking an account in your arsenal of assets could result in that account's not having a named beneficiary, causing it to go through probate—and, perhaps, winding up in the hands of the one person on the planet you *didn't* want to inherit it, ultimately creating a family feud where only the lawyers end up making any money.

This inventory serves as a safety net in the care and feeding of your retirement nest egg. It may even eliminate the possibility of any posthumous family arguments, costly attorney fees, and probate costs occurring as the result of confusion over your holdings and intentions.

Instructions

Fill out a general information sheet for each account you own or have inherited so that you don't forget one later (it happens!). Then summarize the general information on all your accounts in the appropriate spaces of the summary information sheet. If you have multiple owned and/or inherited accounts, photocopy additional inventory sheets and keep them in this section of the book after filling them out. [Your spouse or domestic partner can photocopy the sheets he or she will need too—or, better yet, can buy a copy of their own!]

Use the space marked "Comments" to make any notes to yourself or to record any additional information you fear might fall through the cracks—for example, forgetting to name a contingent beneficiary in the event, however unlikely it may seem to you, that your primary beneficiary dies before you do. If it's all down in black and white for fast, easy reference, there are no cracks or fissures in your care solution. [After each information sheet, I have included an example—for guidance purposes only—of how each sheet may look once you have filled it out.]

Ask Ed . . .

Q: What should I do with this information once I have pulled it together?

A: Put it in a safe place that you can locate easily—and that any family member who will need access to it will be able to locate easily, as well. Better yet, make copies and give them to family members or advisors for referral. Do not store it in a safety-deposit box since the box will be hard to access after your death.

GENERAL INFORMATION

EACH OWNED ACCOUNT

Survey each account for which you are the owner not an inheritor.

ACCOUNT OWNER: ______________________________

TYPE OF ACCOUNT: ______________________________
IRA, Roth, SEP, 401(k), 403(b), Keogh, etc.

ACCOUNT _____ **OF** _____ **ACCOUNTS**

INSTITUTION OR COMPANY ______________________________

ACCOUNT # ______________________________

BALANCE $ ____________________ **AS OF** ___/___/___

AMOUNT OF BASIS (AFTER-TAX FUNDS) IN ACCOUNT $ ____________________

PRIMARY BENEFICIARY % should = 100		%
		%
		%
		%
CONTINGENT BENEFICIARY % should = 100		%
		%
		%
		%
		%

COMMENTS: ______________________________

____

____

____

____

DATE ____________________

EXAMPLE

GENERAL INFORMATION

EACH OWNED ACCOUNT

Survey each account for which you are the owner not an inheritor.

ACCOUNT OWNER: John Smith

TYPE OF ACCOUNT: IRA
IRA, Roth, SEP, 401(k), 403(b), Keogh, etc.

ACCOUNT 1 OF 5 ACCOUNTS

INSTITUTION OR COMPANY The Brokerage Firm

ACCOUNT # 1234567

BALANCE $ 552,687 AS OF 12 / 31 / 05

AMOUNT OF BASIS (AFTER-TAX FUNDS) IN ACCOUNT $ 10,000

PRIMARY BENEFICIARY % should = 100	Mary Smith	100 %
		%
		%
		%
CONTINGENT BENEFICIARY % should = 100	Ann	25 %
	Bill	25 %
	Carl	25 %
	Donna	25 %

COMMENTS: Mary is my spouse
After-tax funds come from IRA nondeductible
contributions made in 1990–1994

DATE 01/15/2006

GENERAL INFORMATION

EACH INHERITED ACCOUNT

Survey each account you have inherited.

ACCOUNT BENEFICIARY: ____________________

ORIGINAL ACCOUNT OWNER: ____________________

TYPE OF ACCOUNT: ____________________
IRA, Roth, SEP, 401(k), 403(b), Keogh, etc.

ACCOUNT _____ **OF** _____ **ACCOUNTS**

INSTITUTION OR COMPANY ____________________

ACCOUNT # ____________________

BALANCE $ ____________________ **AS OF** ____/____/____

AMOUNT OF BASIS (AFTER-TAX FUNDS) IN ACCOUNT $ ____________________

BENEFICIARY IS: PRIMARY ____________ **OR SUCCESSOR** ____________

YEAR OF ACCOUNT OWNER'S DEATH ______ **PRIMARY BENEFICIARY'S DATE OF BIRTH** ______

YEAR OF FIRST DISTRIBUTION TO PRIMARY BENEFICIARY ____________________

PRIMARY BENEFICIARY'S LIFE EXPECTANCY FACTOR BASED ON AGE IN YEAR AFTER OWNER'S DEATH ____________________

SUCCESSOR BENEFICIARY % should = 100		%
		%
		%
		%
		%
		%

COMMENTS: ____________________

____

____

DATE ____________________

EXAMPLE 1

GENERAL INFORMATION

EACH INHERITED ACCOUNT

Survey each account you have inherited.

ACCOUNT BENEFICIARY: *John Smith*

ORIGINAL ACCOUNT OWNER: *Ben Jones*

TYPE OF ACCOUNT: *401 (k)*
IRA, Roth, SEP, 401(k), 403(b), Keogh, etc.

ACCOUNT *4* OF *5* ACCOUNTS

INSTITUTION OR COMPANY *ABC Widget Co.*

ACCOUNT # *123456*

BALANCE $ *96,857* AS OF *12 / 31 / 05*

AMOUNT OF BASIS (AFTER-TAX FUNDS) IN ACCOUNT $ *12, 386*

BENEFICIARY IS: PRIMARY *X* OR SUCCESSOR ______

YEAR OF ACCOUNT OWNER'S DEATH *2005*

PRIMARY BENEFICIARY'S DATE OF BIRTH *01/02/1955*

YEAR OF FIRST DISTRIBUTION TO PRIMARY BENEFICIARY *2006*

PRIMARY BENEFICIARY'S LIFE EXPECTANCY FACTOR BASED ON AGE IN YEAR AFTER OWNER'S DEATH *33.3*

SUCCESSOR BENEFICIARY % should = 100		
		%
		%
		%
		%
		%
		%

COMMENTS: *Even though the IRS Single Life Table allows a 33.3 year payout, the company says I have to take the full amount out by 12/31/06 and that I will have to pay income tax on everything but the $12,386 after-tax amount. See if company will let me wait until 2007 and transfer balance to inherited IRA.*

DATE *11/15/2006*

EXAMPLE 2

GENERAL INFORMATION

EACH INHERITED ACCOUNT

Survey each account you have inherited.

ACCOUNT BENEFICIARY: John Smith

ORIGINAL ACCOUNT OWNER: Sue Brown (Mother-in-law)

TYPE OF ACCOUNT: IRA
IRA, Roth, SEP, 401(k), 403(b), Keogh, etc.

ACCOUNT 5 OF 5 ACCOUNTS

INSTITUTION OR COMPANY The Credit Union

ACCOUNT # 11556699

BALANCE $ 123,682 AS OF 12 / 31 / 05

AMOUNT OF BASIS (AFTER-TAX FUNDS) IN ACCOUNT $ 0

BENEFICIARY IS: PRIMARY ______ OR SUCCESSOR X

YEAR OF ACCOUNT OWNER'S DEATH 2004 PRIMARY BENEFICIARY'S DATE OF BIRTH 1952

YEAR OF FIRST DISTRIBUTION TO PRIMARY BENEFICIARY 2005

PRIMARY BENEFICIARY'S LIFE EXPECTANCY FACTOR BASED ON AGE IN YEAR AFTER OWNER'S DEATH 31.4

SUCCESSOR BENEFICIARY % should = 100		
	Jennifer	33.3 %
	Victoria	33.3 %
	Kaitlyn	33.3 %
		%
		%
		%

COMMENTS: Account was my mother-in-law's and inherited by my wife. I inherited from my wife at her death in 2006.

DATE 11/15/2006

SUMMARY INFORMATION

ALL ACCOUNTS FOR

MY NAME: ______________________ **DATE:** ____________

SPECIAL INSTRUCTIONS: Summarize the basic data you have collected on each owned or inherited account. Note in the space marked "Comments" any after-tax funds held in accounts listed in your own or inherited general information sheets.

#	INSTITUTION	BALANCE	AS OF	TYPE	OWNER

COMMENTS: ______________________

SUMMARY INFORMATION

ALL ACCOUNTS FOR

MY NAME: *John Smith* **DATE:** *1/15/2006*

SPECIAL INSTRUCTIONS: Summarize the basic data you have collected on each owned or inherited account. Note in the space marked "Comments" any after-tax funds held in accounts listed in your own or inherited general information sheets.

#	INSTITUTION	BALANCE	AS OF	TYPE	OWNER
1	*The Brokerage Firm*	*552,687*	*12/31/05*	*IRA*	*John*
2	*The Bank*	*186,981*	*12/31/05*	*Roth*	*John*
3	*The Brokerage Firm*	*72,159*	*12/31/05*	*IRA*	*W. Jones*
4	*The ABC Widget Co*	*96,857*	*12/31/05*	*401 (k)*	*B. Jones*
5	*The Credit Union*	*123,682*	*12/31/05*	*IRA*	*S. Brown*

COMMENTS: *$10,000 basis in IRA #1*

$12,386 basis in 401 (k) & I have to take a full withdrawal before year-end

Section II

THE ACCOUNT OWNER'S CARE SOLUTION

This section addresses planning items that apply if you are the *original owner* (not an inheritor) of any type of retirement account. Most of you reading this book will fall into this category.

A Word to the Wise

Keep your beneficiaries in the loop as you plan your decisions in this section. Remember, your beneficiaries will be stuck with those decisions. Inviting their input now will help to ensure a smooth transition down the road and a nest egg that can keep growing by not being substantially lost to taxes early on.

As the original owner, you will want to make sure you cover such critical items as updating your beneficiary forms and custodial documents, integrating your retirement account(s) into your estate plan, and knowing how to make the right choices when it comes to decisions involving movement of funds from your company plan into an IRA, and so on.

You'll also want to make sure your beneficiaries can stretch distributions from the IRAs they inherit from you, an option that might require looking at other options such as naming a trust as your IRA beneficiary for postdeath control. All of this and more are covered in the six parts of **"The Account Owner's Care Solution."**

At the end of each part, you will have space to make notes of any important items you may have questions on, want to discuss with family members, your attorney, or financial advisor—or simply items that you may want to revisit later on in the event you want to alter your decision.

Completing this section will also help you to create important "To Do" lists for following up on items you have not yet addressed or have found to be improperly addressed. This will give you an action plan that puts you, the original owner of the account(s), well on your way to completing a thorough retirement plan checkup.

Account Owner Alert!

A HERO Is Not Just a Sandwich. Our government found another way to honor our service men and women who are serving in combat zones when it enacted the Heroes Earned Retirement Opportunities Act (HERO) in May 2006. The act provides a rare opportunity for service personnel to make IRA or Roth IRA contributions (even for their spouses) for tax years that are closed. The HERO Act allows excluded combat zone pay to be included in earned income, for the purpose of making an IRA contribution, for compensation earned from January 1, 2004 through May 28, 2006. You have a three-year period in which to make your contribution. (Example: A 2004 contribution would have to be made by 2007.) The period ends on May 28, 2009. If you don't have the funds, all is not lost. Parents and grandparents and any other interested parties can gift the necessary funds to the serviceperson for the IRA contribution. The maximum contribution for 2004 was $3,000 (plus $500 if you were 50 or older), the contribution limit for 2005 was $4,000 (plus $500 if you were 50 or older), and the contribution limit for 2006 was $4,000 (plus $1,000 if you were 50 or older).

Part 1

MY BENEFICIARY FORM CHECKLIST

What It Does

Your retirement account beneficiary form is the single most important document in your estate plan because it *guarantees* that the person you name as beneficiary of what may be the single largest asset you own—your retirement savings—will indeed get that asset when you are gone.

Your beneficiary form has a huge impact on the amount and timing of required distributions that your beneficiaries must take and in turn impacts the ultimate value of the account. It also is a key distribution-planning document because the person you name as your beneficiary can affect the required minimum distributions you must take during your lifetime, which, in turn, can impact the potential growth of your savings. So, who to name is one of many important questions that will emerge for you to answer as you complete this form. And completing that task will put you on the path to being able to respond knowledgably to many other planning questions that pop up as you work your way through your complete road map.

So, do I have your attention? THIS FORM IS CRUCIAL! And filling it out—as well as updating it periodically to reflect any changing circumstances in your life, such as a birth, a death, or a divorce that may affect your wishes—is the first thing you should do.

Typically, you will fill out a beneficiary form for each retirement account you open when you open it—and it will remain on file with your account custodian (bank or other financial institution holding the funds). You and your family should also have copies tucked away in a safe place just in case the original is lost. Your work here will guarantee that won't happen. So, read on.

What's In It for Me?

Actually, nothing—since you will be dead. But seriously, for your own peace of mind until that day comes, if you care at all who will wind up with your hard-earned cash after you die—your family or, heaven help you, the Taxman—and want to know that your family will be able to take advantage of every tax opportunity available to them to keep your hard-earned nest egg growing for decades, *you will want to have an up-to-date beneficiary form on file for every single retirement account you own.* A retirement account beneficiary form is the only way to make absolutely certain that your retirement funds will go to the people you intend—and with the most favorable tax benefits.

What If I Don't?

A recent story in the *New York Post* highlighted the case of Bruce and Anne Friedman from Brooklyn, New York. Anne worked several decades for the New York City school system and accumulated almost one million dollars in her retirement account. When she died, her husband Bruce received not one single penny of it even though she had wanted him to. It turned out that she had never designated him as her beneficiary on her beneficiary form. Whom did she name?

When she first took the job many years ago and opened her retirement account, she was not yet married and so she named her mother, her uncle, and her sister as primary and contingent beneficiaries. Well, her mother and her uncle had long since died, but her sister is still living, and so sis got the whole kit and caboodle. The late Anne's widower husband complained that his sis-in-law "won't give me a cent." Apparently she's either very greedy or she and her brother-in-law never got along too well. Whichever, the fact remains that she doesn't have to give him a red cent, and she has the law to back her up.

If your beneficiary form for each account cannot be found when you die, or does not reflect your current wishes at the time of your death, all bets are off. Your family or other beneficiaries will then have to begin an expensive and time-consuming game of legal hide-and-seek. First, they will have to contact the account custodian to examine the custodial document (see this Section, Part 2) to find out who becomes the beneficiary under the default provision, which kicks in only when there is no beneficiary named. Unfortunately, most default provisions stipulate that the account goes to your estate. This means it passes through your will—if you have one or, if not, through intestacy. Both turn your account or multiple accounts into a probate asset subject to fees and additional legal scrutiny; your will may even be contested by family members who suddenly pop up out of nowhere to claim some of the proceeds as their due even though you barely saw them much and wouldn't recognize them if you tripped over them in a lighted room.

If that isn't enough to give you the cold sweats at night, consider this: If your beneficiary form is not current (as the late Anne Friedman's wasn't) and, for example, lists your spouse—who is now your *ex*-spouse—as beneficiary, guess what? The beneficiary form trumps all other documents, including a will, in determining where the money goes after you die, no matter how up-to-date your will may be. So, your current spouse or children would be left out in the cold, while your ex-spouse (perhaps for the first time) could think fondly of you because he or she is rolling in your dough.

Ask Ed . . .

Q: What if I do not want to name my children as beneficiaries? Do I have to?

A: No. You can name anyone you wish as beneficiary of your retirement nest egg. If you are in a company plan, you generally must name your spouse (though a spouse can waive the benefits in favor of some other beneficiary if he or she desires). But with an IRA you can name a minor, a charity, or a trust if you wish (see Section IV "The Special Issues Care Solution"). But if you want to name a charity, which does not pay taxes on inherited assets, you should still do so through a beneficiary form and not just a will, or the bequest will pass through your estate and thus be subject to probate and to potential contesting by irate family members. Also, if the charitable bequest is not funded properly in your will—as a pecuniary bequest funded with your retirement account, for example—this would subject your estate to income tax on the amount of the retirement assets going to the charity.

Not naming a beneficiary for each account or not keeping beneficiary forms up-to-date also could disqualify your heirs from being able to take advantage of the stretch option [see this Section, Part 3] after you are gone. This option would allow them to keep growing the money you wanted to leave them for decades, building your bequest into a family fortune in tax-deferred funds.

Last but not least, failure to keep your beneficiary form(s) up-to-date can also cause some of your grandchildren to be disinherited. For example, if you name your children as co-beneficiaries of your account and one of your children dies before you, but you don't update the form to name the deceased's child or children as co-beneficiaries of that person's share, the share passes to your other children after you die, disinheriting the deceased's offspring—i.e., some of your own grandchildren.

Bottom line: A properly filled out and up-to-date beneficiary form for each of your accounts that you, your heirs, and your account custodian can always find easily at any time is the way to avoid completely all of these pitfalls.

Ask Ed . . .

Q: What if I want to name a charity as co-beneficiary with my kids? Can I do that?

A: Yes, you can leave a portion of your retirement account to your children and a portion to charity by splitting the account, naming the charity as beneficiary of one account and your children as co-beneficiaries of the other (see the Naming a Charity-As-Beneficiary Checklist, Section IV, Part 1). You can do this yourself now to make sure everything goes smoothly so that your kids and grandkids don't lose out on the "stretch" opportunity you may have set up for them in this section, Part 3, or you can leave the split for your children to handle after they inherit—when special rules will apply that may make things a bit more complicated. If you decide to do the latter, be sure to tell your kids ahead of time to go over the Multiple Beneficiaries' Checklist (Section III, Part 3).

Instructions

Fill out the beneficiary checklist in this section—or make multiple copies if needed for multiple accounts, filling out one checklist for each retirement account you own. This will guarantee the following:

1. You have not overlooked or neglected this critical part of the retirement-planning process.
2. You (your beneficiaries and account custodian for whom you will make copies) will be able locate your beneficiary form(s) at a moment's notice.

3. Your beneficiary forms for each account are fully up-to-date and express your most current wishes as to how your retirement nest egg will be distributed after you are gone.

As you complete each item, make notes of issues you may need to fix or address. If there are any items you do not understand, you should go over them with your financial advisor. For example, Item 8 asks if your overall estate plan takes your retirement assets into consideration—meaning, as part of your estate plan—do your 401(k), IRA, and/or other account beneficiaries fit in with your other estate planning document forms and your will? If they do not figure into your overall estate plan, you will want to review that plan to make sure they do.

Be sure to include primary and contingent beneficiaries. And if there are multiple beneficiaries in either category (say, three children) stipulate how much each is to inherit by writing in the word "equally" (if that is your wish) or the fraction or percentage you desire each

Ask Ed . . .

Q: What should I do if I can't fit the names of all my beneficiaries in the space provided on the beneficiary form?

A: Write the phrase "See Attached" in the space, and on a separate piece of paper list all your beneficiaries and contingent beneficiaries with the shares each one is entitled to (make sure the shares add up to 100 percent). Then staple that piece of paper to the beneficiary form, not once, but several times across the top or down the side of the pages to make sure it doesn't become detached no matter how many people ultimately handle the form. Never, ever, ever list added beneficiaries on, say, the back of the form. You can't be sure someone will actually turn the form over and see them.

child to get so that it is clear who gets what; "equally" will not automatically be assumed if the word is not on the form and there is no mention of what share each beneficiary is to receive.

Ask Ed . . .

Q: Once I have completed my beneficiary checklist, how do I keep it updated?

A: You can either do this through your financial advisor or on your own by contacting the custodian (bank, broker, fund, or insurance company where you have your retirement assets invested) and asking for a new beneficiary form to make the changes. Be sure the advisor or custodian acknowledges that the updated form voids all previous ones, and that he or she, as well as your family, has copies of the new form(s) and has destroyed the old ones. My rule of thumb in making sure account custodians stay current is to contact them a week or two after you've made the changes, and ask them to send you a memo verifying the beneficiaries listed on your form. If they send you a list of the outdated beneficiaries, raise hell. Make sure your estate-planning attorney also has copies of your updated beneficiary form(s) on hand and destroyed all previous ones, as well. You don't want copies of an outdated beneficiary form for any of your retirement accounts popping up later to create potential headaches.

MY BENEFICIARY FORM CHECKLIST

MY NAME: ______________________ DATE: __________

MY ADVISOR'S NAME: ______________________ PLAN #: __________

Follow-ups should be added to the To Do lists at the end of this checklist.

1. Where do I keep copies of my beneficiary form?

____

____

- Can I produce the copies and are they current? (Do they match what is on file with the plan? If not, I should request copies from the plan or update the plan forms.) __________
- Do my beneficiaries or the executor of my estate know where to find a copy of my beneficiary form? __________

Comments: ______________________________________

____

____

____

2. Is my beneficiary form current?

- Does it consider any recent changes in the IRS rules? (e.g., the correct life-expectancy table is being used for required minimum distributions calculations; see Appendices) __________
- Does it consider state or federal estate and tax law changes? (e.g., state estate tax decoupling that could mean estate tax due at my death) __________
- Does it consider plan limitations? (e.g., no stretch opportunity; see checklist this section, Part 3) __________
- Does it consider life events that could change my beneficiary elections? __________

adoption	______	beneficiaries to eliminate	______
births—child or grandchild	______	deaths	______
divorces	______	marriages	______
special needs beneficiaries	______	other life events	______

____

3. **Have I named a contingent beneficiary on my beneficiary form? What would be the effect of disclaiming?** (See The Disclaimer Planning Checklist in Part 3 of Section IV)

___

4. **Is my signed beneficiary form on file with the trustee/custodian/plan provider?** ___

5. **Do I have an acknowledged copy of my most recent signed beneficiary form?** (In case the plan provider "loses" its copy; may not be able to get a copy from an employer plan) ___

6. **Does my advisor have a copy of my most recent signed beneficiary form?** ___

7. **Can my trustee/custodian/plan provider locate and/or produce its copy of my most recent signed beneficiary form?** ___

Comments: ___

___

___

___

8. **When my estate plan was drafted, did it take into account my retirement assets?** (Retirement assets will pass according to my beneficiary form, not my will; see My Retirement Assets and Estate Plan Checklist this section, Part 4)

___

9. **My beneficiary form should name a person not an entity as beneficiary unless I am leaving my retirement assets in whole or in part to a charity or a trust.** ___

10. **Does my beneficiary form allow my beneficiaries to stretch payouts?** (See checklist this section, Part 3) ___

11. **Does my beneficiary form allow "per stirpes" language?** ___

Comments: ___

___

___

___

12. Who are my primary beneficiaries and what % do they inherit?
(Should = 100%)

____

____

____

13. Who are my contingent beneficiaries and what % does each inherit?
(Should = 100%)

____

____

____

14. If there are multiple beneficiaries, make sure I have clearly stated each beneficiary's share on the beneficiary form. ______

15. If I have multiple beneficiaries, is there a need for me to create separate accounts for them now? ______

Comments: ____

____

____

Follow-Up

My To Do List	Date Completed
1	
2	
3	
4	
5	
6	
7	
8	
9	
10	

______________________________ ______________

My Signature Date

Part 2

MY CUSTODIAL AGREEMENT CHECKLIST

What It Does

If you have an IRA, then the IRA custodial agreement at the bank or other financial institution where your funds are kept is the *rulebook* for it. By that I mean the agreement lays out all the investment, distribution, and estate-planning options available to you and those who will be inheriting your IRA. Every IRA owner agrees in writing to the provisions of the IRA custodial agreement upon opening the account (though most IRA owners probably have no memory of ever even signing this key document).

Similarly, company plans such as a 401(k) come with their own custodial rulebook called the "Summary Plan Description," or more commonly the "Plan Agreement." All employees receive this when they begin participating in a company retirement plan. Few company plan agreements offer participants any flexibility—they are pretty much stuck with the investment, distribution, and estate-planning options dictated by their company's plan agreement since they can't go shopping for another 401(k) unless they change jobs. But IRA participants are not stuck—even after they sign on the dotted line—because they do have the option of shopping around for the allowed options they want. That's why it is important to know going in what options your IRA custodian will and will not allow, which is where your custodial agreement checklist comes in.

This checklist addresses the key provisions you want to make sure are in your IRA custodial agreement—and should be asking about when opening an IRA or contemplating a change to another custodian.

Ask Ed . . .

Q: What if my IRA custodian cannot tell me whether my agreement includes all the items you advise?

A: This is quite possible. You may even be looked at as if you had sprouted another head because it is unlikely anyone there has ever asked about this before and so whoever you're talking to will probably not know the answer. But don't give up the ship. This is an important document with a set of rules you will be stuck with. So, persist until you find someone at the custodial institution who can answer your questions. If you start to lose confidence there is such a someone, just put a bug in the institution's ear that you may move your funds elsewhere. That's usually enough to track down the person who knows what's going on. But if even this does not do the trick, get your IRA money out of there fast and into the hands of another IRA custodian who can tell you at all times the allowed provisions in its agreement.

What's In It for Me?

You will know right away how the funds in your IRA will be distributed both during your lifetime and after your death. This way, you will know in advance whether the custodian offers all the investment, distribution, and estate-planning options that you want—or would want—and will be able to choose wisely. If the agreement contains all the provisions you want, you are all set. If not, you've got a heads-up to move your IRA to another, more enlightened or cooperative custodian. By checking all of this out now, you won't saddle yourself or your beneficiaries with restrictive distribution provisions later on.

Ask Ed . . .

Q: Is my IRA custodial agreement something I can actually read and understand (like this book), or is it all inscrutable legalese?

A: Pretty much all legalese, but many times the agreement comes with subject headings that help you locate what you need without having to plow through and decipher the entire document. For example, if you want to look over the agreement's default provision should you die without naming a beneficiary (of course, that won't happen because you've taken care of your beneficiary form, right?) you may see a heading that reads, "Provisions that apply when there is no beneficiary," and will find your answer there—albeit in legalese. Helpful headings or not, if you find the legalese just too much mumbo jumbo to comprehend, run your questions by your financial advisor, who should not only have a copy of your custodial agreement but the answers as well (see Section V).

What If I Don't?

Interestingly, the IRS rules governing IRA distributions are more liberal than what many IRA custodians themselves will permit. But even if the IRS allows it, if the provisions of your custodial agreement don't, the document rules, and you and your beneficiaries pay up.

For example, does your IRA document allow your beneficiaries to stretch distributions from your IRA when they inherit? Most custodians now offer this option, but if you happen to have your IRA funds with a bank, broker, or other fund company that doesn't, your beneficiaries will be stuck taking distributions over a shorter time period, thereby forking over more of their inheritance (your remaining nest egg) to the government, faster.

Your IRA beneficiaries have nowhere near the leverage you have now once they inherit. Let's say that your children (nonspouse beneficiaries) would prefer certain provisions once they inherit, but those provisions aren't in the agreement. Unlike you, they cannot just pull money out and transfer it to another IRA custodian (unless the agreement permits this) or they will trigger a tax on the entire amount of the withdrawal. Bingo, a big chunk of their inherited IRA goes right into the coffers of Uncle Sam.

Ask Ed . . .

Q: What if I cannot find my original IRA custodial agreement?

A: Just call your IRA custodian and ask for a copy or to see a typical agreement form. This way, you will be able to ascertain what's typically allowed and what isn't in that custodian's agreement. In fact, some IRA custodians actually post their custodial agreement forms on their websites. Others will simply mail one to you or you can pick one up the next time you stop in at the bank or wherever your IRA is held. Your financial advisor should have copies of your agreement as well.

Here's another example: Let's say you go through the time and expense of working with an attorney to name a trust as beneficiary of your IRA. But if the custodian does not accept a trust as beneficiary, the devil knows what will happen to your money once you are gone—it may become available to people like your children's spouses or to creditors you specifically wanted to avoid by naming a trust in the first place. The whole point of naming a trust as beneficiary (see Section IV,

Part 2) is to retain some degree of control over what happens to your money after you die, so your planning will not be out the window.

Your IRA custodial agreement is not like your beneficiary form, which allows you to make changes. Only the custodian can make changes in your agreement and probably won't do that just for you. So, all you are left with as an alternative is to complain or to move your IRA funds elsewhere. But by finding the potential problem spots in the agreement ahead of time (by which I mean before you die, or as attorneys put it, "before your will *matures*") you can move your money to a custodian offering the options you want.

Ask Ed . . .

Q: One of the provisions you say to look for is whether the agreement permits a beneficiary to name a beneficiary? Why do I care about that now?

A: Here's why. Let's say your beneficiary George has a thirty-six-year life expectancy and dies five years into the payout of the inherited IRA. That means there are thirty-one years left on the life-expectancy payout (the stretch IRA option, see Part 3). If George had named his son Bill as his successor beneficiary, Bill can complete the thirty-one years remaining on what would have been George's life expectancy, thus preserving the stretch option. In addition, by allowing the beneficiary to name a beneficiary, if your first beneficiary dies with funds still remaining in the inherited IRA, then the account will pass directly to the successor beneficiary and not through the estate, thereby avoiding costly complications like probate.

Instructions

Review each item in the checklist to see if your IRA custodian allows it. If all the important provisions I've noted here are permitted, then you and your beneficiaries are in fine shape for the future. If just a few are allowed, consider carefully whether and how much each disallowed one may affect you and your beneficiaries. For instance, if your IRA custodian doesn't allow a trust as your IRA beneficiary, and you have no intention of naming a trust, then there is no problem. (Of course if you subsequently decide that you do need to name a trust, then your only alternative would be to move your IRA funds to another custodian offering that option.)

Apply this checklist to the custodial agreement for each IRA you own or are considering.

A Word to the Wise

Participants in a company plan such as a 401(k) should go through this checklist too as way of comparing how well the provisions allowed in your plan agreement stack up against the checklist—even though you won't be able to do anything about it unless or until the time comes when you decide to roll your company plan funds over into an IRA.

MY CUSTODIAL AGREEMENT CHECKLIST

MY NAME: ______________________ DATE: __________

MY ADVISOR'S NAME: ______________________ PLAN # __________

Follow-ups should be added to the To Do lists at the end of this checklist.

1. Are stretch distributions permitted? __________

2. What are the default provisions when there is no beneficiary named? __________

3. Will my custodial agreement accept a trust as my beneficiary? __________

4. Will my power of attorney form be accepted?

Comments: ______________________

5. Can my beneficiary name a successor beneficiary? __________

6. Can my nonspouse beneficiary move investments via a trustee-to-trustee transfer? __________

Comments: ______________________

Follow-Up

My To Do List	Date Completed
1	
2	
3	
4	
5	
6	

7 ______

8 ______

9 ______

10 ______

______ ______
My Signature Date

Part 3

MY STRETCH OPPORTUNITY CHECKLIST

What It Does

You won't find the words "Stretch IRA" or "Stretch Retirement Plan" in the tax code because it is a made-up term, one that describes over how long a period of time your beneficiaries can withdraw funds from the account you are passing on to them and pay tax on the withdrawals—in other words, how long they can extend (stretch) payouts of those funds, enabling the balance to grow.

Some financial institutions use made-up terms of their own to describe this extended tax deferral, such as the "Extended IRA," the "Multigenerational IRA," and the "Legacy IRA" to name a few. But don't get caught up in names. It's the option to "stretch" that counts—an option that offers a big tax break that's part of the IRC (Internal Revenue Code) and thus completely legal!

I always say that the only surefire way to build wealth is to eliminate the government as a partner. The more you have to fork over in taxes, the less money you will have. And the longer you can keep the Taxman waiting for his money, the more time it can grow for you and your family and build into a fortune. That's what the stretch option does, and this checklist makes sure you don't blow the opportunity. It sees to it that you set your account up properly so your beneficiaries will be able to seize the stretch option.

Ask Ed . . .

Q: I have a 401(k) with my company. Is there a stretch 401(k)? I never see any mention of this.

A: Yes, there is such a thing as a stretch 401(k), but it is more rare than a rookie Mickey Mantle baseball card. The tax rules specifically allow the stretch option to beneficiaries of all retirement plans, including company plans like the 401(k), as well as 403(b) and 457 plans. But company plans are not required to offer it, and most don't because they really do not want to be bothered with the administrative work involved in paying out distributions to your beneficiaries for decades. The priority with most companies is to get you off their books as soon as you die. To find out if your company plan offers the stretch to beneficiaries, check the plan's "Summary Plan Description" referred to in Part 2 of this section on custodial agreements. If it is not allowed, you should consider rolling your company plan funds into an IRA as soon as you are able. That way, you can *guarantee* the stretch option for your beneficiaries, since non-spouse beneficiaries will not be able to do a rollover after you die. In 2007, for the first time, a non-spouse beneficiary, including a qualified trust, will be able to do a direct transfer to a properly titled inherited IRA, but the plan still has to allow this.

What's In It for Me?

Nothing—except the peace of mind of knowing that whatever funds are left in your account(s) after all that skydiving, bungee jumping, and world traveling you've done in your retirement years will go to your beneficiaries (rather than to the government) in a way that allows those funds to continue to grow and flourish.

To set up the stretch, you simply name a person (as opposed to a "thing" such as an estate or charity) as beneficiary on your beneficiary form. This will allow the named person to spread required distributions on the inherited account over his/her remaining life expectancy, according to the actuarial numbers in the IRS's Single Life Expectancy Table (Appendix I).

The younger the person named, the longer his or her life expectancy, thus the greater the financial value of the stretch option. This is because while your IRA and other plan beneficiaries will be subject to Required Minimum Distributions (aka RMDs, see this section, Part 5) just as you are, their RMDs will be based on their ages and life expectancies, not yours. The result, especially with a younger beneficiary, is that very little must actually be withdrawn each year, allowing the bulk of the inherited account to keep growing tax-deferred. It will take decades before all of that money will be forced out through distributions and by then, your children or grandchildren will have had the benefit of a tax-deferred fortune that dwarfs the actual amount you left them.

Ask Ed . . .

Q: Does the stretch concept apply also to Roth IRAs, which are tax-free at withdrawal?

A: Yes, and a Roth Stretch IRA is as good as it gets because although you are taxed up front on contributions, the money you put in grows exponentially and is never again subject to taxes. So not only do you pay no tax on distributions, your children or grandchildren don't either; they can benefit over time from growth in the inherited Roth IRA, all of it tax-free. Uncle Sam gets cut out completely, which is the way to build real wealth (see The Roth IRA Conversion Checklist, Section IV, Part 11).

The numbers are exponential. For example, a $100,000 IRA left to your eleven-year-old granddaughter—whose life expectancy is 71.8 years according to the IRS's Single Life Expectancy Table—could be parlayed into as much as a $4,500,000 fortune (yes that's 4.5 *million*), which is one nice legacy, if you ask me.

Of course, many people leave their retirement plan money to their spouse (The Spouse Beneficiary's Checklist, Section III, Part 2). That works with the stretch option too, and will yield other tax benefits as well.

The bottom line is that you set up the stretch mostly to make life better for your children, your grandchildren, or whomever you love for the rest of their lives—so that the money you earned during your lifetime (unless you spend it all, which is fun too, and means you can skip this checklist) has the opportunity to grow exponentially and benefit them, rather than Uncle Sam—and with Uncle Sam's blessing to boot!

What If I Don't?

Your beneficiaries will hate you. But seriously (I hope), the world won't end if you don't; it's just that very soon after your passing, the tax shelter your retirement account provides will disappear as funds are distributed, and the IRS gets its mitts on your money faster, leaving your beneficiaries no opportunity to continue to grow the account tax-deferred (even tax-free if it's a Roth IRA) for many more decades.

For your beneficiaries to get the stretch option, you must see if your custodial agreement allows stretch distributions—and then make sure you have designated your beneficiary (or beneficiaries) on your beneficiary form. If you designate no beneficiary, and your account passes through your will, then your inheritors are stuck with the distribution rules under that scenario. Those rules depend on whether you pass away before or after your Required Beginning Date (RBD), which is the date you are required to begin taking minimum distributions from your retirement account; with an IRA and most other plans, the RBD is April 1 of the year following the year you turn 70½.

If you die before your RBD, your beneficiaries must withdraw all the funds in your account by the end of the fifth year following the year of your death (the so-called 5-year rule), and the tax deferral is gone forever. If you die on or after your RBD, then the payout to your heirs will be your remaining life expectancy based on the IRS Single Life Expectancy Table. Since the inherited funds will be forced out much earlier than if they were stretched, the taxes your heirs will pay will be higher, and they will be paid sooner, building a savings account for Uncle Sam rather than your family.

Ask Ed . . .

Q: As great as all this sounds, I cannot see my kids taking distributions over 50 years. They will probably want all the money at once and not care about all these fantastic tax benefits. Can I make sure they stretch?

A: Yes—by naming a trust as your beneficiary for your kids' benefit (see The Naming a Trust-As-Beneficiary Checklist, Section IV, Part 2).

Instructions

Having named your beneficiaries on your beneficiary form in Part 1 and reviewed your custodial agreement in Part 2 to determine if your plan allows the stretch option (if not, this checklist is moot and you can move to Section IV), use the checklist to set up your IRA, Roth IRA, or company plan properly and to make sure *you* make no mistakes in the stretch setup that may haunt your heirs later on. Conversely, you can use this checklist as a reminder to go over your stretch plans with your designated beneficiaries and refer them to Section III so they can go over what *they* must do once they inherit to ensure they will not blow the stretch opportunity you've created for them.

MY STRETCH OPPORTUNITY CHECKLIST

MY NAME: ______________________________ **DATE:** ____________

MY ADVISOR'S NAME: ______________________________ **PLAN #:** ____________

Follow-ups should be added to the To Do lists at the end of this checklist.

A stretch retirement plan will allow payouts to stretch over my beneficiary's own life expectancy, if done correctly.

1. **Have I checked my custodial agreement (see previous checklist) to see if it permits stretch distributions? (Most company plans will not permit stretch distributions to nonspouse beneficiaries.)** ____________
2. **Have I checked my beneficiary form (see checklist this section, Part 1) to see if it allows a stretch payout?** ____________
3. **Have I named a person—spouse, children, grandchildren, life partner, etc. (as opposed to a trust or charity) as my designated beneficiary, or beneficiaries, to take advantage of the stretch option?** ____________
4. **Does my nonspouse beneficiary (if applicable) know how to properly retitle my account when he/she inherits—i.e., John Jones (deceased, date of death) IRA fbo Sam Jones** ____________
5. **Does my spouse beneficiary know that when she inherits my account and rolls it over to her own account, there is no stretch until she dies and the account goes to her designated beneficiaries (the Nonspouse Beneficiary's Checklist, Section III, Part 1)? (It is always a possibility that the spouse will spend down the account and leave nothing for beneficiaries to stretch.)** ____________
6. **If I have multiple beneficiaries and each one wants to use their own life expectancy to stretch, do they know the separate account rules (The Multiple Beneficiaries' Checklist, Section III, Part 3)? (I can separate the account now to make sure nothing goes wrong.)** ____________
7. **Will all my beneficiaries want to stretch my account?** ____________
8. **Will I need to force my beneficiaries through a trust to stretch the account so I can maintain some form of control even after my death?** ____________

9. **Have I made sure my beneficiaries know what they must do, how to do it, and when, in order to implement the stretch opportunity I have set up? (Refer them to Section III.)** ____________

Comments: ____

____

____

____

____

Follow-Up

My To Do List	Date Completed
1 ______________________	
2 ______________________	
3 ______________________	
4 ______________________	
5 ______________________	
6 ______________________	
7 ______________________	
8 ______________________	
9 ______________________	
10 ______________________	

______________________________ ______________

My Signature Date

Part 4

MY RETIREMENT ASSETS AND ESTATE PLAN CHECKLIST

What It Does

Up to this point, you have been focusing exclusively on your retirement assets because they typically make up the largest chunk of your estate. But if you are like most people, you will have accumulated other assets too, such as a home and other property. So, here is where you inventory what you have in other assets in order to coordinate them with your retirement funds as part of your overall estate plan.

Given the state of current estate tax law, which seems to have no certainty to it at all these days, the federal estate tax exemption is already high enough to eliminate most estates from taxation (for 2007 $2 million for singles, $4 million for married couples). If your IRA or other retirement assets combined with your home and other property will add up to an estate valued higher than those figures and thus subject to federal estate taxes (as of this writing), then you need to get serious here and make sure that you title your assets and bequeath them in a manner that will permit most or all of those assets to pass to your heirs estate tax–free.

Even if estate tax is not an issue, however, you still will want your property to go to the people you wish and not to the people you don't wish. That means leaving nothing open to interpretation after you are gone. This inventory and planning assessment checklist will start you off on the right path and keep you there.

Ask Ed . . .

Q: What if I want to leave my retirement account(s) to certain beneficiaries and my other assets to others? Can I do that?

A: Sure you can, and it is advisable in many cases, which is why you want to coordinate your retirement account with your overall estate plan. For example, you may have a younger brother you want to inherit the family business and a child you want to inherit your IRA and get to stretch it over his or her lifetime. Or you might want to leave your IRAs to your grandchildren to gain the biggest hit on the stretch option and leave other assets to your spouse (assuming your spouse will have all he or she needs—you never want to leave a spouse with too little in the name of tax planning). Or your kids might be so successful that they don't want you to add to their own estates, so they would rather have you pass certain assets directly on to their children (your grandkids) instead. These are all issues that come up in the estate-planning process.

What's In It for Me?

Estate planning is not just about saving on or eliminating estate taxes; it is also about finding ways to leverage what you have accumulated in overall assets into even greater wealth by using the tax code to keep more of that wealth in the hands of your family. In other words, even if there is no estate tax to worry about, why not seize the opportunity to leave behind an estate that can be of much greater value than it is now?

Life insurance, for example, is a method that can be used to accomplish this, which is why a life insurance assessment is part of this checklist. You may not have thought of it, but life insurance is THE biggest tax break ever created by Congress—bigger even than the stretch option—because properly owned *life insurance in an estate passes entirely* ***tax-free,*** no matter what the overall value of the estate. Thus, life insurance proceeds can be used by your heirs to pay any estate taxes (should they kick in) without their having to dip into your account and depleting it prematurely.

So, here again, what's in it for you is the knowledge that by going through this checklist, you will once more be doing all you can to make your estate, large or small, as valuable as it can be for your children and grandchildren.

Ask Ed . . .

Q: You stress life insurance as such a big deal. Do you get a kickback from the insurance industry?

A: Let me be very clear about this. I am not now nor have I ever been a shill for the insurance industry. But I strongly believe in life insurance as a surefire way of seeing to it that your family receives tons of tax-free cash after you die—cash that, among other things, they can use to offset estate tax or other financial difficulties without having to sell the family home, business, or other assets to raise cash. Even people who say they can make more profitable investments than life insurance should consider this: The policy generally pays off as soon as you die. No other investment can beat that kind of return as quickly. The amount of life insurance you will need is the amount of wealth you want to create for your family. You pay a relatively small amount of money now for a tax-free windfall forever. That to me is what estate planning is all about and why life insurance is the centerpiece of my own estate plan, and a key part of this checklist.

What If I Don't?

If you are like most people, you have probably put off estate planning for as long as possible. After all, who likes contemplating death, except maybe Woody Allen? But the fact is, YOU are the architect of your estate plan, and if you don't get involved or you don't do it right, you will potentially leave your family one hell of a financial mess at a very emotional and vulnerable time. On the other hand, your government will love you because you will be putting money in its coffers that your family might not have had to pay out so quickly, if at all. So, put yourself in your family's shoes and ask yourself this, "How would I like that to happen to me?"

Furthermore, having no estate plan—or setting one up too willy-nilly—means not only that your family will have to deal with the fallout later on, but also that they will be sorting things out according to their terms, not yours. This could result in the tearing apart of your family over disagreements that YOU could have avoided had you provided them with some guidance in the form of an estate plan.

A Word to the Wise

If your IRA or other retirement account is the bulk of your estate and you do not have other funds from which to buy life insurance, it may pay to withdraw the funds from your retirement account, pay the tax (and, in some cases, even the penalty if you withdraw prematurely), and put those funds into a life insurance policy that can be set up by your insurance professional to be estate- and income-tax-free. Simply by leveraging your taxable retirement assets into buying tax-free life insurance, you have the ability to turn a highly taxed asset like your retirement account into many times its current value, totally tax-free.

Instructions

If you can't remember all the nonretirement account assets you have, or you and/or your estate-planning attorney have overlooked or not considered certain assets as even being part of your estate, this checklist will tip you off to them ("Don't forget to include . . ."). It's impossible for me to suggest every conceivable possibility, however, because each of you has a unique lifestyle and thus will have a wide variety of different types of assets in addition to those I'm suggesting here.

Ask Ed . . .

Q: Should I ever consider leaving my retirement account(s) to my estate?

A: As I've written elsewhere in this section, you should always do *everything* you can to *prevent* your retirement funds from passing through your estate—well, *almost* always. There are situations where you might want to do this—for example if you have no children or grandchildren or anyone other than relatives who are so distant you can't remember their names let alone their faces. I had a client like that. His only potential heirs were fourteen distant nephews and nieces. His plan was to spend most of his funds anyway, and then, rather than naming fourteen distant relatives individually to get whatever might be left, he named his estate and left everything to the fourteen equally. That was the easiest route for him to take. But as a general rule, leaving your money to your estate is a BIG no-no.

Use this checklist also to help you locate all your current estate-planning documents—such as your will, powers of attorney and health care proxies, and so on—for informational purposes, and to make any changes.

If you do not have these documents, it is time to pay a visit to an estate-planning attorney and have them drawn up. And when you make the appointment, be sure to bring your retirement plan beneficiary forms and custodial documents with you—and to clearly express your desire to enable your plan beneficiaries to stretch (if allowable)—so that the attorney can help you put together an overall estate plan that takes *everything* into consideration.

A Word to the Wise

Estate planning is about communicating with your family. It can be a wonderful experience you'll wish you had sooner. The dilemma is that someone has to bring the topic up. Your children may be uneasy about doing so, and you may be just as uneasy about addressing your own mortality. The result is a Mexican standoff, and the planning goes undone because important family conversations never take place. Don't let this happen in your family. Use this checklist to start the ball rolling, and that conversation will quickly fall into place.

MY RETIREMENT ASSETS AND ESTATE PLAN CHECKLIST

MY NAME: ______________________ **DATE:** __________

MY ADVISOR'S NAME: ______________________ **PLAN #:** __________

Follow-ups should be added to the To Do Lists at the end of this checklist.

Use the first section to determine if your estate will be subject to estate tax; if yes, complete the remainder of the checklist.

1. I have inventoried ALL my assets. __________

Don't forget to include:

- Annuities (that have postdeath value) __________
- Other real estate (list location, deeds, and insurance information) __________
- Rental real estate (list tenants and leases) __________
- Investment real estate __________
- Vacation homes __________
- Boat/recreational vehicle/motor home __________
- Club memberships __________
- Ownership interests in a business (a valuation/appraisal will be needed) __________
- Inheritances or gifts __________
- Valuables (hidden or stored) __________

2. Group property by ownership. (Mine, my spouse's, joint, in a trust, etc.)

- Are there rollover possibilities? (Employer plans) __________
- Have I looked at the titling of my assets to determine how they will pass at my death—e.g., which assets will pass through probate, and so on? (Assets with beneficiary forms, such as retirement plans, do not pass through my will and are not subject to probate as long as I do not name my estate as beneficiary on the forms.) __________

3. I have collected all my planning documents. __________

- Tax returns __________
- Wills, trusts, powers of attorney, health care proxies, living wills __________
- Beneficiary forms (retirement plans, insurance policies, annuities) __________

4. I have completed my Custodial Agreement checklist. __________

5. I have completed a liquidity analysis (a listing of all my assets in order of their liquidity) to assess life insurance needs for paying estate taxes and other expenses postdeath. __________

Comments: ____

____

____

____

____

6. I have gathered all my personal information. __________

Family tree:

- Parents, children, grandchildren __________
- Prior marriages __________
- Children of prior marriages __________
- Distant relatives __________
- Ages, health, birthdays, residency, and future residency __________
- Will my surviving spouse need the money? __________
- Liability issues __________
- Medicaid issues __________
- Family dynamics—who gets along with whom, and who does not __________

7. What do I want to accomplish?

- The stretch opportunity __________
- Secure the estate tax exemption (a.k.a. the credit shelter amount) __________
- Postdeath control (beneficiaries are minors, disabled, incompetent, unsophisticated, trust may be needed. (See the Naming a Trust-As-Beneficiary, Section IV, Part 2.) __________
- Creditor protection (The Bankruptcy Reform Act passed by Congress in 2005 gives IRAs widespread protections in Bankruptcy Court.) __________
- Benefit charity __________
- Build estate for my beneficiaries __________
- Reduce taxes my beneficiaries will pay (including generation-skipping tax) __________
- Other __________

8. When will my lifetime distributions begin? ______________

- I am still working. (See checklist this section, Part 5.) ______________
- Will I need my required minimum distributions to live on? (If not, consider converting to a Roth IRA—see checklist Section IV, Part 11.) ______________

Comments: ____

____

____

____

9. Have I assessed the tax and estate planning ramifications of my choice of beneficiary? ______________

- Beneficiary vs. designated beneficiary ______________
- Primary and contingent beneficiaries ______________
- Successor beneficiaries ______________

10. Have I assessed estate tax issues? ______________

- Would there be estate tax (federal or state) if I died now? ______________
- Would there be a projected estate tax (federal or state) based on the asset value and my projected life expectancy as of now? ______________
- Who will pay the estate tax? ______________
- What funds will be available to pay the estate tax? ______________

11. Have I assessed all income tax issues? ______________

- Who will pay the income tax on postdeath distributions (exceptions—Roth IRAs, nondeductible contributions, after-tax funds in company plans)? Will it be an individual beneficiary or trust beneficiary? (Evaluate trust tax rates vs. individual income tax rates.) (State income tax rules will vary.) (Consider a Roth trust solution.) ______________
- What funds will be available to pay the income tax? ______________
- Do I qualify for any special tax breaks? (Section IV, Part 7) ______________

Comments: ____

____

____

____

____

12. I have developed my beneficiary plan based on the information I have obtained from evaluating all the options. ____________

- I have named my primary and contingent beneficiaries on my beneficiary form and shared this information with them. ____________
- I have considered the effect of a possible disclaimer (see The Disclaimer Planning Checklist in Section IV, Part 3). ____________
- I have updated my beneficiary form for each retirement plan, naming both primary and contingent beneficiaries. ____________
- I have obtained acknowledged copies of my updated beneficiary forms from each retirement plan provider and given copies to my financial advisor. ____________

Comments: ____

____

____

____

Follow-Up

My To Do List	Date Completed
1 ______________	
2 ______________	
3 ______________	
4 ______________	
5 ______________	
6 ______________	
7 ______________	
8 ______________	
9 ______________	
10 ______________	

______________________ My Signature

______________ Date

Part 5

MY RMD CALCULATIONS CHECKLIST

What It Does

This checklist takes you through all the steps needed to make sure you calculate your Required Minimum Distributions (RMDs) correctly and take them at the right time, especially if you have funds in several different types of retirement plans, as many people do.

Ask Ed . . .

Q: You say I must take my RMD even if I do not need the money. OK, so let's say I don't need the money, but I take the distribution anyway like I am supposed to and I pay the tax. Now that I did everything I am required to, can I just roll the distributed funds back into my account to keep them growing tax-deferred?

A: No. The tax law specifically prohibits you from rolling RMDs back into a retirement account.

You must begin taking your RMD by what is called your Required Beginning Date (RBD), which is generally April 1 of the year following the year you turn age 70½. There are some exceptions to that rule for distributions from company plans, and these exceptions are covered in this checklist, as well.

Even if you don't need the money, you still must take the distribution. This is not voluntary. The RMD is required under the law.

Roth IRA owners are not subject to RMDs, but beneficiaries of Roth IRAs are, and those details will be covered in Section III.

What's In It for Me?

By using this handy checklist, you will be assured of not messing up this crucial component of retirement account distribution planning. And, believe me, you don't want to mess up or the you-know-what will really hit the fan. But I'll get to that in a moment.

Furthermore, this checklist will show you when you can add all your plans together (if you have more than one) and take RMDs from any one or a combination of the accounts to make calculating easier. You cannot satisfy an RMD from an IRA by withdrawing from your 401(k) plan, however. Nor can you can satisfy an RMD from a Keogh plan with a distribution from an IRA. But for RMD calculations, SEP and SIMPLE IRAs are included with IRAs.

Ask Ed . . .

Q: What is my "first distribution year"?

A: Not what you think. It sounds like it's the year you take your first distribution, which would make sense if the tax code were in English, but it isn't. Your "first distribution year" is not always the year you actually take your RMD, but the first year that an RMD *is required.* Here's an example: Say you turn 70 on April 23,

2007. That means you will turn 70½ on October 23, 2007 (six months later). Since you turn 70½ in 2007, then that is your "first distribution year," but you do not have to take your first distribution until your Required Beginning Date, which is not until April 1, 2008. So in this case, your "first distribution year" is 2007, but the year you take your first RMD can be 2008. Even if you wait until April 1, 2008 to take your first RMD, the year-end balance you will use to calculate your RMD is December 31, 2006 (the year prior to your "first distribution year" of 2007). It is only the first year's RMD that has these twists and turns. Afterward each RMD must be taken by December 31 of that year, which, following on this example, means your second RMD must be taken by December 31, 2008, based on the balance in your IRA or other plan on December 31, 2007. You use the age you turn on your birthday in each distribution year to calculate RMDs. Here, having turned 70 on your birthday (April 23, 2007), you will look up the life expectancy for a 70-year-old in 2007 on the Uniform Lifetime Table (Appendix II) and divide your December 31, 2006 account balance by that number (27.4 years) to determine your RMD. Now, if you turn 70 on, say, November 12, 2007, this means you will not turn 70½ until 2008, and your Required Beginning Date would be April 1, 2009—so your first RMD will be based on your account balance as of December 31, 2007. If you are unsure of any of this, don't go it alone. Any trained financial advisor (see Section V) should be able to help you with your RMD calculations. Your IRA custodian can help you as well.

What If I Don't?

You will lose your money pretty quickly because the government levies a 50 percent penalty for any RMDs not taken. That's one of the stiffest fines in the whole tax code. And believe me, Big Brother is watching and will know if you missed an RMD because your plan custodian is required by law to rat you out by notifying the IRS of your RMDs. With all this watching and ratting out, it is now extremely difficult to plead ignorance of an RMD as many people did in the past when they missed one. It remains to be seen just how lenient the IRS may be now since it will know that your own plan custodian has given you a timely heads-up.

A Word to the Wise

Don't risk the 50 percent penalty by waiting until the last minute to take your RMD. The banks and other financial institutions are flooded with these year-end requests and as a result your RMD might not get distributed in time. Since RMDs are based on the December 31 balance in your account as of the prior year, you can actually compute your RMD early in the year to avoid the year-end rush—and you should do that if only for the peace of mind in knowing that the calculation is done. Then you can take your RMD a bit later in the year (around November for example, though not later). Keep your inventory of owned accounts [Section I, Part 1] up to date so that you will have the most current information on your balances when you begin making calculations and taking RMDs.

Instructions

Refer to the list you made of all owned (not inherited) accounts (Section I, Part 1) to make sure you include all of them here. You also will need your IRA and/or other plan statements handy showing the balance in each plan as of the end of the prior year. For example, you will need your December 31, 2006 balance to calculate a 2007 RMD. Then follow the checklist right through the calculations of each RMD for each account you own, and you won't go wrong.

Ask Ed . . .

Q: If I qualify for the still-working exception referenced in the checklist, does this mean I do not have to take any RMDs from any of my retirement accounts until I actually retire?

A: No! The still-working exception applies only to distributions from your company plan if you are still working for that company—in which case you do not have to begin talking RMDs (from *that* plan), until April 1 of the year following the year you retire. You still must take your RMDs from all other plans and IRAs you have. The still-working exception never applies to IRAs, nor does it apply to a company plan if you own more than 5 percent of the company or are self-employed.

Lifetime RMDs for most IRA and other plan owners are based on the Uniform Lifetime Table (Appendix II) unless the "Spousal Exception" applies. This exception allows IRA and other plan owners to use the Joint Life Expectancy Table to calculate RMDs if the sole beneficiary of the plan for the entire RMD year is a spouse more than ten years younger than you. The Joint Life Expectancy Tables (Appendix III) will give you a lower RMD.

A Word to the Wise

Your trickiest RMD may be the first one because you can take it either in the year you turn 70½ or up to April 1 of the following year. For example, if you turned 70½ in 2006, then your Required Beginning Date (RBD) is April 1, 2007—and you can take your RMD either in 2006 or up to April 1, 2007. In many cases, it might be better to take your first RMD in 2006 rather than waiting to take it in 2007, however. In this way, you will not have to take your first two RMDs in one tax year (2007 in this example) as your 2007 RMD would also be due in 2007. If you take your first RMD in 2006, you can separate the income from both of your first two RMDs into two separate tax years and probably pay a lower tax in each year.

MY RMD CALCULATIONS CHECKLIST

MY NAME: ______________________ DATE: __________

MY ADVISOR'S NAME: ______________________ PLAN #: __________

Follow-ups should be added to the To Do lists at the end of this checklist.

1. I am subject to required distributions because I am or will be age 70½ or older by 12/31 of this year. __________

2. Does an exception apply to my required distributions? __________

- Roth IRAs have no required distributions __________
- My first-year distribution can be delayed until 4/1 of the following year (second distribution must be taken by 12/31 of that year also). __________
- I am still working (company plans only); if I am less than a 5 percent owner of the company, distributions are not required until 4/1 of the year after my retirement. __________
- 403(b) plan balances prior to 1987 are not subject to required distributions until I am age 75. __________

Comments: ______________________

____

____

____

____

3. Determine my distribution year (if turning 73 this year, the distribution year is the current year. If prior year's age 70½ distribution was deferred to current year 4/1, distribution year is prior year). __________

4. What is the balance in each of my retirement plans? __________

- Balance as of 12/31 of the year prior to the distribution year __________

Comments: ______________________

____

____

____

____

5. I have looked up my life-expectancy factor (my age on the last day of the distribution year) in the Uniform Lifetime Table (Appendix II) and it is: ____________

- EXCEPTION: If my spouse is my sole beneficiary for the entire year and is more than ten years younger than me, I will use Joint Life Expectancy Table (Appendix III) to look up my life-expectancy factor, which is: ____________

6. Divide the account balance by my life expectancy factor to calculate RMDs. ____________

Comments: ____

____

____

____

7. Take my RMD by 12/31 of the distribution year (unless it is the first-year distribution delayed until 4/1). ____________

8. I know there is a 50 percent penalty on any required distribution not taken. ____________

9. I know that if I have multiple accounts, distributions can sometimes be taken from any one or a combination of those accounts. ____________

- Owned IRAs (including SEP and SIMPLE IRAs but not including Roth IRAs) or IRAs inherited from the same person can be added together. ____________
- 403(b) plans can be added together. ____________
- All other company or employer plans can*not* be added together. ____________

10. I know that if I have pre-tax (deductible) and after-tax (nondeductible) amounts in my IRA that the pro-rata rule will apply. ____________

- I must file Form 8606 with my tax return. This form will track my after-tax basis amount and give me the calculation for the taxable and non-taxable amounts of my distribution. ____________
- I cannot take after-tax-only amounts out of my IRA(s), even if they are in a separate account. ____________

Follow-Up

My To Do List | Date Completed

1 __________

2 __________

3 __________

4 __________

5 __________

6 __________

7 __________

8 __________

9 __________

10 __________

My Signature | Date

Part 6

MY ROLLOVER/LUMP-SUM DECISION CHECKLIST

What It Does

My daughter Ilana began driving last year, and as any parent knows, that's when the worrying really begins. Whenever she takes the car, I usually say to her, "Call me when you get there" so that I know she arrived safely.

You should do the same thing whenever your retirement funds leave the nest—and that's the short answer to what this checklist does.

The longer answer is this: When you retire or leave the company you work for to take another job (or for any other reason), you will be asked by your current employer what to do with the retirement benefits you have accrued in your 401(k), 403(b), 457, or other company plan. There are four options: (1) Roll the funds over into an IRA; (2) Take them as a lump sum; (3) Keep them in the current plan for the time being, then transfer them into your new employer's plan when you get settled; (4) Leave them in the employer plan. Each option comes with many considerations that must be weighed carefully to make the right decision for you. As these funds represent every penny you have saved from working over the past however many years—the largest check you will ever get—you will want to make sure nothing bad happens to them due to your making the wrong decision here. Because you may only get one chance.

Ask Ed . . .

Q: What if I do an IRA rollover, but then decide I would like to roll those funds back to my company's plan. Can I do that?

A: The IRS says yes, but it is up to your company plan whether to accept your money back or not. In any case, only taxable IRA funds can be rolled back to a company plan. You cannot roll after-tax funds (funds you have already paid tax on) from an IRA to a company plan. But I would think twice before considering a reverse rollover because once your funds are in the IRA most of your company plan benefits (like NUA or 10-year averaging, see Section IV, Part 7, for example) are no longer available on those funds. So that tilts the scales toward leaving the funds in the IRA where you control them. As you go through the checklist, you will find plenty of benefits from having funds in your company plan, such as federal creditor protection, the ability to delay RMDs if you are still working, the age 55 exception from the 10 percent penalty for early withdrawals to name just the big ones. But the distribution options in an IRA are far better than in a company plan—especially for a nonspouse beneficiary who will be able to stretch IRA funds over his or her lifetime, an option that probably won't be available in the company plan and if your beneficiaries inherit from that plan (as opposed to an IRA), they will probably be hit with the full distribution, which will all be taxable. Presto, no more retirement account. This is not the way to leverage your wealth and keep it building for and by your heirs. However, under the Pension Protection

Act, as of 2007 nonspouse beneficiaries can transfer inherited company plan funds to properly titled inherited IRAs maintaining the tax deferral over their lifetime. As far as federal creditor protection is concerned, virtually all IRAs are protected from bankruptcy (not all judgments, only bankruptcy) under the recent Bankruptcy Act, and many states now protect IRAs too—another reason to stay with the IRA. To find out if your state is one of them, ask your estate-planning attorney or expert financial advisor.

What's In It for Me?

You will have all the facts at hand to make the best—and safest—decision possible regarding the rollover or lump-sum distribution of your company plan retirement funds. You won't have to worry about missing any possible tax breaks or wonder whether your funds will indeed get where they're supposed to go (and I don't just mean to your named beneficiaries) when they leave the nest, but to their actual transfer destination. This last concern may strike you as a bit far-fetched—after all, in our age of computerization how could a check as sizable as a rollover or lump sum distribution NOT safely arrive where it's to be transferred? Well, read on, MacDuff.

Ask Ed . . .

Q: Part of my plan balance is after-tax funds. Can these funds be rolled over to an IRA? And, after that, be converted to a Roth IRA tax-free?

A: Yes to the first part of your question—the Economic Growth and Tax Relief Reconciliation Act of 2001 (known as "EGTRRA") does allow that. But no to the second part, at least until 2008, when that will change. But as of this writing, you cannot just convert the tax-free funds and pay no tax at all, unless you have no IRA funds even in other accounts. If you do, then you will have to factor those funds in. This will result in some of the converted funds being taxable—the so-called pro-rata rule. You see, when an IRA contains both after-tax and taxable funds, then each dollar withdrawn from the IRA will contain a tax-free and taxable percentage. That percentage is based on the percentage of after-tax funds to the entire balance in all your IRAs. Let's say you rolled over $50,000 of after-tax funds from your 401(k) to your IRA. There was $450,000 in your IRA and now with this additional $50,000 of after-tax funds, your total IRA balance is $500,000. If you now want to withdraw $50,000 and convert those funds to a Roth IRA, you will still pay tax on $45,000, and the other 10 percent, the $5,000, will be tax-free. The $50,000 of after-tax funds now in your IRA is 10 percent of the total $500,000 IRA balance, so each dollar withdrawn from your IRA will be 10 percent tax-free and 90 percent taxable. If you withdraw the entire $500,000, then all of the $50,000 will be tax-free (since that is 10 percent of the total IRA balance) and the other $450,000 will be taxable. Can you roll that $50,000 of after-tax money into a separate IRA (with no other money in it) and then withdraw tax-free? The answer is still no. Once after-tax funds are rolled into an IRA, they can only be withdrawn under the pro-rata rule where each dollar withdrawn is part taxable and part tax-free based on the percentage of after-tax money in the account. However, beginning in 2008, things will change, and you will be able to roll funds directly from a company plan to a Roth IRA. If your company issues a separate check for your after-tax funds, you can roll the after-tax funds only into a Roth IRA and pay no tax on the conversion.

What If I Don't?

Whenever distributed funds come out of your retirement account, you should follow the money (as the message of Watergate goes) to make sure it arrives at its destination intact. This may sound simple, but many of these transactions end up in the wrong place. And when the error is discovered (typically at tax time), it is often too late to do anything to correct it. You might just as well have signed those funds over to the IRS. All your accountant may be able to say to you at this point is, "Well, at least I do have *some* good news. I saved a fortune on my car insurance by switching to GEICO."

One situation was brought to my attention where the bank rolled more than $200,000 from an account owner's IRA into someone else's account, and the error was not discovered until five years later. The challenge became how to get those funds back into the right account, which might not even be possible at that point. By the way, in case you are wondering how rich a person must be not to miss a sudden drop of $200,000 in his IRA, the answer is—not rich at all. It turns out that for some still-unknown explanation—either a 1099-R form on the erroneous distribution was not sent to the IRA owner, or, like the funds themselves, it went to the wrong account—no red flag went up. Also, you will recall that 2000, the year this mistake occurred, was a year when most people invested in the market saw their portfolios plunge (the so-called "dot.com collapse"). When the owner of the account saw the sudden drop in the value of his holdings on his statement, he simply assumed he'd gotten killed on paper like everyone else in the market and didn't say anything about it to his accountant or custodian until he wanted to start taking distributions and wondered where most of his nest egg went!

Botched rollovers are so prevalent that more than 300 Private Letter Rulings (PLRs)—requests to the IRS from plan owners requesting relief from a botched distribution—have been issued by the IRS in recent years. In the majority of such cases, the cause of the problem was financial advisor error or a mistake made by the financial institution either in providing proper guidance or by moving the money to a taxable account instead of an IRA. In these cases, the IRS granted the victims relief. But a PLR is an expensive process and it can take nine months or more to get an answer—with no guarantee the answer will be a favorable one. Do you want to take that chance? This is YOUR life savings we're talking about.

What else could happen if you ignore this checklist? You will never know until it's too late if you made the right distribution decisions. You will never know until it's too late if you left any big tax breaks on the table simply because you did not know you were entitled to them. You will never know until it's too late that you are paying a lot more tax on the distribution of your tax-deferred funds than you probably should be. Are all of these not reasons enough?

Ask Ed . . .

Q: How best can I avoid a rollover horror story like those mentioned?

A: Easy. When moving money, don't do a *literal* rollover (where the money is issued to you and thus temporarily in your possession until you put it in an IRA or other plan). Do a trustee-to-trustee transfer where the funds move *directly* from your 401(k) or other plan into an IRA or other plan without touching your sticky little fingers, and thus becoming vulnerable to the Taxman. The rollover process has three problems. The first is the 60-day rule, which gives you just 60 days from the date you receive the distribution to roll it into another plan. That deadline comes very quickly and people often miss it. The second problem is the once-a-year rollover limitation rule, which prohibits you from doing more than one rollover every twelve months. Why should you care about this? Let's say you have $500,000 in your IRA at Mutual Fund A and you roll $1,000 of that to another IRA at Bank B. You must then wait at least a year before you can roll over any of the remaining $499,000 from your IRA at Mutual Fund A. And you also must wait a year before you can roll the $1,000 in Bank B over to another IRA. And the final problem with a rollover distribution is that it may be subject to a mandatory 20 percent withholding tax if it comes from a company plan. A trustee-to-trustee transfer avoids all these issues. The 60-day rule does not kick in since the money transfers directly. There is no limit on the number of trustee-to-trustee transfers you can do in a year. And there is no 20 percent mandatory withholding tax.

Instructions

Even if you have made a decision about how you want your money distributed, go through each item in this checklist, ticking off those that apply to you; then prioritize them 1, 2, 3 and so forth according to which applicable item is most important to you (1 being most important and 3 being of lesser importance). By going through the entire checklist and rating your priorities, you will expose any conflicts or potential conflicts in your decision-making, and be able to resolve the problem now.

For example, let's say you know you want to get those 401(k) funds into a Roth IRA so they can begin to grow tax-free. You also know that to do this you must first roll those funds into an IRA because you cannot convert from a 401(k) directly to a Roth IRA until the law changes in 2008. So, you mark the line after "ability to convert to a Roth IRA" under the "My reasons to do an IRA rollover" section with a 1, since that is important to you. But you might find other items offering other choices that may also rate a 1 to you now that you think about them, such as "qualifying for tax breaks on the distribution—10-year averaging and NUA" under "My reasons to do a lump-sum distribution." Thus, you find yourself torn because that's important to you, too. Now you have a conflict. By going over every applicable item and rating it, you will know what you will have to resolve ahead of time with your financial advisor, spouse, even your beneficiaries in order to make the right decision for you and your family.

After you make your decision, you will fill out the required paperwork at your employer to actually get the distribution. Here again, you should work closely with an expert financial advisor to avoid any slip-ups. Although many companies have people on staff in the Benefits Department to work on distributions, these people are usually not financial professionals and thus can easily make mistakes. Furthermore, while they may be nice people and very helpful, the bottom line is they work for your employer, not for you. That's why you want an expert financial advisor for guidance here. You want someone who works for *you* and is thus 100 percent accountable to you.

In the end, an IRA rollover will probably be your best choice, but there are so many factors to look at first, and you will find them all here. So, if your advisor—or any of those financial experts you encounter down at the local gym—tells you just to do an IRA rollover without considering anything else, you are getting the wrong advice.

A Word to the Wise

If you are going to roll over your 401(k) or other plan balance to an IRA and request a trustee-to-trustee transfer, but your Benefits Department does not do this and says it must issue you a check instead—with the check made out to *you*—then the IRS will consider you to be in receipt of the money, thereby triggering the three rollover problems I've mentioned. Insist that the check be made out instead to **"ABC Bank as trustee of Individual Retirement Account of (Your Name)."** This way, the check can only be cashed by ABC Bank to go into your IRA, thus qualifying as a direct transfer [IRS Regulation § 1.401(a)(31)-1].

MY ROLLOVER/LUMP-SUM DECISION CHECKLIST

MY NAME: ______________________ **DATE:** __________

MY ADVISOR'S NAME: ______________________ **PLAN #:** __________

Follow-ups should be added to the To Do Lists at the end of this checklist.

My distribution options available from a company plan are:

1. Rollover to an IRA
2. Lump-sum distribution
3. Move it to my new employer's plan
4. Leave it in my current plan.

1. My reasons to do a rollover to an IRA are:

- I don't need the money now ______
- Ability to create a stretch IRA for my beneficiaries. As of 2007 my beneficiaries will be able to directly transfer company plan funds to an inherited IRA, if the company plan allows ______
- Estate planning with an IRA is easier ______
- Wider choice of investment options ______
- Ability to convert to a Roth IRA. As of 2008, I will be able to convert plan funds directly to a Roth IRA ______
- Ability to invest in an annuity ______
- No withdrawal restrictions (after age 59½) ______
- Ability to consolidate accounts ______
- No withholding taxes on a trustee-to-trustee transfer ______
- Access to professional advice (IRA funds can be placed with a manager accountable to me) ______

Comments: ______________________

____

____

How to do a Rollover

2. Trustee-to-trustee transfer

- Unlimited number of transfers per year ______
- Exempt from 20 percent withholding (applies to transfers from employer plans only) ______
- No opportunity for me to use tax-deferred funds ______

3. 60-day rule

- I will have 60 days from the receipt of my funds to contribute them to an IRA or company plan without penalty ______
- When distributed from company plan, funds are subject to 20 percent withholding (the withheld amount can be rolled over but I must pay out of pocket) ______
- Funds not deposited within 60 days are considered income and subject to tax ______
- IRS now has the power to grant relief and allow completion of the rollover after the 60 days under "special circumstances" ______
- For IRAs only—one rollover per year per account ______
- Roth conversions—60-day rule applies, one per year rule does not apply ______
- 60-day IRA loans—funds are removed from the IRA for personal use and returned within 60 days. (IRS is reluctant to grant relief if the funds are not returned on time) ______

Comments: ______

______

______

______

4. Funds eligible for rollover: ______

- RMDs *No*
- Distributions that are part of a substantially equal payment plan *No*
- Hardship distributions *No*
- Distributions to nonspouse beneficiaries *No*
- After-tax funds:

  To an IRA *Yes*

  Between the same types of plans if the plan agreements allow (Must be a trustee-to-trustee transfer) *Yes*

  Between different types of plans if the plan agreements allow (Must be a trustee-to-trustee transfer) *Yes*
- The same property received—i.e. if I receive cash, I must roll over cash; if I receive ABC stock, I must roll over ABC stock—except for a distribution from a company plan, where I can sell the asset received and roll over the cash from the sale *Yes*

- Funds from plans of other countries—e.g. assets in a Canadian plan cannot be rolled over to a US plan — *No*

Comments: ______________________________

____

____

____

____

The lump-sum distribution

5. My reasons to do a lump-sum distribution are:

- I need the money now. ______
- I will qualify for tax breaks on the distribution (i.e., NUA and 10-year averaging, see The Tax Breaks for Lump-Sum Distributions Checklist—Section IV, part 7). ______
- My tax bracket is lower now than it will be in retirement when I start taking withdrawals and paying tax on them. ______
- No future taxes will be due (they are paid at the time of distribution). ______
- Source of liquidity for estate planning ______

Comments: ______________________________

____

____

____

6. Qualifying as a lump-sum distribution:

- Entire balance(s) credited for all like plans of the employer must be distributed in the same tax year — *Yes*
- The distribution must take place after a triggering event: separation from service (except for self-employed individuals), attainment of age 59½, death, or disability (Disability is only for self-employed individuals) — *Yes*
- I have taken no other distributions from the plan between the triggering event and the lump-sum distribution unless they are in the same tax year as the lump-sum distribution — *Yes (I took no other distributions)*

7. **Distribution can be split between funds I keep and funds rolled over to an IRA or another company plan.** ______

Comments: ____________________

____

____

____

Leave in my company plan or move to my new employer's plan.

8. My reasons to leave my funds in my company plan are:

- I will be working again ______
- No taxes are due ______
- Federal creditor protection ______
- Loan provisions (may not apply to terminated or retired employees) ______
- Plan holds life insurance that cannot be transferred or replaced ______
- I can defer required distributions if still working and not a 5 percent owner of the business (see checklist this section, Part 5) ______
- I am exempt from 10 percent early-distribution penalty if I was at least age 55 when I separated from service ______

Comments: ____________________

____

____

____

Follow-Up

My To Do List	Date Completed
1	
2	
3	
4	
5	

6 ______________________________

7 ______________________________

8 ______________________________

9 ______________________________

10 ______________________________

______________________________ ______________

My Signature Date

Section III

THE ACCOUNT BENEFICIARY'S CARE SOLUTION

"A son can bear with composure the death of his father,
but the loss of his inheritance might drive him to despair."

—Niccolo Machiavelli (1469–1527)

Even if the person you have inherited or will be inheriting from does everything correctly to enable you to inherit with all stretch and other tax opportunities intact, it can all be for nothing if you make a mistake on your end by not knowing what to do *when* you inherit. So, this section tackles all the critical items all types of beneficiaries must take care of and do (or not do) in order to inherit the maximum amount possible and keep their inheritance growing tax-deferred (or even tax-free) for as long as the law allows. In other words, for beneficiaries, this section can spell the difference between Uncle Sam's beating you out as the biggest beneficiary of all.

When it comes to company retirement plans and IRAs, beneficiaries are divided into two distinct camps. No, it's not good beneficiaries and evil beneficiaries (that's the theme of an earlier work about two well-known beneficiaries named Cain and Abel). The types I am referring to are beneficiaries who are spouses and beneficiaries who are nonspouses. There are distinct tax law differences in the ways these two beneficiaries can inherit retirement plans.

I thought the difference between a nonspouse beneficiary and a spouse beneficiary was obvious until I received the following question from a client a few years ago: "Dear Ed," she wrote, "I am the benefi-

A Word to the Wise

If your benefactor has not kept you in the loop, and it's not too late to alert him to some of the things he can and should do for your benefit when you inherit, this section will tip you off to those key opportunities to grab and pitfalls to avoid—because when you inherit it may be too late to do anything about them. Once you have inherited and assumed legal ownership as a beneficiary of the account(s), thereafter **you** are treated as the owner (with some exceptions) and you will use Section II (for account owners) to plan opportunities for your own beneficiaries.

ciary of my dad's IRA, but I am also married. Am I a spouse beneficiary or a nonspouse beneficiary?" Signed Susan Confused.

"Dear Susan," I wrote back. "You are a nonspouse beneficiary, even though, yes indeed, you are someone's spouse."

The type of beneficiary you are is based on your relationship with the *deceased owner* of the account you have inherited. If you were married to him or her, then you are a spouse beneficiary (even though you are now a widow or widower and no longer married). If you are not the widow or widower of the deceased owner and you inherit, then you are a nonspouse beneficiary (even though you may be someone else's spouse). Got it?

In addition, nonspouse beneficiaries don't always have to be people. An estate, a charity, or a trust that inherits is also a nonspouse beneficiary.

So, this section offers different checklists of what to do when you inherit, depending upon which type of beneficiary you are. It also provides a third checklist for multiple beneficiaries that covers a very common inheritance situation—where an IRA, for example, is left to two children, or to three grandchildren, or to a child and a spouse, or any other combination of multiple (or multiple types) of beneficiaries.

Part 1

THE NONSPOUSE BENEFICIARY'S (AN INDIVIDUAL) CHECKLIST

For a child, grandchild, relative, family friend, or other individual who inherits

What It Does

If you are a living, breathing (unlike a charity or trust) nonspouse beneficiary of an IRA or company plan (or will be), this checklist is for you. It shows you everything you must do to inherit an IRA or company plan correctly. By *correctly,* I mean in order to maximize the tax deferral of the inherited account for as long as legally possible and to be aware and able to take advantage of every possible tax benefit available to you that has been set up for you in the bequest.

This checklist covers IRAs, Roth IRAs, 401(k)s, 403(b)s, 457 plans, and all other types of "inherited accounts," a term that in tax lingo means an account that is inherited by someone (or something) other than a spouse. What's the distinction? When a spouse inherits, he or she can do a rollover or a trustee-to-trustee transfer, and from that point the account is treated as his or her own, not as an inherited one. To add to the confusion, if a spouse is one of several beneficiaries and the account is not split by 12/31 of the year after the account owner's death (the spouse is still one of several beneficiaries) then he or she is considered to be a nonspouse beneficiary. In such a circumstance, this Nonspouse Beneficiary's Checklist is what to use.

In addition, it is common for nonspouse beneficiaries to inherit several different types of retirement plans from one person—for example, your dad could leave you a 401(k) and an IRA—so you'll need to know your distribution options for each plan. They are probably very different. This checklist provides an easy-to-use chart that lays out in one page ALL of the distribution options available to you as a nonspouse beneficiary of the human type. (Charities or trusts get their own separate checklists in this section.)

Everything covered here applies equally to nonspouse beneficiaries of Roth IRAs, as well. The only difference is that distributions from inherited Roth IRAs will generally be income tax-free.

Ask Ed . . .

Q: I just inherited an IRA from my mom, but I am under 59½ years old. Will I pay a penalty on any distributions I take now?

A: No. The 10 percent penalty on early withdrawals before age 59½ ***NEVER*** applies to a beneficiary.

What's In It for Me?

Using this checklist to make all the right moves with your newly inherited account(s) will ensure that you maximize your inherited dollars for the rest of your life by not missing out on any tax benefits to which you are entitled. This is your inheritance, but because it is a retirement account—unlike, say, an antique automobile—it can provide a lifetime legacy of *income* to you and your own heirs. What you make of this incredible opportunity is up to you, but everything you will need to seize that opportunity is here for you.

Ask Ed . . .

Q: I inherited retirement accounts from two different people. Can I combine them into one inherited IRA?

A: No. Each inherited account must be kept separate and in the name of the deceased original owner but with your social security number on it. This does not mean it is not your money. It means that the account must always be recognized as an inherited one—but you still control the distributions and investments the same as on any accounts you possess in your own name. However, you can combine two or more inherited accounts that you inherited from the *same* person into one IRA. For example, if you inherited two accounts from your brother, you can combine those into one inherited IRA that is maintained in his name but under your social security number.

What If I Don't?

You'll blow your inheritance. The money will go quickly to Uncle Sam, leaving you with little more than a memory of what could have been. This is a common occurrence because most beneficiaries do not realize the long-term potential of an inherited account such as an IRA. It is the goose that keeps laying the golden egg, and this is your one chance to have it.

You will see many items in this checklist that may strike you as seeming unimportant or even ridiculous. But I assure you they are not. Missing any one of them could cause your golden goose to break its neck.

For example, something as simple as titling the inherited account in your own name is considered a complete distribution subject to tax. What happens then? The entire IRA balance becomes taxable to you, and the stretch opportunity is over. You'll have to withdraw the funds and pay the tax all in one year, giving you a large amount of added income that not only may bump you into a higher tax bracket that year, but also prompt other tax increases that may result in your giving more money to the IRS than you would have had to. You see, when you pile on a lot of income in a year, you start to exceed certain income limitations that cause you to lose exemptions for your family and deductions based on a percentage of your income. A loss of tax deductions is the same as a tax increase.

Ask Ed . . .

Q: How do I find out how long (for how many years) I can stretch the IRA I inherited and calculate my Required Minimum Distributions?

A: You would look up your age as of your birthday in the year *after* your benefactor's death in the IRS Single Life Expectancy Table (Appendix I) and note the life-expectancy factor that corresponds to your age. That is your stretch period. For example, if you turned age 50 in 2006 when the person you inherited the account from died, you will be 51 in 2007 (the year after the account owner died) with a life expectancy—stretch period—of 33.3 years. Your first RMD is due for 2007. To determine the amount, divide the account balance at the end of 2006 by 33.3. The 2007 RMD must be taken by the end of 2007. For each succeeding year you cannot go back to the Table to calculate your RMD for that year—just reduce the life expectancy factor by one each time—so that in 2008, you'll use 32.3, then in 2009 you'll use 31.3 and so on. The RMD is what it says—the *minimum* you must take. You can always withdraw more than that if you wish, but you will owe tax on whatever you withdraw. Each year's RMD is due by the end of that year.

A financial advisor shared this story with me. A client of his died naming a son the beneficiary of a $560,000 IRA. The son did not like the conservative investments that this advisor and his late father had in the IRA, and basically said, "I am taking the money and moving it to an account where I can do my own trading and investments." The son withdrew the $560,000 and went to move it to a discount broker, but as soon as he took the check to the broker's company, he was told that they could not open an inherited IRA for him. When he asked why, the company told him the bad news. The minute he took the distribution from the inherited IRA, the entire $560,000 became taxable, and the error could not be corrected. The son did not know that a nonspouse beneficiary cannot do a rollover.

His dad might have spent a lifetime conservatively investing this money to grow it to $560,000, but his son wiped it out in seconds—and furthermore had to add the $560,000 distribution to his own income for the year, putting him in the highest tax bracket and causing all of his other income for that year to be taxed at higher rates, not to mention losing many deductions and exemptions because his income was now too high.

So, here's the message: Messing up a single step in the inheriting of a retirement account can result in very bad news all around. But

Ask Ed . . .

Q: My mom died late in the year and did not take her RMD for the year when she died. What happens now? Who takes her year of death distribution or is she exempt since she died?

A: Death gets you out of pretty much everything under the tax code, but not RMDs. You, as the beneficiary, must take her year of death RMD, and you also must pay tax on the distribution on your own tax return. The following year, you will start taking RMDs based on your own life expectancy.

you can avoid that bad news by putting this checklist to good use and not missing a beat.

Instructions

This checklist takes you through every critical step in the inheriting-an-account process, beginning with the most important step of all, "Touch Nothing!" Do not move or touch a red cent of that money until you have carefully reviewed all the points in this checklist relevant to your situation, and discussed them with your *expert* financial advisor (Section V). This is an area where just any advisor won't do. Even the advisor your parent or whomever you inherited from used may not be up to the task—because most financial advisors are not trained in what to do with a client's retirement account *after* the client dies. A mistake made by the untrained can end your inherited account; it happens all the time.

It is critical that the inherited account be set up and titled correctly. It is also important that you immediately name your own beneficiary so that if you die while there are still funds remaining in the inherited account—an IRA, for example—your children will be able

Ask Ed . . .

Q: Can I disclaim an inherited account so that it will go to my children?

A: Once you disclaim (refuse) an inherited account, you have no say where it goes. It will go to the contingent beneficiary named by the deceased original owner of the account. Of course, if the deceased owner named your children as contingent beneficiaries, then they will inherit the account you have disclaimed—but not on your say-so. (See The Disclaimer Planning Checklist, Section IV, Part 3.)

to continue the stretch you would have been entitled to had you lived (assuming, of course, the IRA custodial agreement [Section II, Part 2] allows that, which hopefully it will because your benefactor has made sure it's there).

If you need funds—to pay estate taxes, for example—after the death of the person you inherited from, and you have not yet had a chance to go through this checklist, then see if it is at all possible to take the money you need from some other asset you may have inherited. The minute you use any inherited retirement account funds, even if it is to pay estate taxes, you will first have to pay income tax on the amount you withdraw and you'll be quickly eroding your inherited funds. Use these funds last. They are too valuable.

THE NONSPOUSE BENEFICIARY'S (AN INDIVIDUAL) CHECKLIST

MY NAME: ______________________ **DATE:** __________

MY ADVISOR'S NAME: ______________________ **PLAN #:** __________

Follow-ups should be added to the To Do lists at the end of this checklist.

1. I will touch nothing! __________

- I have obtained or will obtain copies of the death certificate (the plan custodian will probably ask for a copy). __________
- I have copies of the beneficiary form. __________
- I have determined the type of retirement account—traditional IRA (including SEP and SIMPLE IRAs), Roth IRA, or company plan (401(k), 403(b), 457 plan), etc.—I am or will be inheriting. __________ Type of plan(s)
- I know that I can make no contributions to the account (nonspouse beneficiaries are prohibited from making contributions to inherited accounts). __________

2. The plan custodian's copy of the beneficiary form names as beneficiary:

- Primary (if spouse is primary beneficiary and elects to roll over account to her own, he/she should go to checklist in Part 2 of this section) __________
  - Designated or nondesignated (a designated beneficiary is an *individual;* a non-designated beneficiary is an *entity,* such as a charity) __________
- Contingent __________
  - Designated or nondesignated __________

3. The distribution options allowed by the plan custodian are:

- Did the account owner die before or after the Required Beginning Date (RBD) for his or her required distributions? (For definition of RBD, see Section II, Part 5.) __________
- The stretch is/is not allowed? __________
- 5-year rule only? __________
- Other? __________

4. I have determined whether to disclaim the account (Checklist Section IV, Part 3). __________

5. If the primary beneficiary is a nondesignated beneficiary, the two payout options are:

- Death before the RBD, 5-year payout option only. Account must be emptied by the end of the fifth year after the account owner's death; there are no required annual distributions. __________
- Death after the RBD, distributions can be stretched over the remaining life expectancy of the account owner. (See chart after item 13) __________

6. As primary beneficiary I should do the following if not disclaiming:

- Change the social security number on the account to my own social security number. __________
- Change the account title to include my name as well as the name of the deceased owner, which must remain in the account title—i.e., John Smith, (deceased, date of death) IRA fbo Charles Smith. __________
- I have named a successor beneficiary (if the account document allows). __________
  —Owner: uses his own age
  —He names a beneficiary: uses her own age
  —She names a successor beneficiary: uses beneficiary's age

7. If the account owner died after his/her RBD, was the RMD satisfied for the year of death? (Does not apply for a Roth IRA.) __________

- If no, have the balance of the account owner's required distribution distributed to me as beneficiary by 12/31 of the year of the account owner's death (distribution is calculated as though the owner were alive for the entire year). I can still disclaim even after I take the year-of-death RMD. __________

8. Pay estate taxes from other assets, not from the inherited account if possible. __________

9. When changing plan providers, I know to move funds via direct transfer only (trustee-to-trustee transfer) because as a nonspouse beneficiary I *cannot* do a rollover, only a direct transfer. __________

Comments: ____

____

____

____

____

10. For multiple beneficiaries—see The Multiple Beneficiaries' Checklist in Part 3 of this section. ______

11. For a trust beneficiary—see The Naming a Trust-as-Beneficiary Checklist in Part 2 of Section IV. ______

12. For tax breaks—see The Tax Breaks for Beneficiaries Checklist in Part 5 of this section. ______

Comments: ____

____

____

____

____

13. I must take my first RMD by 12/31 of the year after the original owner's death. (10 percent early-distribution penalty does not apply to distributions to beneficiaries.) ______

- Determine age to use for stretch payouts (see chart following this item): ______
- Look up life expectancy factor from Single Life Expectancy Table (Appendix I). It is: ______
- Use the balance in the decedent's account as of 12/31 of the year of death. If the account was split after that, use only the proportionate share of the balance applicable to each beneficiary. ______
- Divide the balance determined above by my life-expectancy factor to determine my RMDs. ______
- If I die after the original owner's death but before 9/30 of year after the owner's death, my age is used for calculating of RMDs going to my successor beneficiary (See The Successor Beneficiary's Checklist in this section, Part 4). ______

The following is a synopsis of options allowed by the IRS final-distribution regulations. All distribution options are subject to the terms of the custodian's agreement in effect at the time of the distribution. The 10 percent early-distribution penalty never applies to beneficiaries taking distributions. All beneficiaries generally have the option of taking a lump-sum distribution and paying income tax on the distribution or choosing to use the 5-year rule. Roth IRA beneficiaries use the Owner Dies Before RBD rules.

	Account Owner Dies Before RBD	Account Owner Dies After RBD
Nonspouse, Designated Beneficiary	Distributions based on the life expectancy of the beneficiary Use **Single Life Expectancy Table,** look up attained age in the year after account owner's death to get factor, factor is **reduced by one in each subsequent year**	Distributions based on life expectancy of the **younger of** the account owner or the beneficiary Use **Single Life Expectancy Table,** look up attained age in the year after account owner's death to get factor, factor is **reduced by one in each subsequent year**
Nondesignated Beneficiary (Charity, Estate or Non-Qualifying Trust)	**5-year rule** No annual required distributions but account must be emptied by the end of the fifth year after the year of the account owner's death	Distributions based on the life expectancy of the **deceased account owner** Use **Single Life Expectancy Table,** look up attained age account owner would have been in the year of death to get factor, factor is **reduced by one in each subsequent year**

14. I know there is a 50 percent penalty on any required distribution that is not taken. __________

15. My required distributions *cannot* be made from any other inherited retirement account unless it is inherited from the same person and is the same type of account (i.e., 2 IRAs inherited from Great-aunt Matilda). __________

16. If I am the nonspouse beneficiary of a Roth IRA inherited in the 5-year period after the account owner established the account, I may be subject to income tax. __________

Comments: ______

______

______

Follow-Up

My To Do List | Date Completed

1 ______

2 ______

3 ______

4 ______

5 ______

6 ______

7 ______

8 ______

9 ______

10 ______

______ ______

My Signature | Date

Part 2

THE SPOUSE BENEFICIARY'S CHECKLIST

For an inheriting spouse who is the sole beneficiary

What It Does

Although I am not a chess player, I do know that in chess, the queen can do anything and go anywhere she pleases. She's downright intimidating. She can move, up, down, across, and even diagonally. She *owns* the chessboard.

When it comes to moving inherited retirement money around, a spouse beneficiary, whether male or female, is very much like that queen. A spouse beneficiary has more flexibility than a nonspouse beneficiary because she (or he) can do almost no wrong—and is usually bailed out by some provision in the tax rules if she (or he) does make some tactical blunder. To paraphrase Mel Brooks, "It's good to be the queen." This checklist shows why.

As most people do name their spouse as sole beneficiary of their assets, including retirement account funds, this checklist will apply to most beneficiaries. To avoid staying gender neutral and having to keep repeating the qualifiers she or he and her or him, I'll go with statistics, where the surviving spouse is typically female, and refer to the female gender.

Generally, when a spouse inherits she does a "spousal rollover" and elects to become the new owner of the inherited account rather than remaining a beneficiary. From that point, the IRS treats her as if she were the original owner of the account, and she follows the same RMD and penalty rules as any other original owner of an IRA or other plan. So, the spousal rollover is typically the best option for her.

Under some circumstances, though, she may want to remain a beneficiary for a time rather than do a spousal rollover right away. This might occur if she were younger than 59½ when she inherits the account and needs some of the funds in it to pay off debts or estate taxes. If she were to do a spousal rollover, then took distributions from the IRA before reaching age 59½, she would be subject to the 10 percent early withdrawal penalty, the same as any account owner. By remaining a beneficiary, however, she avoids the penalty because IRA and other plan beneficiaries are never subject to the 10 percent early withdrawal penalty (she will, of course, have to pay tax on any withdrawals). Then, when she reaches 59½, and the penalty is no longer an issue, she can still do the spousal rollover to her own IRA as there is no deadline for a spousal rollover and choosing to remain a beneficiary does not stop her from changing her mind later because she is the queen and can do as she pleases.

Ask Ed . . .

Q: If I do the spousal rollover and become the IRA owner, can I later change my mind and go back to being a beneficiary?

A: No. That is one of the few moves the queen cannot make on this particular chessboard. Once you take ownership of the account, it is, in all respects, yours, so you cannot go back and make it a beneficiary account again.

Well, almost as she pleases. Even the queen has to address some issues in making her spousal rollover vs. remain a beneficiary decision—and this checklist takes her through them.

What's In It for Me?

By designating a spouse as beneficiary of his retirement funds, the original owner (see Section I) has set the account up to provide the best opportunities for growth and longevity. He has also made sure that his grieving (one assumes) spouse—YOU—is not suddenly overwhelmed with having to make a slew of choices involving the inheritance at a very emotional and vulnerable time. Therefore, much advance planning and spadework has already been done for you. However, if your deceased husband did not take advantage of Section I to do much advance planning on your behalf, you can still seize the advantage with this checklist of your own.

Ask Ed . . .

Q: Can I contribute to an IRA for my deceased spouse? He would have qualified had he lived (he was still working).

A: No. The IRS ruled many years ago that you couldn't make an IRA or any other plan contribution for a deceased person even if that person would have qualified to make a contribution had he or she lived. You can argue with the IRS's logic on many things, but not here. It reasoned in its ruling that it saw no point in funding a retirement account for a dead person since that person is clearly retired . . . for good.

What If I Don't?

For the most part, all you have to do as a spouse beneficiary to take ownership of an inherited account is a spousal rollover—and even if you forget or miss out on doing that right away, you can always do it later on. So, it's hard for you as a spouse beneficiary to get hit with a monkey wrench even if you do mess up. But your own beneficiaries will get hit with a monkey wrench if you don't follow this checklist—so if you care about *their* future, that's why this checklist is here.

For example, let's say you mess up by not naming a beneficiary of your own as soon as you inherit, which the checklist urges. If you never get around to this step or die prematurely, the likelihood is the fund will go to your estate, and your children and grandchildren may lose out on the stretch option, or even be disinherited. Furthermore, if you remarry, the fund might go to your new spouse instead of your children and grandchildren as I'm sure your late first husband and you would have preferred. Even worse, the fund might wind up going to your new spouse's kids and grandkids, shutting out yours and your first husband's altogether.

So, if not for yourself, use this checklist for the benefit of your heirs.

Ask Ed . . .

Q: My spouse died with all his money in a 401(k). Can I roll that over to my IRA, even though he did not have his funds in an IRA when he died?

A: Yes. As a spouse, you can roll over 401(k) or other plan balances to your own IRA. The IRS has even ruled that a spouse beneficiary can roll a deceased spouse's 401(k) plan into an inherited IRA in the name of the deceased so that the surviving spouse can choose to remain a beneficiary instead of doing a rollover.

Instructions

Use this checklist to decide the best way for you, as a spouse beneficiary, to inherit—do a spousal rollover or elect to remain a beneficiary, and make other important choices. You have all the options for making your decisions here, but remember, because you are the spouse, you can change your decisions later on. Once you make a decision, be sure to follow the distribution rules that apply to the option you have chosen.

For example, the IRS likes the spouse beneficiary so much that it doesn't want her to have to share her inheritance. That is why there are different rules for when the spouse is the sole beneficiary (no sharing) and when the spouse is one of several beneficiaries (sharing the inherited account with co-beneficiaries—see checklist this section, Part 3). The spouse who is the sole beneficiary has the most flexibility and can take advantage of the distribution benefits available to her. But when a spouse is not the sole beneficiary, she lowers her status to that of a pawn, and is relegated to following the distribution rules that apply to other lowly nonspouse beneficiaries. The difference, though, is that she is usually able to remove her share and go back to being the sole beneficiary of her separate share and thus resume her royal status, regaining all the benefits of being a sole beneficiary (see The Multiple Beneficiaries' Checklist in this section, Part 3).

Ask Ed . . .

Q: If I were 45 in the year my husband died and left me his account, what RMDs must I take if I choose to remain a beneficiary because I am under age 59½ and do not want to get hit with a 10 percent penalty on any withdrawals?

A: This depends on how old your spouse was when he died. Let's say he was the same age as you, 45. If you choose to remain a beneficiary you do not have to withdraw anything from the inherited account until twenty-five years from now when he would have turned 70½ (the age when he would have to start taking his RMDs). So, any withdrawals you make during those twenty-five years are voluntary on your part, not required. But let's assume he was 75 when he died and you are 45. In this case, since he had already reached age 70½ when he died, you must begin taking RMDs in the first required distribution year (the year after his death). You will look up the life-expectancy factor in the Single Life Table [see Appendix I) for a 46-year-old (37.9 years), and then divide the account balance as of December 31 of the prior year by 37.9 to calculate your first-year RMD as spouse beneficiary. This distribution is subject to income tax, but no penalty because you have chosen to remain a beneficiary as opposed to taking ownership of the account with a spousal rollover. To calculate the next year's RMD as a beneficiary, see the chart following item 11 in the checklist.

THE SPOUSE BENEFICIARY'S CHECKLIST

MY NAME: ______________________ **DATE:** __________

MY ADVISOR'S NAME: ______________________ **PLAN #:** __________

Follow-ups should be added to the To Do lists at the end of this checklist.

1. I will touch nothing! __________

- I have obtained or will obtain copies of the death certificate (the plan custodian will probably ask me for a copy). __________
- I have found copies of the beneficiary form. __________
- I have, or will, inherit through a trust or a will. __________
  - If I am the sole beneficiary of the trust or will and entitled to the entire account, I may be able to do a rollover based on numerous Private Letter Rulings and be treated as a spouse. __________
  - If I am not the sole beneficiary and I choose to remain a beneficiary, I will be treated as a nonspouse beneficiary if I am one of multiple beneficiaries and the account is not timely split (see The Nonspouse Beneficiary's Checklist in Part 1 of this section). __________
- I have determined the type of retirement account(s) I have inherited or will be inheriting—traditional IRA (including SEP and SIMPLE IRAs), Roth IRA, or company plan (401(k), 403(b), 457 plan), etc. __________ Type of plan(s)
- Did the deceased (original owner spouse) die before or after his Required Beginning Date for taking Required Minimum Distributions (for definitions of these terms, see The RMD Calculations Checklist in Part 5 of Section II). __________
- I will make no contributions to the account (if I do, I will be deemed to be treating the account as my own). __________

2. The distribution options available to me as a spouse beneficiary are:

- Spousal rollover __________
- Treat as my own account __________
- Elect to "remain a beneficiary" __________
- 5-year rule only __________
- Lump-sum distribution __________

Comments: ______________________________

____

____

____

____

3. Determine if I should disclaim. (If yes, see The Disclaimer Planning Checklist in Section IV, Part 3.) ______

4. If not disclaiming, I must change the social security number on the account to my own social security number and name successor beneficiaries as soon as possible, even if I am planning on doing a spousal rollover. ______

5. If the original owner spouse died after his RBD, was the distribution satisfied for the year of death? (Does not apply for a Roth IRA.) ______

- If not, take the balance of the deceased owner's required distribution (if any) by 12/31 of the year of death (distribution is calculated as though the deceased were alive for the entire year, see Section II, Part 5). ______

6. Pay estate taxes from other assets, not from the inherited account if possible. ______

Comments: ______________________________

____

____

____

____

____

7. If I am not the only beneficiary, see The Multiple Beneficiaries' Checklist in this section, Part 3. ______

8. Am I entitled to any tax breaks? (See The Tax Breaks for Beneficiaries Checklist in this section, Part 5.) If so, they are: ______

Comments: ____

____

____

____

____

____

9. If I treat the account as my own or if I do a spousal rollover, I become the new owner and I can:

- Make contributions to the account. ______
- Have Required Minimum Distributions made to me as the account owner. (See the chart following item 11 and the My RMD Calculations Checklist, Section II, Part 5.) ______

10. If I do *not* do a spousal rollover but elect to remain a beneficiary (see chart following item 11 for distribution options if I die with a balance remaining in the account), I can:

- Take distributions before age 59½ with no 10 percent early distribution penalty (penalty does not apply to beneficiaries). (I should do a spousal rollover after attaining age 59½.) ______
- Do a spousal rollover at any time after inheriting the account. ______

11. As spouse beneficiary I must take an RMD in the year the deceased owner would have been 70½. (See chart following this item.)

- Determine the age I must use for calculating my RMDs: ______
- Use that age to look up my life expectancy factor from appropriate table (See chart following this Item and refer to appropriate appendix). ______
- Find the balance in the account as of 12/31 of the prior year and divide that by my life-expectancy factor. (For all subsequent years I will use the same method.) ______

12. I know there is a 50 percent penalty on any required distribution not taken. ______

13. **I know that required distributions from an account inherited from my spouse *cannot* be satisfied by distributions made to me from any other inherited account unless it came from my spouse and is the same type of inherited account (e.g., 2 IRAs or 2 Roth IRAs.)** ________

The following is a synopsis of options allowed by the IRS's final distribution regulations. All distribution options are subject to the terms of the plan agreement in effect at the time of the distribution. The 10 percent early distribution penalty never applies to beneficiaries taking distributions. All beneficiaries generally have the option of taking a lump-sum distribution and paying income tax on the distribution or choosing to use the 5-year rule. Roth IRA beneficiaries use the Owner Dies Before RBD rules. A spouse is considered the sole beneficiary of the plan when he or she is the sole designated primary beneficiary on the account as of 12/31 of the year after the original account owner's death.

Spouse as Sole Beneficiary

	ACCOUNT OWNER DIES BEFORE RBD	ACCOUNT OWNER DIES AFTER RBD
Remain as Beneficiary	I use the **Single Life Expectancy Table** (Appendix I) and look up my attained age **each year** a distribution is required (recalculation) to get the life expectancy factor	
	I can delay taking my distributions until account owner would have been 70½	I must take my first distribution by 12/31 of the year after the account owner's death
	I am not subject to the 10 percent early distribution penalty	I am not subject to the 10 percent early distribution penalty
Spousal Rollover	I take my first distribution at my RBD I use the **Uniform Lifetime Table** (Appendix II) and look up my attained age **each year** to get the life-expectancy factor	
Take Account as Own	I take my first distribution at my RBD I use the **Uniform Lifetime Table** (Appendix II) and look up my attained age **each year** to get the life-expectancy factor	

Spouse Is Not Sole Beneficiary

	ACCOUNT OWNER DIES BEFORE RBD	ACCOUNT OWNER DIES AFTER RBD
Remain as Beneficiary	I use the **Single Life Expectancy Table** (Appendix I) to look up attained age in the year after account owner's death to get factor; factor is **reduced by one in each subsequent year** I MUST take my first distribution by 12/31 of the year after the account owner's death I am not subject to the 10 percent early distribution penalty	

14. If I inherited a Roth IRA, I realize that distributions of earnings made to me within 5 years of the establishment of the account by my deceased spouse (original owner) may be subject to income tax. ______

Comments: ______________________________

____

____

Follow-Up

My To Do List	Date Completed
1	
2	
3	
4	
5	
6	
7	
8	
9	
10	

______________________________ ______________

My Signature Date

Part 3

THE MULTIPLE BENEFICIARIES' CHECKLIST

For spouse and nonspouse co-beneficiaries

What It Does

United we stand, divided . . . we are better off—as beneficiaries that is. If you are one of several co-beneficiaries of an inherited account, this checklist is for you.

When there are multiple beneficiaries of an inherited account, all

A Word to the Wise

Make sure your co-beneficiaries go through this checklist with you so that you will all understand what to do and how to do it (and when) if you mutually agree that you want to separate the shared inherited account. Then create the separate accounts as soon as possible after the inheritance with the help of an expert financial advisor (Section V) to ensure that everything goes smoothly.

must use the age of the *eldest* beneficiary for calculating their own RMDs. So what? Here's what: Let's say you are one of three people named as co-beneficiary of an IRA or other plan. If you are all very close in age, using the age of the eldest in taking RMDs may not be such a big deal. But what if you are 35 years old, and your co-beneficiaries are your 9-year-old niece and your 90-year-old aunt? According to the IRS's Single Life Expectancy Table (Appendix I), your life expectancy is 48.5 years, your niece's is 73.8 years, and your aunt's is 5.5 years. That means you are stuck with using the life expectancy of the eldest to calculate RMDs for all three of you, and the account's stretch and growth potential for the younger of you goes out the window because all the money in the account has to be withdrawn in 5.5 years.

The situation gets even worse if one of your co-beneficiaries is not a person but a charity or a trust, for example. Since neither is a living being, it has no life expectancy; thus, there is no stretch option at all for any of you.

These are situations you want to avoid as a co-beneficiary, and it can be done by creating what the tax rules call "separate accounts" so that each beneficiary can take RMDs based on his or her own age. This

Ask Ed . . .

Q: I inherited my dad's IRA with my mom. We are each named as 50–50 beneficiaries. Do I still get the stretch?

A: Yes, if you split the inherited account no later than the end of the year following the year of your dad's death. If your dad died in 2007, then you must split the account into separate inherited IRAs by December 31, 2008. But I would not wait that long. You should split up your shares as soon as possible after you inherit. Then both of you should each name successor beneficiaries immediately.

checklist is about how to do that so that each beneficiary can be treated as the *sole beneficiary* of his or her own share and thus maximize the stretch potential individually.

What's In It for Me?

If you are one of several co-beneficiaries of an inherited retirement account and don't want to be stuck with another co-beneficiary's life expectancy in taking your own RMDs, you can be rid of that obstacle for good by using the steps in this checklist to create your own separate account and increase your own payout period, thereby adding greater longevity to your account and maximizing its growth possibilities. Here's why: By extending the term of your lifetime payout, you can take lower RMDs each year, pay less tax each year on those lower RMDs, and build more money tax-deferred for you over your longer-term payout period term—all because the calculations you use will be based on your age alone, not the eldest among your co-beneficiaries.

Ask Ed . . .

Q: What if three children inherit a parent's 401(k)? Do the separate account rules apply here?

A: Yes, they apply the same as with an inherited IRA, but the difference is that the co-beneficiaries will probably not get the chance to use them because most 401(k) plans will just send the co-beneficiaries a lump-sum check subject to tax, thereby killing the need to create separate accounts because there won't be enough money left to stretch even if the option were offered, which is unlikely since few 401(k)s will allow one beneficiary to stretch, let alone two, three, or more.

What If I Don't?

You'll likely be stuck with someone else's life expectancy in determining your RMDs and end up giving more of your inheritance to Uncle Sam faster than you had to. Or, you may not even be able to seize the stretch opportunity in the first place if one of your co-beneficiaries lacks a pulse—is a trust, for example. In either case, you will wind up paying more tax, more quickly. This happens to many people because they are unaware that they can create their own separate inherited IRAs from the big one they've inherited mutually.

Ask Ed . . .

Q: If the original owner of the account dies before taking a RMD for the year and there are several co-beneficiaries, who takes the RMD for the deceased?

A: Each co-beneficiary takes a proportionate share. For example, if three children inherit a third each, then each would take one-third of the RMD the deceased owner would have had to take had he or she lived—and each beneficiary will pay the income tax on their one-third RMD on their own tax return. But the IRS doesn't care who takes the RMD as long as someone takes it. If one of the beneficiaries wants to cash out their share and the IRA has not been split yet, the distribution to the beneficiary that is cashing out can be used to satisfy the RMD and the other beneficiaries can wait until the following year before they have to take any distributions.

Instructions

The first thing you will want to do in this checklist is to identify your fellow co-beneficiaries and enlist their cooperation in separating ac-

A Word to the Wise

As I pointed out in Part 1 of this section, a nonspouse beneficiary cannot do a rollover, so if you are one of three nonspouse co-beneficiaries, separate accounts can only be set up by doing a trustee-to-trustee transfer, where you do not touch or withdraw the funds. Imagine, for example, that you and your two siblings inherited a $300,000 IRA from your mother and withdrew the $300,000 to deposit in your separate inherited accounts of $100,000 each. The result would be a tax on all $300,000 in one shot—and you would no longer need separate accounts because none of you will have an inherited account.

counts for your mutual benefit. Even most surviving spouses who squabble with their children or children who squabble with each other about everything will see the value in agreeing with each other here.

Make sure the account custodian (financial institution holding the fund) knows that you wish to create separate accounts from the one inherited—otherwise, the custodian might just cash all of you out. Although you have until the end of the year following the year of the original owner's death to create separate accounts, this is one reason why you shouldn't wait that long. Bad things can happen. And that's one of them.

If part of your planning involves a disclaimer (where you, or your co-beneficiaries, wish to refuse your respective share so that it can pass to the contingent beneficiaries), *do not set up the separate accounts until the disclaimers are completed* (see The Disclaimer Planning Checklist in Section IV, Part 3). Once you take possession, you can generally not disclaim anymore, and creating separate accounts could be deemed as taking possession.

The biggest issue presented in separating accounts is when there are any nondesignated beneficiaries—those nonhuman beneficiaries I've mentioned called charities, trusts or estates—that are co-beneficiaries with you. So as not to turn you into a nondesig-

Ask Ed . . .

Q: If I plan to disclaim my share (so it can pass to my children) but there are other co-beneficiaries on the account with me, how do I make sure that my share goes to my children and not to my siblings?

A: The original owner of the account will have to have planned to pass the account to his or her named beneficiaries "per stirpes" so that when you as one of those beneficiaries disclaim, your share goes to your children, not your siblings. You cannot put your children in as contingent beneficiaries after you inherit. So, if you intend to disclaim but don't know whether the account is set up for you to do that once you inherit, alert the account owner now because this is an item he or she must set up for you.

Q: What happens if the inherited account is not split by the deadline? Can it be split later?

A: There is no time limit for splitting up an inherited account, but if it is not split by the deadline (the end of the year following the year of the original owner's death), then the separate account treatment option will expire. This means that while you can still physically separate accounts after the deadline, the chief advantage of doing so is lost because you will forever be stuck with having to use the age of the eldest co-beneficiary for calculating your RMDs.

nated beneficiary on paper as well, they must be removed from the inherited account by September 30 of the year following the year of the original owner's death. By removed I don't mean having them "whacked." This is not *The Sopranos* (and besides, how do you *whack* a trust?). I mean having them removed as a co-beneficiary by splitting the account or cashing them out (paying out their share in full) BEFORE the September 30 deadline.

THE MULTIPLE BENEFICIARIES' CHECKLIST

MY NAME: ______________________ DATE: __________

MY ADVISOR'S NAME: ______________________ PLAN #: __________

Follow-ups should be added to the To Do lists at the end of this checklist.

1. Who are my named co-beneficiaries as listed on the beneficiary form?

____

- Are all my listed co-beneficiaries designated? (A designated beneficiary is an *individual* named on the beneficiary form not an entity, such as a charity.) __________
- If not, these are the nondesignated co-beneficiaries: __________

Comments: ______________________________

____

____

____

____

____

The period between the plan owner's death and 9/30 of the following year is called the "gap period." Designated beneficiaries, for RMD calculation purposes, are those named as of the date of death and who remain beneficiaries as of that 9/30 milestone.

2. I have evaluated my tax and income situation—and those of my designated co-beneficiaries—to determine if I should disclaim. (See the Disclaimer Planning Checklist in Section IV, Part 3.) __________

3. I know that all nondesignated beneficiaries' shares must be distributed before 9/30 of the year after the account owner's death. __________

4. As co-beneficiaries, we understand that if one of us dies during the gap period, our respective life expectancy will be used to calculate distributions to our successor beneficiary. __________

Comments: ______________________________

____

____

____

____

____

5. As co-beneficiaries of an inherited account that has not been split into separate accounts, if I/we wish to split them and use our respective individual life expectancies in calculating RMDs, this must be done by 12/31 of the year after the original owner's death. (And preferably earlier to simplify bookkeeping when making withdrawals and investment decisions.) ______

- Properly title the separate accounts to include the original owner's name with my/our own to avoid making the entire inherited account balance subject to income tax—i.e., "John Smith (deceased, date of death) IRA fbo Jane Smith" ______
- Assets can be moved into the new, properly titled inherited accounts by a trustee-to-trustee transfer only. A nonspouse beneficiary can NEVER do a rollover. ______
- Change the original owner's social security number on my separate account to my social security number. ______
- Name my successor beneficiaries (if the plan allows). ______
- See checklists in Parts I or 2 of this section for instructions on calculating my RMDs. ______

Comments: ______________________________

____

____

____

____

____

6. I understand that if there are multiple beneficiaries of a trust that is the beneficiary of an inherited account, there can be no separate accounts and all distributions will be calculated using the life expectancy of the eldest of the trust beneficiaries. ______

7. **I understand that if there are multiple beneficiaries, I/we can split accounts after the 12/31 deadline, but will be forced to continue using the life expectancy of the eldest for calculating required distributions even after the account is split.** ____________

Comments: ____

____

____

____

Follow-Up

My To Do List | Date Completed

1 ____

2 ____

3 ____

4 ____

5 ____

6 ____

7 ____

8 ____

9 ____

10 ____

____________________________ ____________

My Signature | Date

Part 4

THE SUCCESSOR BENEFICIARY'S CHECKLIST

What It Does

You may be asking, "What the heck is a successor beneficiary anyway, and why should *I* care? This better be good because it looks like a chapter I could skip."

The short answer is this: For retirement planning purposes, a successor beneficiary is simply the beneficiary's beneficiary. And you should care for the same reason the original owner of the account you have inherited or will be inheriting cared about naming a beneficiary—YOU—in the first place: to keep whatever funds may be left in the account growing and out of the Taxman's pocket for as long as possible after death. Especially if your death were premature, in which case there could be quite a sizable chunk of change left in the account—and quite a long stretch period remaining in which those funds could continue to grow that will be lost.

The premature death of a beneficiary need not be—and should not be—the death of the inherited account itself. But generally that is what happens because most people and many financial institutions do not know what to do when a beneficiary dies, and the account is just cashed out and taxed. The point of planning is to prevent that from happening and to keep the original owner's wealth in the family and building for as long as possible. This checklist takes you through the steps that you as the beneficiary of an inherited account need to follow to ensure that happens, and what the beneficiary's beneficiary needs to be aware of when inheriting so that the best-laid plans of your benefactors do not go awry.

Ask Ed . . .

Q: Should the successor beneficiary also name a beneficiary as soon as he or she inherits?

A: Yes. Though it may be unlikely that two beneficiaries—the original and the successor—will die prematurely, it's always better to be safe than sorry. Then the account will go to the "successor, successor beneficiary," who can then complete the remaining term on the stretch that was available to the first successor beneficiary.

What's In It for Me?

If you are the beneficiary of an account that the original owner beneficently set up for you to stretch, isn't it equally beneficent for you to extend the same opportunity to your own heirs? Here, you will learn how to do that and keep what's left in your inherited account growing and away from taxes even after your death. Think of this as creating both a memorial to the original owner's intentions and a satisfying way to fulfill those intentions while making them your own.

And if you are (or may be in the future) a successor beneficiary (the beneficiary's beneficiary), what's in this checklist for you is that which you must know when you inherit in order to keep the balance in your inherited account alive and working for you and your family as long as you can.

Ask Ed . . .

Q: **What if there are two or more successor beneficiaries—for instance, two children inherit their father's inherited IRA? What happens then?**

A: They share the remaining payout on the inherited IRA based on how many years were remaining on their father's stretch period. It makes no difference how many successor beneficiaries there are or whether they split the inherited IRA into separate accounts because whatever they do, they cannot use their own life expectancy. They can only use their father's remaining term of years had he lived. But they also do not have to cash it out and end the inherited IRA, unless they have a very uncooperative IRA custodian.

What If I Don't?

The account will likely be cashed out on your death as the original beneficiary, providing a potential windfall for Uncle Sam, especially, as I've written, if your death is premature and there is a substantial sum left in the account and a long stretch period (your remaining life expectancy had you lived) to go.

For example, let's say you are the sole beneficiary of an IRA inherited from the original owner, and you have a thirty-seven-year life-expectancy payout term on the stretch. But you die prematurely five years into the payout period. If you have named a successor beneficiary on your beneficiary form, your account will not go to your estate, wind up in probate, and be subjected to all the costly bad things that go with probating retirement plans as discussed earlier in this section and in Section II. Instead the balance in the account will go *directly to your successor beneficiary* who can take distributions over the thirty-two years left on the payout schedule based on your life expectancy had you lived. If your estate inherits, yes it could keep the stretch going (if the custodian agreement allows) for the same length of time to the beneficiary of your estate named in your will (who might even be the same person), but the beneficiary will wind up having much less in the account to stretch due to losses incurred by paying taxes and other expenses. So, to prevent the remaining stretch period from being lost, it is always wise for a beneficiary to name a successor beneficiary as soon as possible after inheriting.

Instructions

As a beneficiary, use this checklist for two purposes: (1) to make sure your own beneficiaries know that even your premature death does not have to mean the end of the inherited account, and (2) to show them why it is so important for them to name a beneficiary of their own as soon as they inherit from you. This way, you will both be covered in preserving the inherited account for as long as legally possible even if one or both of you dies prematurely.

What follows are the two most common successor beneficiary situations—and *darn,* wouldn't you just know it, there's a different set of distribution rules for each of them to make things complicated? Apply the checklist to find out if you are using the right set of rules.

1. The IRA owner names his child as beneficiary. The child inherits. As soon as the child inherits, she names her child (his grandchild) as her successor beneficiary just in case there are still funds left in the inherited IRA to be distributed when she dies.
2. The IRA owner names his spouse as IRA beneficiary. When she inherits, she chooses to remain a beneficiary, rather than becoming an owner. She immediately names her child as successor beneficiary just in case there are still funds left in the account to be distributed when she dies. When she passes on, her child can become either a

beneficiary or a successor beneficiary; depending on whether or not she was taking required distributions when she died. If she died after her required distributions began, the child becomes a successor beneficiary.

In each of these cases, the IRA can pass from the first beneficiary to the beneficiary's beneficiary (the successor beneficiary). But what happens then?

Let's say Mike has a $500,000 IRA and dies at age 45. He named his wife Mary as his beneficiary. Mary is 41 years old and decides to remain a beneficiary (not do a spousal rollover) because she may need to withdraw funds and does not want to get hit with a 10 percent penalty for early withdrawal (under age 59½).

Mary immediately names her 1-year-old daughter Rachel as her successor beneficiary, but Mary dies prematurely just nine years later at age 50, and her daughter Rachel, who is 10 at the time, inherits then. What are Rachel's distribution options? Does the entire $500,000 account have to be cashed out in one year? No. The key here is that her mom, Mary, immediately named a beneficiary (Rachel) of her own upon inheriting the account from her husband Mike. That changes everything for the good.

Because Mary's husband Mike died at 45 and she dies at 50 (before Mike would have reached age 70½ if he had lived) then she is treated as if she were the IRA owner (even though she is a beneficiary). Because Mary named her daughter Rachel as her successor beneficiary, when Rachel inherits she is treated not as the successor beneficiary under this special rule, but as if she were the original beneficiary, and can thus stretch distributions over her own life expectancy of 71.8 years (the life expectancy for an 11-year-old—Rachel's age the year after her mother's death—according to the Single Life Table in Appendix I).

If Rachel were not named as Mary's successor beneficiary here, then the IRA would have had to be distributed under the 5-year rule (assuming the IRA went to Mary's estate). But much more happily, a $500,000 inherited IRA that could have been wiped out from being taxed in one year (if it were cashed out because no one knew what to do) can now be stretched over 71.8 years, potentially providing millions of dollars to Rachel over her lifetime, because Mary had known to name her own beneficiary early on.

Ask Ed . . .

Q: What would happen if Mike had died *after* reaching his Required Beginning Date?

A: Rachel would be considered the successor beneficiary and would have to withdraw over Mary's remaining single life expectancy had Mary not died—which is 33.2 years,* according to the Single Life Table (Appendix I) and still a decent stretch period. A successor beneficiary can never use his or her *own life expectancy* to extend distributions on an inherited account. The successor beneficiary can only complete the remaining term based on the age of the original beneficiary—in this case Mary—at death.

* Because Mary is a beneficiary, you look up her attained age (50) in the year of her death. The factor is 34.2 which is then reduced by one for each subsequent year.

THE SUCCESSOR BENEFICIARY'S CHECKLIST

MY NAME: ______________________ **DATE:** __________

MY ADVISOR'S NAME: ______________________ **PLAN #:** __________

Follow-ups should be added to the To Do lists at the end of this checklist.

A successor beneficiary inherits the remaining retirement plan assets, including Roth IRA assets, at the death of the retirement plan beneficiary—and is thus defined as the "beneficiary's beneficiary."

1. I have named a successor beneficiary (or beneficiaries) to inherit my retirement assets at my death. He, she or they are:

____

____

- **Note:** If I have not named a successor beneficiary or the plan custodian does not allow me to name one, then at my death any remaining retirement plan assets will pass to the default beneficiary named in the plan document. That is generally the estate, which would make the retirement plan subject to probate. It may get cashed out and be subject to income tax, it could be contested, and may end up not going to the beneficiary of my choice. __________
- My successor beneficiary can continue to stretch the remaining required distributions over my life expectancy. __________
- My successor beneficiary can accelerate distributions or liquidate the account. But if there are multiple successor beneficiaries, this could create an accounting problem for the financial advisor trying to keep track of each beneficiary's share. __________

2. If my successor beneficiary does not disclaim the inherited account or cash out, he or she (or they) must:

- Change the social security number on the account to his or her social security number. __________
- Change the account title (the name of the original deceased account owner must remain in the account title) __________
- e.g. John Smith (deceased, date of death) IRA fbo Charles Smith __________
- Name a successor beneficiary of their own (if the custodian allows). __________

Comments: ____

____

____

____

____

____

3. If there is more than one successor beneficiary named, and the account is not split, all beneficiaries share the required distribution each year. ________

4. Successor beneficiaries can move the assets from one custodian to another but ONLY by using a trustee-to-trustee transfer. ________

5. Guidelines for a successor beneficiary of a nonspouse:

- Name a successor beneficiary of your own as soon as you inherit (if the plan custodian allows). ________
- Take the remaining required distributions of the deceased beneficiary by continuing to use the deceased's life expectancy factor (Appendix I) and reducing that factor by one each subsequent year in calculating RMDs. ________
- **Note:** As a successor beneficiary, you cannot use your own age or life expectancy to replace the deceased beneficiary's payout period. The payout period will continue to be based on the age of the original beneficiary. The age of the successor beneficiary has no effect on the remaining payout term.
- **Example:** Chris is the beneficiary of an IRA. Her first RMD is taken using a life expectancy factor of 37. She names her son James as the successor beneficiary. Chris dies 5 years later when her factor would have been 32. James can continue taking distributions using Chris's factor of 32 and reducing it by one in each subsequent year in calculating his subsequent RMDs.

Comments: ____

____

____

____

6. Guidelines for a successor beneficiary of a spouse beneficiary:

- Name a successor beneficiary of your own as soon as you inherit (if the plan custodian allows). __________
- If the spouse dies before the original owner of the plan would have been 70½, the successor beneficiary inherits as a beneficiary and can use his/her own life expectancy in calculating the remaining RMDs. __________
- **Note:** This is the only time that the successor beneficiary's age is used in calculating the remaining RMDs.
- If the spouse dies after the original owner of the plan would have been 70½, the successor beneficiary continues to use the spouse's life expectancy factor in calculating RMDs, reducing the factor by one each year. (See example above.) __________

Comments: ____

____

____

____

____

Follow-Up

My To Do List	Date Completed
1	
2	
3	
4	
5	
6	
7	
8	
9	
10	

____________________ __________

My Signature Date

Part 5

THE TAX BREAKS FOR BENEFICIARIES CHECKLIST

What It Does

As an IRA or company plan beneficiary, you may be in line for big tax benefits, but you cannot rely on the average financial advisor or tax professional to point them out to you or even ask you if you might qualify. So, you will use this checklist to uncover those tax breaks, then go to your tax preparer or financial advisor and make sure they know to take advantage of them for you.

This checklist covers all the tax-saving opportunities that apply to you as the beneficiary of an IRA or company plan. Although one can find all kinds of tax breaks for account owners listed on the Internet and covered in tax books and magazine articles, one almost never sees any listed for beneficiaries of an IRA or company plan. As a result, beneficiaries tend to miss out.

Under old tax law, since a nonspouse beneficiary could not do a rollover, once that check was in hand, the ball game was over. The tax deferral ended as the entire distribution became taxable. But as of the year this book comes out (2007), nonspouse beneficiaries can do a direct rollover (a trustee-to-trustee transfer) of employer plan balances to a properly titled inherited IRA account, if the plan allows. This will allow nonspouse beneficiaries to stretch distributions over their own life expectancies. This checklist highlights some of the biggest, but largely unknown, tax breaks available to beneficiaries of an inherited IRA or company plan. But they do not come automatically. These must be asked for, or they're not given. And to ask for them, you need to know they exist.

You may not even be able to rely on your tax planner or financial advisor to be aware of them. In fact, when I cover them in my training programs for advisors here is where I really see my trainees taking notes at a frenzied pace, all the while mouthing the words, "Wow, I didn't know any of this!" For example, has your tax preparer or financial advisor ever asked you, "Did any of that stock you inherited from your dad in his 401(k) contain any Net Unrealized Appreciation?" Hardly likely. But the answer to that question can yield a huge tax break for beneficiaries, which I will get to later in this chapter. This checklist DOES ask that question, and others, so that you will know enough to seek out the answers.

Ask Ed . . .

Q: I inherited an IRA from my brother. How would I know if he had ever made nondeductible IRA contributions?

A: You would have to look at his tax return to see if there is Form 8606 ("Nondeductible IRAs"). Or you can check his IRA statements to see if he made IRA contributions and then cross-check that with his tax return to see if he took a deduction for those contributions. If he did not, then you know he made nondeductible IRA contributions and a portion of each distribution you take from your inherited IRA will be tax-free. You will then have to file Form 8606 yourself to calculate the portion of each IRA distribution that will be tax-free to you.

What's In It for Me?

Even after your tax preparer may have told you there was nothing else you could do to keep more of your inherited IRA or company plan out of the hands of the government, it is likely you will find some goody-goody tax break in here for you. And even if just one of these goodies applies to your situation, this may be enough to cut down seriously on your inherited account tax bill.

For example, let's say you receive a lump-sum distribution from your late dad's 401(k). The plan balance is in company stock and other assets and you put them in your own brokerage account. Now, assume the entire plan balance is $500,000 and $400,000 of that is in company stock with a Net Unrealized Appreciation (NUA) of $300,000. For the tax year of the lump-sum distribution, the plan will send you a 1099-R form for the full $500,000. When you have your taxes prepared, your accountant will tell you that you owe tax on the full $500,000 at ordinary income tax rates. That's what

Ask Ed . . .

Q: How would I know if there was NUA in a 401(k) plan I inherited?

A: It would show that on the 1099-R form you received when the plan assets were distributed to you. Look in Box 6 (titled "Net Unrealized Appreciation in Employer's Securities") of the form. The number in that box is the NUA, and that amount is not taxed at the time of distribution if it is a qualifying lump-sum distribution to you as a plan beneficiary. You do not pay tax on the NUA until you sell the stock. When you sell it, you pay only capital gains taxes on the NUA amount regardless of how long you held the stock. This box is often overlooked by tax preparers, so be sure to look yourself and to alert your tax preparer.

the form says, so why would your accountant, let alone you, question it? So, you will pay the tax and walk away grumbling about what a huge tax hit you had to take. But you would really have something to grumble about if you found out later that you didn't have to take such a big hit—because you did not have to pay tax on the $300,000 of NUA since you had not sold the stock yet. Even when you do get around to selling the stock, which you can sell at any pace you wish, you will automatically qualify for long-term capital gains rates that will probably be less than half of ordinary income tax rates.

What If I Don't?

The items in this checklist are aimed exclusively at cutting your tax bill. And so not taking advantage of them will cost you. You will pay the highest tax possible on the IRA or company plan you have inherited. It's as simple as that.

Instructions

Review each of the items in this checklist to see which tax savers apply to you. It is likely that you may qualify for more than one of them. Very often you will find that what is good for the goose (the original owner) is good for you too. For example, if you inherit a Roth IRA, you may not know that the distributions you take are not taxable either.

Ask Ed . . .

Q: How would I know if the IRA I inherited is a Roth IRA?

A: Roth IRAs have only been available since 1998 and so they are relatively young, just like most of their owners. But it is not impossible for a Roth IRA to get passed on, and if you do inherit one it should be clearly titled as such—though I have seen cases where an inherited Roth IRA was titled as a traditional IRA because the financial institution did not have the proper titling in its system yet for an inherited Roth IRA. What happens then? You'll most likely pay tax on the distributions of the inherited Roth that should be tax-free. So, don't just trust what the title says (or doesn't say). If you are unsure, check the account statements sent to the account owner during his lifetime. They should clearly state that an account is a Roth IRA. If you are still unsure, you can also check tax returns (you only have to go back to 1998, which was the first year you could have a Roth) of the person you inherited from. If he or she converted a traditional IRA to a Roth IRA you will see the conversion income on the deceased's tax returns. If the deceased had made Roth IRA contributions that information would not show up on the tax return, but the financial institution would have records of them. The financial advisor and/or tax preparer for the deceased owner should also know if your inherited account is a Roth or traditional IRA. So, ask them as well.

In a different instance, you may be entitled to tax breaks on the state level that you didn't know about. For example, some states do not allow deductions for plan contributions, even if the deduction is allowed federally. So, if you inherit an IRA, for example, from your dad, who did not receive a state tax deduction for his IRA contributions, then you do not have to pay state income tax on the distributions you take from that inherited IRA. How will you know to ask about this? This and many other reminders are on the checklist.

A Word to the Wise

The biggest and most complex tax break available to plan beneficiaries is the Income in Respect of a Decedent (IRD) deduction. There is so much to be aware of with the IRD deduction alone that I am only reminding you here to check whether you may qualify for it or not, but have created a separate checklist (see this section, Part 6) that goes into the details. Likewise, among the biggest—and most involved—tax breaks available to plan owners AND to beneficiaries (if the owner qualified) are NUA and 10-year averaging on lump-sum distributions. Again, I am only alerting you here to check if you qualify for these breaks. Look for the details in The Tax Breaks for Lump-Sum Distribution Checklist, Section IV, Part 7.

THE TAX BREAKS FOR BENEFICIARIES CHECKLIST

MY NAME: ______________________________ DATE: ____________

MY ADVISOR'S NAME: ______________________________ PLAN #: ____________

Follow-ups should be added to the To Do lists at the end of this checklist.

1. Are all inherited accounts titled properly and identified correctly (i.e., a Roth as an inherited Roth)? ____________

2. Am I eligible to claim the IRD deduction? To be eligible, the inherited IRA or plan must have been subject to federal estate taxes in the estate I inherited from. (See checklist this section, Part 6.) ____________

3. Does my state allow any tax breaks for distributions from inherited IRAs or employer plans? (Some states exempt all or a portion of retirement plan distributions from state taxes even when those distributions are made to beneficiaries.) ____________

Comments: ____

____

____

____

____

4. Does my inherited IRA hold after-tax contributions (basis)? Distributions of basis will reduce the income tax I owe on the distribution. Note: Basis can include nondeductible IRA contributions made by the deceased IRA owner (after 1986) and after-tax contributions made to an employer plan that were rolled into an IRA (after 2001). ____________

- Look for Form 8606 (Nondeductible IRAs) attached to the decedent's tax returns. ____________
- If there is no Form 8606 and I think there are after-tax contributions, I can look for Form 5498 (IRA Contribution Information) or IRA statements to see when contributions were made and check the corresponding tax returns to see if a deduction was taken. ____________
- Figure the tax-free portion of the distribution using the calculation on Form 8606, which must be filed with my tax return. ____________

Comments: ______

______

______

______

5. Does my inherited IRA have a different basis for state taxes than it has for federal taxes? ______

- Did the deceased IRA owner live in a state that does not allow deductions for contributions to IRAs? ______
- If yes, for state tax purposes, are distributions partially tax-free? ______

Comments: ______

______

______

______

______

6. Did I inherit a Roth IRA? ______

- If the account has been established for more than 5 years (counting the time the Roth IRA was held by the deceased owner) then all distributions from the Roth are income-tax-free. ______
- If the account has been established for less than 5 years then distributions of contributions and conversions are income-tax-free. Distributions of earnings will be subject to income tax (but never a 10 percent penalty since that does not apply to beneficiaries). ______

Comments: ______

______

______

______

7. Did I inherit an employer plan? ______

- Do I have to take a lump-sum distribution? ______
  - If there is company stock in the plan, I am eligible to use the NUA tax break (See The Tax Breaks for Lump Sum Distribution Checklist in Section IV, Part 7) ______

- If the deceased owner was born before 1936, I am eligible to use the 10-year averaging tax break (see The Tax Breaks for Lump-Sum Distribution Checklist in Section IV, Part 7). ____________
- If any of the lump-sum distribution is from plan participation before 1974, I am eligible for the capital gain election (see The Tax Breaks for Lump-Sum Distribution Checklist in Section IV, Part 7). ____________

- 10-year averaging and the distribution of pre-74 balances are reported on Form 4972. ____________
- Lump-sum distributions from an employer plan using either 10-year averaging or NUA can qualify for the full IRD deduction. (See The IRD Checklist in this section, Part 6.) ____________
- As of 2007, funds in an employer plan can be transferred directly to a properly titled inherited IRA. If a check is made payable to me, I cannot put the funds in an inherited IRA. ____________

Comments: ____________

____

____

____

____

Follow-Up

My To Do List	Date Completed
1	
2	
3	
4	
5	
6	
7	
8	
9	
10	

My Signature ____________ Date ____________

Part 6

THE IRD CHECKLIST

What It Does

The IRD deduction is number one on my list of the most overlooked tax breaks available to beneficiaries of inherited retirement accounts and other property. In fact, it is one of the oldest provisions in the tax code, dating back to the early 1940s. With so many baby boomers inheriting larger retirement plans and other assets than ever these days as their WWII-generation parents pass on, more people are in a position to qualify for this deduction than ever before. But they may not receive it due to their ignorance of its existence, which is why this checklist is here.

IRD stands for Income in Respect of a Decedent, an IRS term (who else could string such words together like this?) that describes inherited income subject to federal tax. An IRA or company plan is probably the most common example. The income in the plan was earned by the decedent during his or her lifetime, but the tax was not yet paid on the funds remaining in the account at death. The beneficiary must pay the income tax as he withdraws from the inherited account.

Ask Ed . . .

Q: How do I know if the IRA or company plan I inherited was subject to federal estate taxes?

A: Easy. You look at the federal estate tax return (Form 706) for the person you inherited from to see if the estate paid federal estate tax. If federal estate tax was paid, and the item you inherited is included in the estate, you qualify for the IRD deduction and can claim it on your personal tax return as you withdraw the assets.

Death does not remove the tax obligation; the plan beneficiary (you) must pay income tax when he or she starts taking withdrawals from the inherited account. But the IRD deduction can whittle down this tax obligation big-time. It is much more valuable than most other itemized deductions because it is not eroded by the 2 percent of adjusted gross income (AGI) limitation nor is it even subject to the dreaded alternative minimum tax (AMT). Not checking to see if you qualify for the IRD deduction could be criminal—you may end up having as much as 80 percent of your inheritance confiscated by Uncle Sam.

Ask Ed . . .

Q: What if the inherited plan is not subject to federal estate tax, but the estate did pay state estate or inheritance taxes? Do I still get the IRD deduction?

A: No. The IRD deduction is only available when the item gets hit with federal estate tax. State estate taxes do not qualify for the IRD deduction, so on a state level the double taxation still exists. This is getting to be a more common situation as more revenue-hungry states institute estate taxes of their own on estates of lower value where there might not otherwise be federal estate tax due.

What's In It for Me?

The IRD deduction is a way for beneficiaries to *offset* the effect of the double taxation that comes with inheriting assets such as tax-deferred retirement accounts that are subject to federal income tax. But most beneficiaries and their financial advisors are woefully unaware of the existence of the IRD deduction to offset this blow. You'll save a fortune in taxes if you spot even one item in this checklist, such as an inherited account, that may qualify you as a beneficiary for the IRD deduction. And many of you may find more than one.

Ask Ed . . .

Q: What if I am one of several beneficiaries who inherit an IRA that qualifies for the IRD deduction? Who gets the deduction?

A: You each take your share of the total IRD deduction in accordance with your share of the inheritance. For example, if the total IRD deduction is $60,000 and there are 3 equal beneficiaries, you are each entitled to a $20,000 IRD deduction as you withdraw the assets. If there are 2 unequal beneficiaries—one inherited 75 percent of the IRA and the other received 25 percent—then the 75 percent beneficiary is entitled to 75 percent of the IRD deduction or $45,000 ($60,000 IRD deduction × 75 percent) and the 25 percent beneficiary is entitled to 25 percent of the IRD deduction or $15,000 ($60,000 IRD deduction × 25 percent).

The IRD tax deduction is large. It often runs as high as 45 percent, meaning that if you inherit an IRA subject to federal estate tax and withdraw $100,000 (on which you must pay tax), your withdrawal also amounts to an approximately $45,000 IRD tax deduction. That can be used to offset your overall tax bill. Imagine someone missing a $45,000 tax deduction because he or she didn't know better! But it happens—all the time.

Ask Ed . . .

Q: Can I take the entire IRD deduction in one year?

A: Only if you withdraw the entire balance of the inherited IRA or plan in one year. The IRD deduction is taken in proportion to how much of the IRD income you have withdrawn during the year. For example, if you and your advisor calculate the IRD deduction to be $100,000 and you only withdraw 6 percent because that is your required minimum distribution for the year, then you can claim 6 percent ($6,000), and you will still have $94,000 of IRD deductions to use for future years. You never run out of time to claim the rest of the IRD deduction until the account is used up.

Q: Is there a dollar limit on the amount of IRD deduction that can be claimed?

A: No. But you can only take the deduction against IRD income that you report. You cannot just make up a number. So, as long as you have IRD income to take (say from inherited IRA distributions) and you qualify for an IRD deduction, you can claim an amount up to the amount allowed. You can never claim more than the IRD deduction, but there is no limit on the actual dollar amount of the IRD deduction itself.

What If I Don't?

You won't have to worry about your successor beneficiaries killing you; you'll do it yourself. Seriously (I hope), if you do nothing, you may (and probably will) lose out substantially by missing this important tax break.

Ask Ed . . .

Q: If I missed taking the IRD deduction in past years can I go back and correct my mistake?

A: Yes, you can go back three years and amend your tax returns to claim the IRD deductions you missed. You'll receive a tax refund plus interest (IRS has to pay you interest even if the mistake was yours). If your state allows the IRD deduction, and you missed taking it in past years, you can go back three years as well to amend your state tax returns and receive even more refund checks. You cannot go back beyond three years (the statute of limitations), but if there are still funds in the IRA or plan balance you inherited, you can keep taking the IRD deduction against your future withdrawals as long as those funds last.

Instructions

Review the checklist to see if you qualify for the IRD deduction. First up, you will find a listing of every conceivable inherited item subject to federal estate tax that will put you in line for this deduction. Many of these items represent income owed to the decedent (your benefactor, the account owner) at death that do not receive a step up in basis. Of course, you'll see IRAs and company plans in the eligible list too, but keep your eye open for receivables, insurance renewal commissions, lottery winnings, legal claims, alimony, and a host of other things you may inherit that can qualify you for the IRD deduction when you withdraw the income.

If you don't qualify, then you can move on to the next section in this book. If you do qualify, use the checklist that follows to find out how to claim the IRD deduction on your tax return. There are different ways to claim the IRD deduction. For example, most beneficiaries will claim it as a miscellaneous itemized deduction, but those who receive a lump-sum distribution may be able to take the deduction on

Form 4972 to directly offset the income if the deceased qualified for 10-year averaging (see The Tax Breaks for Lump-Sum Distribution Checklist in Section IV, Part 7).

Ask Ed . . .

Q: Why should I care about the IRD elimination strategies on this checklist?

A: To eliminate the income tax burden on your own heirs by withdrawing more during your lifetime when you become the plan owner. Due to the high combined tax on IRAs, even after the IRD deduction, it can often pay to reduce your IRA and plan balances during your lifetime and leverage those funds into more-tax-efficient vehicles such as life insurance, for example, or for charitable planning, or by converting to a tax-free Roth IRA. This is something you should alert your benefactor to now, if it's not too late.

A Word to the Wise

After you complete the checklist and run your IRD calculations, you should run them by your tax or financial advisor. There may be some items, such as basis, that you may even need your advisor to help you with, so you may wish to consult with him or her beforehand. Then you will be assured you are doing everything right.

Qualifying IRD Items

Use this list to identify Income in Respect of a Decedent (IRD) in an estate that you have inherited or may be inheriting. IRD is income earned by the decedent during his or her lifetime, but unpaid (owed to the decedent) at death. IRD items do NOT receive a step up in basis, but if the estate was subject to federal estate tax, then beneficiaries who inherit any of these items will be able to claim an IRD deduction as they collect the income.

1. Investment Income
    - Interest income—accrued to date of death
    - US savings bonds interest (unrecognized)
    - Dividend income
    - Rental income
    - Royalty income
2. Employee Compensation (Postdeath payments from employers)
    - Regular wages
    - Vacation pay
    - Sick pay
    - Deferred Compensation
    - Employee death benefit
    - Voluntary payments from employer
    - Stock options
    - Postdeath bonus
3. Independent Contractor Income (sole proprietors, professionals, contractors, consultants, etc.)
    - Receivables for services (professional fees, commissions, etc.)
    - Partnership income
    - Insurance renewal commissions
    - Fiduciary fees (due to Fiduciary)
    - Director fees
4. Retirement and Pension Income
    - All tax-deferred retirement plans (qualified pension & profit-sharing plans and IRAs [but generally not Roth IRAs]; including 401(k)s, 403(b)s, Keoghs, etc.)
    - Joint and survivor annuities
    - Deferred compensation
    - Net Unrealized Appreciation (NUA) in employer stock

5. Sales Area
    - Sale of a partnership interest—IRC Sec.736(a) payments
    - Installment sales—Income portion of installment payments received by beneficiary is IRD
    - Executory Contracts—if seller dies between contract and closing, there may be IRD depending on how much of the sale was completed at death.
    - Proceeds of property sales owed to the decedent at death are IRD. Examples:
        - Stocks, bonds, funds
        - Land, buildings, equipment
        - Home
        - Business interests
6. Other Income Owed to the Decedent at Death
    - Income owed to deceased beneficiary from trust or estate
    - Legal claims, lawsuits, damages
    - Medical insurance reimbursements
    - Alimony
    - Tax refunds
    - Lottery winnings
    - Other refunds or amounts due decedent at death

THE IRD CHECKLIST

MY NAME: ______________________ **DATE:** __________

MY ADVISOR'S NAME: ______________________ **PLAN #:** __________

Follow-ups should be added to the To Do lists at the end of this checklist.

IRD is income earned by a decedent during his or her lifetime but not received or taxed until after death.

For Beneficiaries

1. Am I eligible to claim the IRD deduction? __________

- Did I inherit assets from an estate that was subject to federal estate tax? __________
- If no, there is no IRD deduction. __________

2. If yes, go through estate assets on US Estate Tax Return and identify IRD items. __________

- NO IRD deduction is allowed for state estate taxes paid. __________
- Lump-sum distributions from an employer plan using 10-year averaging (found on Form 4972) can qualify for the full IRD deduction and the deduction is not reduced by the 3 percent overall itemized deduction limitation. __________
- IRD items subject to generation-skipping transfer taxes can still qualify for the IRD deduction. __________

Comments: ______________________

____

____

____

____

3. Has a distribution been made from the IRA or any other IRD item? (There is NO IRD deduction unless there is a distribution.) __________

Look for distributions: __________

- on Form 1099-R, box 7, code 4 __________
- of interest or dividends __________
- of receivables __________
- on W-2 forms (e.g. deferred comp) __________

- of lump sums from employer plans including Net Unrealized Appreciation (NUA) ______
- from inherited Roth IRAs where earnings might be taxable ______

4. The IRD deduction is taken on my tax return (even if I did not pay the estate tax):

- As a miscellaneous itemized deduction, NOT subject to the 2 percent AGI limits and NOT subject to AMT ______
- On Form 4972, Tax on Lump-Sum Distributions (if I took a lump-sum distribution from an employer plan and am using 10-year-averaging) ______

5. Was there any basis in my inherited account? Distributions of these funds do not qualify for the IRD deduction. ______

- Check prior year tax returns for Form 8606, Nondeductible IRAs and Coverdell ESAs. IRA amounts withdrawn tax-free do not qualify for the IRD deduction. ______
- Do any of the balances include after-tax funds rolled over from a company plan? ______

Comments: ______

______

______

______

______

6. Calculate the IRD deduction: ______

1. Take the federal estate tax amount from page one of Form 706. ______
2. Calculate the estate tax again without including any of the IRD items in the estate. ______
3. Subtract the estate tax in Step 2 from the estate tax in Step 1. The result is the total amount of the IRD deduction. ______
4. Divide the amount from Step 3 by the amount of the IRA included in the estate. This will give me the percentage of the deduction I will be able to claim. ______
5. Multiply the amount of the IRA distribution (if any) I have taken during the year by the percentage from Step 4 to get the deduction amount for the year. ______

7. Calculate how much of the IRD deduction is unused and available for future years. ______

Comments: ____________________

____

____

____

____

8. Did I miss the IRD deduction in past years? ______

- If yes, amend tax returns (federal statute of limitations is 3 years) or take from future distributions. ______
- Check state tax returns if my state allows the IRD deduction for federal estate taxes (ask advisor) and also allows the deduction even if the income is exempt from state income tax. ______

9. Did I inherit assets that were IRD assets in a prior estate? ______

- Were the assets subject to federal estate tax in both prior estates? ______
- If yes, I can take a double IRD deduction, one for each estate in which the asset was subject to federal estate taxes. **Note:** §2013, the double IRD deduction, could be reduced by credits for estate taxes paid on prior transfers. The credit is on a sliding scale. ______

Comments: ____________________

____

____

____

____

For Beneficiaries-To-Be (Alert My Potential Benefactors to These IRD Preplanning Measures on My Behalf)

10. What types of assets are included in the estate that could become IRD? ______

- Notify beneficiary, family, and tax advisors of potential double taxation of IRD items after death ______

11. Explore IRD elimination strategies:

- Leverage IRAs/life insurance ____________
- Charitable planning/leave IRD asset to charity ____________
- Income acceleration strategies ____________

  IRA distributions ____________

  Roth IRA conversions ____________

  Executory contracts ____________

  Tax elections ____________

  S corp income §1377(a) ____________

  US savings bond interest §454(a) ____________

  Installment sale income §453(d) ____________

Comments: ____

Follow-Up

My To Do List | Date Completed

1 ____

2 ____

3 ____

4 ____

5 ____

6 ____

7 ____

8 ____

9 ____

10 ____

My Signature ____________ Date ____________

Section IV

THE SPECIAL ISSUES CARE SOLUTION

The entire purpose behind this book is to make sure everything goes according to plan with your retirement savings bequest—whether you are on the giving or the receiving end of that bequest. To further that goal, this section addresses those out-of-the-box issues and concerns that affect those of you who do not fit the exact account owner or beneficiary mold. Thus, the section is not for everyone—which is to say, it is not for ALL account owners or ALL account beneficiaries. But I will bet my own life savings that one or more of these special situations will apply to either or, perhaps, even both of you at some point. That's why I have included this section. It is for those situations specific to YOU.

For example, as an account owner with company stock in a 401(k) you will need to be aware of the tax breaks known as Net Unrealized Appreciation in setting up your account to best advantage for passing on to your beneficiaries. Or you may need to tap your retirement funds early and want to avoid the 10 percent penalty for early withdrawals, have financial or bankruptcy issues, are divorced, or perhaps want to leave some of your funds to charity. Conversely, if you are or will be the beneficiary of an inherited account, and thus on the receiving end of the issues sparked by these special care situations, you will need and want to know what to do, as well.

Part 1

THE NAMING A CHARITY-AS-BENEFICIARY CHECKLIST

For account owners only

What It Does

Every once in a while in my line of work, I run across an individual or a couple who have no beneficiaries—at least none they care about leaving anything to, especially something as important as a retirement account. I would offer myself as beneficiary just for them to have one, but I doubt this would work because there are much better causes than mine to leave retirement money to, and charity is a big one.

If your heirs don't need the money, bequeathing your IRA or company plan to them could push them into a higher tax bracket and may even trigger estate tax. Under those circumstances, some account owners decide that donating this asset to charity is the better route. A charity does not have to pay income tax when it cashes out the inherited IRA. There is no loser here because our tax laws encourage charitable giving so that the government does not have to provide as much to those in need as it would otherwise.

In addition to sparing your well-to-do heirs some potential grief with the Taxman, you may just want to make a difference in the

Ask Ed . . .

Q: I know that in leaving a retirement account to charity, the charity pays no tax when it cashes out, but do I receive a tax deduction for the gift?

A: No. But your estate does—for the amount in the account that passes to the charity, provided it is an IRS-qualified charity, which generally includes religious, charitable, educational, scientific, or literary groups or those organizations that work to prevent cruelty to children or animals. Not sure if the charity you are considering qualifies? You can either call the IRS at 1-877-829-5500 for the answer, or find it in IRS Publication 78 (available online at www.irs.gov or in your local library.

world, one that will endure after you are gone. There's nothing wrong with that. And in such a case, this is the checklist for you. It will take you through the most tax-efficient and family-friendly ways to leave all or part of your IRA or company plan to a charity hassle-free.

It will show you the various ways to structure your plan ahead of time and tip you off to the most common errors that are made in that process. It will also cover family issues relating to your charity planning here that you should *make sure your loved ones are aware of (assuming you want them to know) in advance so they can put in their 2 cents.*

What's In It for Me?

You'll be able to leave all or part of your retirement account balance to charity and reap the best tax benefits while also doing a good deed. Or, you will be able to cut taxes for your heirs by leaving the entire account to charity and your other property (nonretirement account assets) to family members. This way, the nonretirement account property that goes to your family receives a step up in basis, and there is no income tax on the appreciation. This is not the case with an IRA or

Ask Ed . . .

Q: Would it be wise to do a conversion to a Roth IRA if I will be leaving those funds to a charity?

A: No. As much as I like Roth IRAs, this makes no sense because unlike a traditional retirement account you pay tax on a Roth when you contribute not when you withdraw. And since a charity pays no tax on withdrawals even from a traditional account, there is no advantage to your funding a Roth that you simply plan to give away—unless, of course, you like paying taxes.

other plan asset. There is no step up in basis for those assets, and family members receiving them will owe income tax when they start withdrawing—unlike a charitable beneficiary, which pays no tax.

So you get a win-win; you will have seen to it that your family pays no tax on the appreciation of its bequest, and the charity has to pay no tax on the retirement account proceeds you have donated.

What If I Don't?

This checklist does not tell you whether to leave your IRA or other plan to charity or not. That's for you to decide with the help of your financial advisor and with (or without) input from your family. But if you do decide to go ahead and leave all or some of your account to charity, be aware that a single mistake you make in this process could wind up making the IRS your BIGGEST charitable beneficiary.

For example, one common mistake is naming the charity in your will rather than on your beneficiary form (see checklist Section II, Part 1) in which case you will have turned a nonprobate asset (your retirement account) into a probate asset, potentially triggering an income tax on the bequest where none existed before. Furthermore, the bequest could be challenged by some remote moneygrubbing family member showing up out of nowhere to contest your will and scuttle your charitable plans. This is just one of the costly errors that might occur if a charitable bequest of your retirement assets is your goal but you don't follow this checklist.

Instructions

Most other types of property can be given to charity during your lifetime, but not IRAs or company retirement plans—unless you cash out and pay the tax on your withdrawal, hoping to qualify for at least a partially offsetting tax deduction on the balance (if any) you give to charity. This is why the only way to give retirement funds in whole or in part to charity in the most advantageous way for all concerned is to bequeath the account at death. So, this checklist takes you through that process.

Under a new tax law, however, you have the ability to make charitable contributions directly from your IRA to a qualified charity for tax years 2006 and 2007. You must be at least age 70½ at the time you make the contribution. The contribution must go directly from your IRA account to the charity, it cannot be paid to you, then you write out a check to the charity. The contribution can be made from taxable funds only, not from any after-tax amounts you have in your IRA accounts. It cannot come from an employer plan or from SEP or SIMPLE IRAs. That sounds like a lot of rules already, but there are more—and all for a provision of the law that exists for less than eighteen months! That's another reason to use this checklist.

If you want to leave your whole IRA or 401(k) to charity, no problem—just spell that out on your beneficiary form (Section II, Part 1). If you want to make sure the charity receives at least some portion of your IRA or 401(k), you will also spell that out on your beneficiary form and can set things up in any of the following ways: (1) Split the account while you are alive, naming the charity as beneficiary of one account and your children as co-beneficiaries of the other account; (2) Leave part of the account to charity and part to your children for them to separate after your death (see The Multiple Beneficiaries Checklist in Section III, Part 3); (3) Leave the account to a charitable remainder trust (see The Naming a Trust-As-Beneficiary Checklist in Part 2 of this Section) where you can dictate the terms so that family members will receive a certain amount of income for a term of years after you're gone and the rest goes to charity.

On the other hand, you might want to name your spouse as your primary beneficiary to make sure she has enough to live on, and then name the charity as a contingent beneficiary. After you die, your spouse can decide how much she can pass to the charity and how much she would like to keep by disclaiming the amount she will not need (see The Disclaimer Planning Checklist in Part 3 of this section) based on her needs at the time.

You should not only involve your financial advisor in your decision-making here, but family members and the charity too so they can all contribute to your vision and your wishes.

Ask Ed . . .

Q: Instead of naming a charity (or charities) on my beneficiary form and separating accounts so my family doesn't have to do it, wouldn't it be much easier for me just to leave my account to my estate and make all my charitable bequests in my will?

A: It might be easier, but it will be much more costly because a tax could be triggered in the estate. That's because the bequest of a specific dollar amount in your will—like a $10,000 bequest to a charity—is known in tax terms as a "pecuniary bequest," and if you satisfy a pecuniary bequest with, for example, an IRA, you trigger immediate taxation on the IRA in the estate under Section 691 (a)(2) of the Internal Revenue Code. It's as if you took the retirement plan money out, paid a tax on it, then made the bequest. That defeats the tax benefit of leaving the account to charity.

THE NAMING A CHARITY-AS-BENEFICIARY CHECKLIST

MY NAME: ______________________ DATE: __________

MY ADVISOR'S NAME: ______________________ PLAN #: __________

Follow-ups should be added to the To Do lists at the end of this checklist.

1. I have a desire to leave funds to charity. __________

2. Make sure the charity I am considering is a qualified charity so there will be a tax deduction for my bequest. Contact IRS at 877-829-5500, check IRS Publication 78 (available in many public libraries), or check on the IRS website at www.irs.gov. __________

3. Should I leave my retirement assets to the charity? Or should I leave other assets to charity? __________

- At my death retirement assets do not get a step up in basis and are subject to both income tax and estate tax. __________
- Other assets do get a step up in basis and are only subject to estate tax at my death. __________
- It is more tax-efficient to leave retirement assets to charity and leave appreciated (nonretirement) assets to individual beneficiaries. __________

4. If I am planning to leave my retirement plan to charity, don't do a Roth conversion as I will have to pay income tax on the conversion when there would be no income tax due at my death. __________

5. As an alternative, use life insurance to fund my charitable bequest. Take funds from my retirement plan to buy insurance. The distributions reduce my taxable estate, and there is more to leave to charity. __________

Comments: ______________________________

6. Should I name both individuals and a charity as beneficiaries of the same retirement plan or split the plan?

- A charity is a nondesignated beneficiary with no life expectancy, which can kill the stretch option if accounts are not split. ____________
- Segregating the portion to go to charity eliminates any postdeath problems for designated beneficiaries with regard to stretch distributions. ____________
- It is more cumbersome to have separate accounts, more paperwork, more fees, and maintaining the balance I want in each account. ____________

7. If I leave my account to be split by my named beneficiaries after my death:

- Beneficiaries must split into separate accounts by no later than 12/31 of the year following my death. ____________
- Charity should be paid out no later than 9/30 of the year following the year of my death. ____________
- If charity is not removed or accounts are not timely split, then there is no designated beneficiary and distributions to beneficiaries will be accelerated. ____________

Comments: ____

____

____

____

____

8. Consider creating a charitable trust as beneficiary. The most common type of trust used is a Charitable Remainder Unitrust.

- At the death of the plan owner, a distribution is made from the IRA to the trust. ____________
- The plan distribution to the trust is not subject to income tax because of the charitable beneficiary. ____________
- The estate gets a partial charitable tax deduction based on the expected trust payouts to the beneficiary. ____________
- Beneficiaries of the trust receive a stream of income (based on a percentage of the trust balance) in accordance with the trust terms but do not have access to principal. ____________

• Distributions to the beneficiaries are included in their income and are taxable to them. ________

• At the death of the last beneficiary or at the end of the trust term, the remaining assets are paid to charity. ________

Comments: ________

10. Keep family and beneficiaries informed of charitable intentions and beneficiary designations so there are no postdeath surprises. ________

11. Name a contingent beneficiary to allow more flexibility in postmortem estate planning by the use of a disclaimer. (See The Disclaimer Planning Checklist in Part 3 of this section.) ________

Comments: ________

The following section applies to tax law changes enacted in 2006 that are effective from August 17, 2006 through December 31, 2007 only.

Qualified Charitable Distributions

12. Consider funding charitable contributions directly from my IRA if:

• I ordinarily cannot take a deduction for the contribution on my income tax return because I use the standard deduction and don't itemize deductions. ________

• I may not receive a full tax deduction for my gift because it exceeds 50 percent of my adjusted gross income. ________

• I live in a state with no income tax. ________

• A distribution would increase my AGI and put me at more risk of losing deductions, exemptions, and tax credits. ________

13. A qualified charitable distribution could satisfy my Required Minimum Distribution (RMD). In effect, my RMD becomes income-tax-free for the year to the extent of my charitable distribution (but limited to $100,000 for the year). __________

14. The distribution does not have to be reported as income in the year of the distribution, and I do not get a charitable deduction. __________

Comments: ____

____

____

____

____

15. I have an opportunity through the end of 2007 to make distributions of any amount up to $100,000 per year directly from a traditional IRA to a charity if:

- I am the account owner (not a beneficiary). __________
- I will be age 70½ (or older) at the time of the distribution. __________
- I do a direct transfer from the IRA to the charity. (I cannot receive the payment, then give it to charity—unless the check I receive is payable to the charity). __________
- The transfer comes from a traditional or a Roth IRA, not from a SEP or SIMPLE IRA. __________

The charity is qualified, which means it: __________

- Cannot be a donor-advised fund. __________
- Cannot be a private foundation. __________
- Cannot be a charitable gift annuity. __________

Only taxable amounts are transferred, in which case: __________

- For the purposes of charitable distributions, all my IRAs are considered one IRA (excluding SEP and SIMPLE IRAs). __________
- Taxable amounts are considered to be distributed first. __________
- A distribution is considered taxable as long as it does not exceed the total taxable amount in all my IRAs. __________
- I must keep track of my basis. __________

- I would have been able to claim a charitable deduction for the qualified charitable distribution. There can be no benefit received (raffle tickets, meals, etc.) and I must have substantiation (a receipt from the charity for the contribution). ______

16. I will need either an IRA custodian or a self-directed IRA custodian willing to make direct transfers from my IRA to the charity, or an IRA checkbook to write the checks directly to the charity. ______

Comments: ______

______

______

______

______

17. A qualified charitable distribution cannot be made from employer plans. ______

18. If the qualified charitable distribution fails, then the regular charitable deduction rules apply. The distribution is included in my income for the year, and I get a charitable deduction if I itemize deductions. ______

Comments: ______

______

______

______

______

Follow-Up

My To Do List	Date Completed
1	
2	
3	
4	
5	
6	
7	
8	
9	
10	

My Signature

Date

Part 2

THE NAMING A TRUST-AS-BENEFICIARY CHECKLIST

For account owners only

What It Does

Most account owners do not need to name a trust as beneficiary. But you won't know if you are one of them until you go through this checklist, where you will determine if you need a trust because you may need some postdeath control over your retirement assets to prevent your beneficiaries from squandering them or because you wish to leave your assets to a minor child (your grandchild, for instance).

If after reading through the reasons to name a trust as your beneficiary you have found no reasons to do so and decide that a trust is not for you and your family (which is by the way what the majority of folks decide), then you stop and move on to the next checklist appropriate to you.

A Word to the Wise

I know that this checklist can be intimidating at first glance—it is even to many professionals. This is because it covers so many arcane areas in the law, such as the Uniform Principal and Income Act, pecuniary bequests, see-through trusts, conduit or discretionary trusts to name just a few. This is why you will need an expert estate-planning lawyer to help you actually set up the trust once you have determined whether you need one or not. And when I say "expert," I mean just that. If the trust is not set up correctly, it may not be properly implemented according to your wishes, and by then it may be too late to do anything about the problems that arise. So, any old lawyer and financial advisor won't do here. You will really need to grill your advisors to make sure they are up to the task, which is why I've included an expert advisor (including estate-planning attorneys) locator tool (Section V, Part 2) for you in this book.

Ask Ed . . .

Q: What if I find that I need to name a trust for one of my three children but not for the other two?

A: You can split your account into three: two for the beneficiaries who do not need the trust and the other for the beneficiary who does. Then on the beneficiary form for the children who don't need the trust, you just name them directly. For the beneficiary who needs the trust, you name the trust on your beneficiary form. Or, if you want to have only one retirement account, on the beneficiary form you can name your two children and the trust for the third child to split the IRA equally (or in any percentage you choose).

What's In It for Me?

This checklist will reveal to you whether you have something to worry about with regard to your retirement plan bequest. In other words, you will learn here whether it is in your interest as well as that of your beneficiaries to name a trust beneficiary as a protective measure. And whichever way you go, you will feel comfortable and secure in the knowledge that you have covered this base in your estate planning as well.

Ask Ed . . .

Q: If I want to leave my IRA to a trust for my children, when can they actually receive the money and who decides that?

A: You decide this when you express your wishes to the attorney who drafts the trust. If it is a discretionary trust, this means you give to the trustee—a corporate trustee, a spouse, sibling, or other person you charge with carrying out your instructions after you're gone—the power to determine how much of the IRA your beneficiaries should be allowed access to and when, in accordance with your wishes.

Q: If I need a trust to inherit my account for the sake of some of my beneficiaries, how long should their shares remain in trust? Does the trust ever end?

A: That is up to you. The trust can go on for their lifetime or end when they reach a certain age. You will decide the term and put that in the trust. For example, if you name a trust as beneficiary of the account because your grandchild is a minor at the time, you might want to put in a provision ending the trust when he or she reaches 21 or whatever age you decide. You can also end the trust in stages; for example, make half of the funds available at age 21 and then have the trust end and all the funds dispersed when the grandchild reaches age 30 or 35 or 40. (Some parents tell me their 50-year-old children are not yet able to handle large sums of money!) Postdeath control is what you wanted, so you have total flexibility to write the rules of your own trust.

Q: If I name a trust as the beneficiary for my IRA, will my children (the trust beneficiaries) still be able to take advantage of the stretch opportunity?

A: Yes, if the trust is a "see-through trust." This means that it treats your kids (your trust beneficiaries) as if they inherited directly. If you wish all your trust beneficiaries to be able to use their individual life expectancy (rather than that of the eldest) for the stretch period, then you would have to leave their shares in separate named trusts. In many estate-planning trusts, the owner lists a spouse as the income beneficiary in order to provide funds for the spouse after their death. If that is the case, the remainder trust beneficiaries (children and grandchildren) will be stuck using the surviving spouse's life expectancy and will not get the full advantage of the stretch. But this may be a trade-off you as the original owner will want to go with depending upon how much postdeath control you seek. (For all the ins and outs of the stretch option, see Section II, Part 3.)

What If I Don't?

Whether you are a control freak or not, if you have accumulated a sizable retirement account (or accounts) that you know you can't possibly go through in your remaining years no matter how many trips you take and other activities you participate in, you will experience a lot of sleepless nights before you're done wondering what will happen to the balance when your spendthrift offspring get their hands on it, or the government does.

Ask Ed . . .

Q: If I name a trust as beneficiary, is the inherited account still subject to Required Minimum Distributions?

A: Yes. The inherited account must pay the RMDs to the trust. Once that happens, it is up to the terms of the trust whether the RMDs paid to the trust are subsequently paid out to your beneficiaries. If not, the trust itself will pay the income tax (at trust tax rates, which are almost always higher than the tax bracket your kids or grandkids are in) on the RMDs it has taken. To avoid the trust tax issue, you might opt for a conduit trust, which pays the RMDs taken by the trust to your individual beneficiaries, who will then be taxed on this income at their (typically) lower rate. Or, you can name the trust as beneficiary of a Roth IRA, which will make income-tax-free distributions to the trust.

Q: What if I want to protect my IRA funds by keeping them in a trust for my kids, but I still want them to have access to the money for emergencies or education or some other prudent reason?

A: You can do that with a trust by inserting what are called "invasion provisions" (i.e., access to the funds in an emergency) into the trust, or you could give the person you name as your trustee the discretion to decide when and for what reason your kids should be permitted early access.

On the other hand, the good news is that you won't actually know, so, in effect, all those sleepless nights will have been for nothing.

Instructions

Unless you have true expertise in this area, most of the items on this checklist will need to be reviewed with a qualified financial advisor

Ask Ed . . .

Q: What if I name a trust and after I die my children or spouse see no need for it and want to end it? Can they do that?

A: Yes, if you give them the authority to do so in the trust itself. But even if you don't, ending the trust may still be possible if all, not just some, of your trust beneficiaries mutually agree. But it will be costly and time-consuming. They'll need a Private Letter Ruling (PLR) from the IRS allowing them to end the trust and have all funds in the inherited IRA transferred directly into their individual inherited IRAs (trustee-to-trustee in order to avoid triggering a tax). A spouse beneficiary who had complete control of the trust could roll the inherited funds from the trust over to her own IRA, but would still likely need an IRS ruling for that as well. The best solution is to name your spouse or children directly as your contingent beneficiaries. This way if they all feel the trust is not necessary, they can easily eliminate the trust after your death by having the trustee disclaim the interest in the trust. The IRA will then pass to them directly without the complications of the trust.

and estate-planning attorney. So, the way to proceed here is to make notes right on the checklist itself of anything you don't understand or will need help with from them. Create your list of questions, then make an appointment with the advisor and/or attorney. Having your questions prepared and ready to go over with them will not only save on time and possibly expense, but will expose very quickly whether they have the "right stuff" or not and if you need to look for advice elsewhere.

A Word to the Wise

If you have named a trust as your IRA beneficiary, do all you can during your lifetime to make that IRA a Roth IRA. Why? Naming a trust as a beneficiary of a Roth IRA removes the trust tax problem. If the trust is an accumulation trust (also known as a discretionary trust) where some or all of the IRA distributions are accumulated instead of paid out to the trust income beneficiary, the distributions will be trapped in the trust and taxed at high trust tax rates. But if a Roth IRA has a trust beneficiary, distributions to the trust have no income tax. Most people who name trusts as IRA beneficiaries do so because there are significant sums at stake and people with that much in an IRA are likely to have incomes in excess of the $100,000 Roth conversion eligibility limit and cannot convert. But under a new tax law provision, they will be eligible to convert their IRAs to Roth IRAs in 2010. Then they can leave Roth IRAs to their trusts and not have to worry about high trust tax rates, because inherited Roth IRA distributions will almost always be income-tax-free.

THE NAMING A TRUST-AS-BENEFICIARY CHECKLIST

MY NAME: ______________________ DATE: __________

MY ADVISOR'S NAME: ______________________ PLAN #: __________

Follow-ups should be added to the To Do lists at the end of this checklist.

Should I name a trust as beneficiary of my account(s)?

1. Reasons Yes:

- My beneficiary is a minor, disabled, incompetent, unsophisticated in money matters __________
- To provide an income stream __________
- A subsequent marriage—to provide income to spouse, remainder to children of prior marriage __________
- To ensure that my beneficiaries do not withdraw more than required distributions __________
- To avoid estate tax inclusion in my beneficiary's estate __________
- Generation skipping—not to exceed generation-skipping transfer tax exclusion amounts __________
- Continuation of distributions after death of beneficiary __________
- Control disposition of large retirement plans __________
- Creditor protection (The Bankruptcy Reform Act passed by Congress in 2005 gives IRAs widespread protections in Bankruptcy Court.) __________
- Divorce protection __________
- Fund charitable bequests through charitable remainder trusts (See The Naming a Charity-As-Beneficiary Checklist in this section, Part 1.) __________

2. Reasons No:

- To save estate or income tax (There is no tax benefit that can be gained with a trust that cannot be gained without a trust.) __________
- You incur trust taxation, payment of trustee fees, and other trust expenses __________
- To preserve the estate tax exemption (required distributions may deplete the plan, particularly QTIP trusts) __________
- The trust may preclude use of the stretch option __________

- Trust must be maintained for its entire term (could be decades): annual trust tax returns must be filed, trustee has fiduciary obligation to invest trust funds, account to beneficiaries, decide invasion requests, interpret terms of trust, and wind up the trust. __________

3. Factors to consider before naming a trust as my beneficiary:

- Coordination of retirement plan and trust with overall estate plan __________
- Will my spouse be the income beneficiary of the trust? __________
- Will my retirement plan be consumed by my spouse (leaving my children with little or no plan to inherit and a wasted estate exemption)? __________
- Will life insurance proceeds be available to my spouse? __________
- Separate trusts must be established before my death if I want my beneficiaries to be able to stretch distributions over their individual life expectancies—or subtrusts must be named on the beneficiary form. __________
- Who will pay the income tax on the postdeath retirement plan distributions—the trust or trust beneficiary? (Evaluate trust tax rates vs. income tax rates.) __________
- What funds will be available to pay the income taxes? __________
- Who will be the trustee (bank or trust company, family member(s), professional advisor, friend)? __________
- Trust provisions to include (e.g., invasion for health, education, emergency reasons; business investments; pay debts or bills; buy a home, etc.) __________
- Coordination with required distribution rules (See The RMD Calculations Checklist in of Section II, Part 5.) __________
- When does the trust terminate? (A trust that terminates as soon as the estate is settled should not be named a beneficiary of retirement funds.) __________
- Consider using a Roth IRA with the trust (no income tax on required distributions) __________

Comments: ____

____

____

____

If I have determined a trust is *not* necessary, STOP HERE. Otherwise, CONTINUE:

4. **I must name the trust as beneficiary on my account beneficiary form. DO NOT have retirement assets transferred to the trust. That is a taxable distribution and ends the tax-deferred status of the assets.** ____________

5. **Will the custodial document provider accept a trust as my beneficiary and make distributions according to the trust terms?** ____________

6. **Does the trust qualify as a "see-through" trust?** ____________

- It must be valid under state law. ____________
- Trust is irrevocable or becomes irrevocable upon my death. ____________
- Those beneficiaries (my trust beneficiaries) with respect to the trust's interest in my retirement plan are identifiable. ____________
- The required trust documentation must be provided by the trustee of the trust to the plan trustee, custodian, or administrator no later than October 31 of the year following the year of my death. ____________

7. **Are all my trust beneficiaries individuals (persons)? (A nonindividual beneficiary may mean an accelerated payout of the account balance—no stretch.)** ____________

8. **Will my estate be considered a trust beneficiary because the trust has language allowing the payment of estate debts and expenses?** ____________

9. **Is the right *type* of trust named?** ____________

- Conduit or discretionary trust? ____________
- Does the trust fit my estate plan? ____________

10. **Evaluate all beneficiaries of the trust to determine which ones will be considered beneficiaries of my retirement plan according to the retirement plan distribution rules. The age of the oldest of those beneficiaries is the one that will be used in calculating required distributions.** ____________

11. **Will the trust have to comply with Uniform Principal and Income Act, Unitrust, or Power of Adjustment provisions? (Has my state adopted any of these acts?)** ____________

12. Is the trust intended to qualify for the marital deduction? __________

13. Does the trust refer to a specific company plan or IRA rather than "retirement accounts" or "retirement benefits"? __________

14. Is my chosen trustee aware of the trust terms and familiar with the regulations regarding distributions from a retirement plan to a trust? __________

- How will my trust beneficiaries be paid? __________
- Who will determine the form and timing of the payouts to my trust beneficiaries? Is it the beneficiary? The trustee? __________
- When does the trust end? (Trust beneficiaries should be informed) __________
- Will my trustee need guidance? (Refer him/her to The Nonspouse Beneficiary's Checklist in Part 1 of Section III) __________
- How much of the required distribution will be subject to trust tax rates? __________

15. Is the trust assignable? __________

16. Does the trust contain any pecuniary bequests? (This will accelerate recognition of IRD) __________

Comments: ____

____

____

____

To ensure the proper implementation of the trust after my death, do the following:

17. Do NOT liquidate the retirement plan and put the resulting funds in the trust. That is a taxable distribution and ends the tax-deferred status of the assets. __________

18. Title the retirement account properly. __________

19. File for a federal identification number for the trust. __________

20. If I do not satisfy any required distribution for the year of my death, any remaining distribution must be made to the trust by 12/31 of that year. __________

21. Determine if trust should disclaim any or all of the retirement benefits within 9 months of my death. The trust can still disclaim the balance in the IRA after taking any required year-of-death distributions per Revenue Ruling 2005-36. (See The Disclaimer Planning Checklist in Part 3 of this section.) __________

22. Determine if the trust or the trust beneficiaries qualify for tax benefits. (IRD, 10-year averaging, NUA; see The IRD Checklist in Section III and The Tax Breaks for Lump-Sum Distribution Checklist in Section IV for 10-year-averaging and NUA.) __________

23. My trustee must provide trust documentation (either a copy of the trust or a list of the beneficiaries and their entitlement) to the retirement plan custodian by 10/31 of the year after my death. __________

24. Evaluate my trust beneficiaries to determine beneficiary with shortest life expectancy. (Required distributions will be based on this life expectancy.) __________

25. Required distributions will begin in the year following my death. Distributions should be made to the trust using the trust tax ID number, then be distributed to my trust beneficiaries in accordance with the trust language. (There is a 50 percent penalty on any required distribution not taken.) __________

Comments: ____

____

____

____

____

Follow-Up

My To Do List	Date Completed
1	
2	
3	
4	
5	
6	
7	
8	
9	
10	

My Signature ________________________ Date ____________

Part 3

THE DISCLAIMER PLANNING CHECKLIST

For account owners and beneficiaries

What It Does

A disclaimer is a written refusal by the beneficiary to receive assets, such as a retirement account, that would otherwise pass to him or her. In effect, it treats the inheritance as if the named beneficiary had died before the account owner so that the assets will go to whoever is named next in line, allowing the assets to be removed from one estate and pass to another without triggering income tax.

Ask Ed . . .

Q: **What is a "renunciation"?**

A: It is the legal term for a disclaimer. It means the same thing—the beneficiary is electing to refuse a gift or inheritance.

Changing beneficiaries on an IRA or company plan is different from changing beneficiaries on most other types of property because it is the age and type of beneficiary that determines the postdeath payout term and the Required Minimum Distributions that must be taken. A change, therefore, can have a huge impact on the eventual value of the inherited account. So, proper planning is important.

Disclaimer planning is one of the best estate-planning strategies available because it enables an account owner to create a contingency scenario that permits his or her beneficiaries to alter the deceased's estate plan on an as-needed basis, allowing them to put Plan B into effect if Plan A is no longer viable.

Of course, disclaiming begs the question: "What sane person would ever refuse an inheritance?" Actually, many people disclaim, and few of them are insane (in this area anyway). For example, if a spouse inherits a large estate and on top of that also inherits an IRA, she can disclaim the IRA, and if the children are named as contingent beneficiaries, the IRA will pass to them, and they can stretch it over their lifetimes. The disclaimer provides the spouse with much-needed flexibility.

Now you might ask, "Well, if the spouse didn't want the IRA herself but wished it to go to her children why didn't her husband (the late IRA owner) just name the children instead of her in the first place?" Good question. And here's the answer: Perhaps when the original planning was done, neither she nor the husband was sure if she would need the money or not to live on when he died. So, he

Ask Ed . . .

Q: How much can I disclaim? Is there a limit?

A: No, there is no limit. You can disclaim a billion-dollar inheritance if you wish and remove that from your estate with no estate or gift tax being assessed.

Q: How do I actually do a disclaimer or renunciation?

A: After inheriting, you should have an estate attorney prepare a disclaimer statement for you, which you will sign and then serve on the plan custodian (the IRA institution holding the funds). I would also file it and have it recorded with the probate court like a property deed simply as further proof that the disclaimer was done within the appropriate 9-month deadline just in case the IRS or anyone else questions you. The stamp of the court on the document is the best proof you can have—especially if the IRA custodian loses your signed statement, which is not uncommon. The executor of the estate should have a copy as well. I would also attach a copy of the disclaimer to the estate tax return if one has to be filed. You should also keep a stamped and dated copy with your permanent tax records—as should the person who receives the property as a result of your disclaimer.

planned for each contingency by giving her the flexibility to disclaim.

In another example, let's say you're an account owner who wants to leave part of your retirement account to charity, but you still want to make sure your spouse has all the money she needs. So, you name your spouse as your primary beneficiary and the charity as contingent beneficiary. After your death, if your spouse finds that she does not need all the funds you left her and wishes to pursue the charitable bequest you had in mind, she can disclaim the share that she wants to go to the charity, and that is where it will go.

So, for account owners, this checklist covers all the points you need to know in order to properly lay out a disclaimer path for your beneficiaries. And for beneficiaries, it alerts you to the fact that a disclaimer plan is in place (assuming the owner hasn't told you already) and points out what you must do on your end if and when you want to disclaim.

Ask Ed . . .

Q: **Can I disclaim for a dead person?**

A: Yes, and in fact this happens frequently. For example if a husband dies and leaves an IRA to his wife and she dies right after that without taking possession, then the executor of her estate (probably the couple's child), can disclaim the inheritance on behalf of the estate so that it passes to the next-in-line beneficiary, allowing distributions to be taken over the child's longer life expectancy.

Q: **My mom has named the three of us as beneficiaries of her IRA. My sister and I have children of our own, my brother does not. I don't need the funds from the IRA. If I disclaim, will my two children get my share, or will it go to my sister and brother?**

A: You can make sure your children get your share of the IRA in two ways. (1) Asking your mom to split her IRA into three separate shares, naming you as her primary beneficiary and your children as her contingent beneficiaries on the share going to you. Or (2) asking your mom to include the phrase "per stirpes" (meaning "per branch" or "by the stem") on her beneficiary form so that if you disclaim, your share follows your branch of the family tree and would go to your children, not to your sister and brother. But you have to be careful; not all IRA custodians allow the use of per stirpes.

What's In It for Me?

As a retirement account owner, you will be at ease knowing that the estate plan you have created for your account has the maneuverability to roll with the punches should your beneficiaries need or want to alter who gets the account and when due to circumstances you could not have foreseen while putting your plan in place. And for a beneficiary, this maneuverability could possibly add years of life and considerably more value to your inheritance. Disclaimer planning can accomplish these goals by laying out a ready-made road map that covers all the bases and contingencies.

Ask Ed . . .

Q: Can I disclaim if there is no contingent beneficiary?

A: Yes, you can always disclaim your inheritance, but if no contingent beneficiary is named, why would you want to? The funds could wind up as a probate asset and never reach the person you would like them to.

What If I Don't?

You may stick your beneficiaries with an inheritance path that may not work out best for them—or for your account—because family and financial issues may change between the time you laid out that path and your death. This roadblock to postdeath flexibility could trigger taxes that might severely diminish the account balance if not wipe it out altogether.

The stretch IRA opportunity for a younger secondary beneficiary could be lost as well if there is a need but no disclaimer plan in place for the primary beneficiary to transfer the account. And a hefty gift tax could be levied on the primary and secondary beneficiaries if they tried to effect this transfer without a proper disclaimer plan in place.

Ask Ed . . .

Q: If the deceased owner has not taken his year-of-death RMD, and I as beneficiary want to disclaim the inherited account, which must come first, taking the year-of-death RMD or the disclaimer?

A: In the past, beneficiaries were advised to disclaim before taking the year-of-death RMD. The reason for this was to make it clear that they have accepted no part of the account. But the disclaiming process sometimes caused them to miss the December 31 deadline for taking the year-of-death RMD, leading to a 50 percent penalty. A recent IRS Revenue Ruling (2005-36) now allows beneficiaries to take the year of death RMD and still be able to disclaim the balance afterward—they just can't disclaim the RMD once it is taken.

Q: My dad died at 78 and had not yet taken his Required Minimum Distribution for the year, so I know that as his primary beneficiary, I must take that distribution. What happens if I want to withdraw more than the RMD, can I still disclaim the balance?

A: Since this was not specifically covered in the IRS Revenue Ruling 2005-36, the unofficial answer is yes, you as the beneficiary can still disclaim the balance of the IRA.

Q: Can a beneficiary always disclaim after taking the year-of-death RMD?

A: Not always. For example, Bill dies in January and Mary is the primary beneficiary. Mary has until October (9 months) to disclaim so her daughter Sarah (the contingent beneficiary) will inherit, but the year-of-death distribution does not have to be taken until December 31. If Mary waits until November to take the year-of-death RMD, she cannot disclaim after that since the nine-month disclaimer deadline has passed. Now, you may ask, "Does the year-of-death distribution have to be taken before making the disclaimer?" And the answer again is, not always. Using the same example, if the disclaimer is made in October, the year of death RMD still does not have to be taken until December. There is no guidance as to which beneficiary (Mary or Sarah) should take the year-of-death distribution, so there is an opportunity here to do some postmortem planning and choose which beneficiary receives that distribution. However, if the primary beneficiary does a complete disclaimer prior to the distribution of the year-of-death RMD, then the contingent beneficiary is required to take that distribution.

Instructions

For a disclaimer to be effective in allowing the change of a previously designated beneficiary to another after the owner's death, the disclaimer must qualify. As with everything else, certain requirements determine whether it qualifies or not:

1. It (the refusal) must be made in writing.
2. The property must be disclaimed within nine months of the date of death. This is a strict rule, but there is an exception for minors, who have nine months from the time they turn age 21 to disclaim.
3. The property cannot already have been taken into possession by the primary beneficiary.
4. Whoever disclaims cannot direct who gets the property. It must pass to the next-in-line beneficiary (the contingent beneficiary, if there is one) named by the deceased owner without any interference or direction by the person disclaiming. Furthermore, the property must pass to someone other than the disclaimant (unless the disclaimant is the spouse of the deceased). In other words, except for a spouse beneficiary, you cannot disclaim an inherited account knowing that you will get it back (through the estate, for example) as a result of the disclaimer.

If you are the account owner, use this checklist to formulate your disclaimer plan for each of your retirement accounts, remembering to name a primary and, most important, a contingent beneficiary on each so that the path will be clear as crystal as to who inherits should the primary beneficiary disclaim. Then share this information with your primary and contingent beneficiaries so they will know that this path is available to them.

If you are a beneficiary-to-be and are concerned about whether your potential benefactor's silence on this issue indicates no disclaimer planning on your behalf, bring the issue up now and thrust this checklist under his or her nose.

Ask Ed . . .

Q: Will changing the title on the account mean that the beneficiary can't disclaim?

A: Although this issue is not directly addressed in Ruling 2005-36, it would appear that changing the account title would not mean the beneficiary has accepted an interest in the account. This is because many custodial institutions are going to automatically change the title on the account when they change the social security number to the beneficiary's social security number in order to pay out the year-of-death RMD.

THE DISCLAIMER PLANNING CHECKLIST

MY NAME: ______________________ DATE: ____________

MY ADVISOR'S NAME: ______________________ PLAN #: ____________

Follow-ups should be added to the To Do lists at the end of this checklist.

A disclaimer is used when an IRA or plan beneficiary wishes to refuse (disclaim) all or part of the inherited asset so it can pass to the next-in-line beneficiary (usually the named contingent beneficiary). The account owner or plan participant chooses the disclaimer path. The choice to disclaim is that of the beneficiary. A disclaimer is a legal document and as such it should only be drawn up by an attorney.

1. Reasons to plan for a disclaimer (why my primary beneficiary might disclaim):

- My primary beneficiary may not want or need the inherited property (it may be better to keep it out of his/her estate). ____________
- It may be better for the asset to go to a younger beneficiary to take advantage of a longer stretch period. ____________
- I want the flexibility to maximize my estate-planning strategies (to fund a credit shelter trust, for example, or make a charitable bequest, etc.). ____________
- There may be a need to adjust my estate plan after my death (for example if I have named a trust as my beneficiary and that no longer may be the best choice). ____________

Comments: ______________________

____

____

____

____

2. Plan ahead for the right outcome of a disclaimer by:

- Naming a contingent beneficiary so I will know where the property will go. ____________
- Including a "per stirpes" provision in my beneficiary form. ____________
- Considering how the disclaimer will affect stretch distributions. ____________

3. Will the disclaimer cause estate tax? If so:

- Who will pay estate taxes on the disclaimed asset (check the tax apportionment clause in my will or trust)? ____________
- Is there life insurance or some other source of money available to pay the tax? ____________
- Will the disclaimer set up a conflict with estate tax provisions in the will or trust, creating an inadvertent result (a larger share of the estate tax being paid by an unintended beneficiary)? ____________

4. Will the disclaimer result in generation-skipping transfer taxes if the asset goes to a grandchild? (The exemption is $2 million for 2006–2008)

5. I have no guarantee that my beneficiary will disclaim. ____________

Comments: ____

____

____

____

____

6. A qualified disclaimer must meet ALL the following tests:

- It must be an irrevocable and unqualified refusal. ____________
- It must be submitted in writing. ____________
- The disclaimer must be received by the transferor of the interest, his/her legal representative, or the holder of the legal title to the property to which the interest relates no later than 9 months after the later of: ____________

  —The day on which the transfer is made ____________

  —Or, the day on which the transferor attains age 21 ____________
- The person disclaiming must not have accepted the interest or any of its benefits. ____________
- As a result of the disclaimer, the interest passes without any direction on the part of the person making the disclaimer. ____________
- The interest passes to the spouse of the decedent or to a person other than the person making the disclaimer. ____________

7. If the account title is changed after the death of the plan owner, the account can still be disclaimed as long as it remains an "inherited account" (see definition, Section III, Part 1). ____________

8. A spousal rollover is considered acceptance of the account, which cannot thereafter be disclaimed. __________

9. Making investment decisions (exercising investment control) is considered acceptance of the account, which thereafter cannot be disclaimed. __________

10. Property cannot be disclaimed in exchange for something else. That is considered acceptance. __________

11. In addition to complying with all the federal laws previously listed, the disclaimer must comply with any other requirements imposed by state law. __________

Comments: ____

____

____

____

____

12. A beneficiary can do a partial disclaimer of a retirement account. __________

13. A beneficiary can disclaim before or after taking any Required Minimum Distribution (RMD) due upon the death of the plan owner. __________

14. A beneficiary can take more than the RMD and still disclaim. __________

15. When the disclaimed amount is a stated dollar figure (e.g. $100,000), earnings accrued on that amount from the date of the plan owner's death are also considered to be disclaimed. __________

16. An executor or personal representative can disclaim for a deceased person. __________

17. A trustee can disclaim on behalf of a trust that inherits the retirement plan, provided the trustee is not the beneficiary next in line to receive the disclaimed bequest unless the next-in-line beneficiary is the spouse. __________

Comments: ____

____

____

____

____

____

18. Steps for doing a disclaimer:

- Provide a list of the account custodian(s) and contact information to the attorney preparing the disclaimer. ______
- Include account number(s). ______
- Provide name and contact information of administrator of employer plan. ______
- Include the date of death of the asset owner. ______
- Determine who will handle the delivery of the disclaimer—beneficiary, attorney, trustee, etc. ______
- File with the court as a precaution to establish the date of the disclaimer. ______
- Make note of when the disclaimer is delivered. If the deadline for making the disclaimer falls on a Saturday, Sunday, or holiday, the deadline is extended to the next business day. Timely mailing is considered timely delivery. ______

Comments: ____

____

____

____

____

____

____

____

____

____

____

Follow-Up

My To Do List | Date Completed

1 ____________________

2 ____________________

3 ____________________

4 ____________________

5 ____________________

6 ____________________

7 ____________________

8 ____________________

9 ____________________

10 ____________________

My Signature | Date

Part 4

THE DIVORCE CHECKLIST

For account owners

What It Does

There is no such thing as a joint retirement account. And because a couple's individual retirement savings—whether his is in a 401(k) and hers is in an IRA or vice versa—is likely to be the single largest asset each owns, it is more likely in a divorce situation to be the asset they will have to split up. How it is split up will determine whether the divorce action turns into a ménage à trois, with the Taxman as trois.

Retirement money is tax-sheltered until the shelter becomes a broken home. That's just what happens in a divorce situation. You cannot just give part (or all) of your retirement account to your ex-spouse as part of a property settlement without properly planning each step of the transaction—otherwise, you could expose your entire plan balance to taxes, which may result in your account being liquidated to pay the IRS.

To add to the problem, many divorce lawyers, accountants, and financial advisors are not as familiar with the steps involved in this type of divorce transaction as they are with how to split ownership of a

Ask Ed . . .

Q: Under the terms of my divorce decree I have agreed that my former spouse will receive my entire IRA in exchange for my receiving a larger share of other assets. How should I transfer the funds in this case?

A: This is probably the easiest transfer to execute since you don't have to actually move the money in your IRA. You simply retitle the IRA with the name and social security number of your former spouse, since he or she is receiving the entire balance in accordance with your divorce decree. But you can also do a trustee-to-trustee (direct) transfer of your entire account into an account of your former spouse's. With either method, the transfer will be tax-free.

house, say, or other kinds of property that don't come with the complex tax baggage retirement accounts do.

This checklist will guide you and your attorney/advisor through the delicate process of splitting either an IRA or a company plan balance in the event that your marriage bond goes the way of Ken and Barbie's or Jen and Brad's. It covers all those critical circumstances you might never even think of, let alone resolve, at such an emotional time.

What's In It for Me?

Splitting up property in a divorce settlement is traumatic enough to go through without having the Taxman also coming in with an outstretched hand. In most cases, it's also a complicated enough task to work out without having to worry about whether you may make a mistake in the language of the settlement that could send your entire account into the welcoming arms of your ex, or the IRS. If you adhere to this checklist, however, your divorce may not be amicable, but it should at least be tax-free to you insofar as the split of your retirement funds is concerned.

Ask Ed . . .

Q: I am getting divorced, but a few years back I needed to tap some of my funds early (before age 59½), so under the tax rules I began taking periodic withdrawals of substantially equal payments* to avoid the 10 percent penalty for early withdrawal. The problem is that under the divorce decree I have agreed that my ex-wife will receive 40 percent of my IRA. How do I do this without breaking my substantially equal payment schedule (which still has several years left) and getting hit retroactively for all the years I withdrew penalty-free?

A: In several private letter rulings (PLRs) the IRS has said that if a soon-to-be-former-spouse—is to receive a certain percentage (in your case 40 percent) of her soon-to-be-ex-husband's IRA as part of the divorce agreement, and hubby is currently taking payments under the substantially equal payment early withdrawal exception, then the 40 percent can be transferred to the ex-wife's account. Furthermore, hubby's remaining payments can be reduced by 40 percent (the percentage of the account transferred to her) and the payment schedule will not be broken by this action. Hubby will not be subject to back penalties as long as he continues taking 60 percent of his original payment amount from the remaining 60 percent in his IRA according to the terms of his payout schedule.

*Also known as 72(t) payments; see The Early Distribution Exceptions—72(t) Payments Checklist in this section, Part 5.

What If I Don't?

You will probably get the shaft. If you are the one with the IRA or plan, you may also have to pay tax and a 10 percent penalty (if you are under age 59½) on the amount you transfer, just at the time when you will probably have little or no money available to pay that tax and penalty because of all the other divorce expenses that have hit you. Of course, if you are the owner's ex-spouse, you may not care if your former wife or husband has to pay taxes and penalties—just as long as you don't. But if you are that former wife or husband who is reading this, you will want to make sure you do everything right so you keep your fair share of the mine and don't end up with the shaft.

Even a seemingly straightforward agreement to split an IRA or company plan in a divorce settlement can become a minefield of potential headaches and gross inequities if the agreement is not properly worded. Here are two very different examples:

In the first, the divorcing couple mutually agreed that the ex-wife would receive $800,000 (or half) of her ex-husband's $1,600,000 IRA. But when the account was finally split in accordance with the divorce agreement, the stock market had tanked and the value of the IRA was now only $1,200,000. Since the wording of the agreement stipulated that the ex-wife was to receive a specified dollar amount ($800,000) rather than a specified percentage (in this case 50 percent) or fraction (½), the ex-wife wound up getting two-thirds ($800,000) of the account, and her ex-husband (the account owner) got the remainder, which was now down to $400,000, or half what he would otherwise have received, just because of the wording of the agreement. If the agreement had simply stated a fraction or percentage rather than a specific dollar amount, this inequity could have been avoided.

Going with a split percentage or fraction settlement doesn't necessarily ensure an equitable outcome though if, as in this second example, the divorcing couple doesn't get its percentages straight. Their agreement said the soon-to-be-ex-husband's 401(k) would be split by the same percentage as all the other assets to be divided between the two. Unfortunately, there was no consistent percentage in the agreement for all assets. So, instead of an easy, straightforward, and relatively amicable split, things got ugly, a court battle ensued, and a team of expensive lawyers went on the dueling duo's payroll to fight it out over who got what. This could all have been avoided with a more carefully considered and more carefully thought-out agreement, or

Ask Ed . . .

Q: If I am under 59½ and in a 401(k) that my former wife is to receive a portion of in accordance with the QDRO, can she roll those funds over to an IRA and would I have to pay a 10 percent early withdrawal penalty on the rollover?

A: The portion of your 401(k) plan that will go to your former wife under the QDRO can be rolled over to her IRA so long as you would have been eligible to roll it to your own IRA if the distribution was made to you. (She can also roll those funds into her own employer plan.) No, there is no penalty; a distribution subject to a QDRO is exempt from the 10 percent early withdrawal tax.

Qualified Domestic Relations Order (QDRO, pronounced "Kwadrow"). This is the order or judgment issued under the domestic relations laws of a state to determine the split of a qualified company plan such as a 401(k) in a divorce settlement. (IRAs are split in accordance with the divorce or separate maintenance decree or a written document related to the decree, not with a QDRO.)

Instructions

If you are going through a divorce, do not—I repeat NOT—move one cent of your IRA or company plan funds without first going through this checklist. Even after you review the checklist, still touch nothing—until you have gone over it again with your financial advisor, accountant, and attorney to make sure that your retirement funds are split according to the QDRO (if you have a qualified company plan) or according to the divorce decree (if you are splitting an IRA). The funds that are split should be moved only by trustee-to-trustee transfer (a rollover to your ex's account must be done within 60 days or there will be tax consequences, a mistake that kills many an IRA for spouses attempting to transfer these assets in a divorce).

Under a QDRO, the account owner's ex-spouse becomes what is known as an "alternate payee" entitled to receive a percentage of the owner's 401(k). But the QDRO cannot force the plan to make a distribution that is against the plan rules, so the ex-spouse may not be able to access these funds immediately. So, all you former spouses out there on the receiving end of a QDRO whose ex is in this position, beware. What good is receiving half your spouse's 401(k) if you cannot get your hands on it because the plan may not allow for withdrawals until many years later? In that case you should negotiate to receive other assets that you can get your hands on *now* in lieu of the 401(k).

Ask Ed . . .

Q: If as a result of my divorce and in accordance with a QDRO I am to receive a portion of my ex-husband's 401(k) plan, can I qualify for the lump-sum distribution NUA (Net Unrealized Appreciation) tax break on company stock in his plan?

A: Yes, but only if he is eligible for a lump-sum distribution due to separation from service, reaching age 59½, death or disability (if self-employed) or similar event. Then you can take the NUA tax break on your portion of the lump-sum distribution the same as he can. (See The Tax Breaks for Lump-Sum Distributions Checklist in Part 7 of this section)

THE DIVORCE CHECKLIST

MY NAME: ________________ **DATE:** ________

MY ADVISOR'S NAME: ________________ **PLAN #:** ________

Follow-ups should be added to the To Do lists at the end of this checklist.

1. Insert Contact Information ________

________________ ________
My attorney—Name Phone Number

________________ ________
My spouse's attorney—Name Phone Number

________________ ________
My company plan contact—Name Phone Number

________________ ________
My IRA contact—Name Phone Number

Comments: ________________

____

____

____

____

2. I understand that any voluntary payments made to my ex-spouse without a QDRO (for an employer plan) or divorce or separation agreement (for an IRA), will be taxable to me (plus a 10 percent early distribution penalty, if applicable) and my ex will not have a tax-deferred account. ________

3. I understand that a prenuptial agreement does not waive spousal benefits available in an employer plan. Benefits can only be waived by a spouse who signs a consent form provided by the employer. ________

4. Is my advisor familiar with the specifics of how a retirement account is split in a divorce? ________

5. Is this an employer plan or an IRA? __________

- I understand that a QDRO cannot force distributions that are not allowed under the terms of the employer plan. __________
- Specify in the agreement or QDRO who will pay fees or penalties related to the splitting of the accounts, if any. __________
- State the specifics clearly: __________

  —If I want my ex-spouse to receive a specific amount, specify a dollar amount or a percentage of a specific account value as of a specified date. __________

  —If I want to limit what my ex receives in the event of a potential change in my account balance (such as a market collapse), specify a percentage or a fraction with no as of date to be received. (**Example:** "My spouse gets 50 percent" would mean he or she gets *no more than 50 percent* no matter what the account balance is on the date of the split.) __________

6. All movement of funds should be done as direct (trustee-to-trustee) transfers rather than rollovers. __________

Comments: ____

____

____

____

____

7. With a QDRO: __________

- After the QDRO is delivered to the company, my ex-spouse's share of the assets are segregated and the company has an obligation to preserve them. __________
- The company has up to 18 months to review and approve the QDRO. __________

Comments: ____

____

____

____

8. With a divorce or separation agreement for splitting an IRA: ____________

- The IRA custodian should get a copy of the divorce decree or separation agreement before I move any funds to my ex-spouse's account. ____________
- I should do a trustee-to-trustee transfer to my ex-spouse's account. ____________

9. If I have a 72(t) payment plan on the account I have to split, I can split it without breaking the 72(t) schedule and incurring penalties. ____________

Note: The IRS has had a major policy shift on this; it is now recommended that you get a PLR if you want to do this.

- I should use a trustee-to-trustee transfer. ____________
- My ex-spouse does not have to continue my 72(t) payments on the portion received from my account. ____________
- I can reduce my payments proportionally (if my spouse gets half of my account, I can reduce my payments by half). ____________

Comments: ____

____

____

____

10. As soon as my ex and I have split my account, update my beneficiary form to make sure my ex does not wind up with the remaining balance at my death. ____________

11. If I have an RMD for the year of the split, the transfer of assets to my spouse does not reduce the RMD amount for the year. I must take the full RMD from the remaining assets in my account. ____________

12. For tax filing purposes, marital status is determined as of 12/31 of the year (if married on 1/1, for retirement plan purposes I am considered to be married for the entire year). ____________

Comments: ______________________________

____

____

____

____

Follow-Up

My To Do List | Date Completed

1 ______________________________

2 ______________________________

3 ______________________________

4 ______________________________

5 ______________________________

6 ______________________________

7 ______________________________

8 ______________________________

9 ______________________________

10 ______________________________

______________________________ ______________

My Signature | Date

Part 5

THE EARLY-DISTRIBUTION EXCEPTIONS—72(t) PAYMENTS CHECKLIST

A Word to the Wise

You should never withdraw funds from your retirement account early for some arbitrary reason like buying a big-screen TV. Withdrawing early is rarely a good idea and should be avoided at all costs—or used as an absolute last resort because you have no other resources you can tap for must-have cash. Remember, you have spent many years of disciplined saving to build the account into what it is, and withdrawing from it early could defeat the very purpose for which you have been saving—a comfortable retirement. It is the hardest money to replace because whether you get hit with the 10 percent early withdrawal penalty or not, you still must pay tax on the withdrawal, and that will eat into the money you can actually spend. So, just because there may be some exceptions to the early distribution penalty rules, don't just jump at them.

What It Does

An early withdrawal under our tax laws is any distribution taken from a company retirement plan or IRA before you reach age 59½. Generally, an early withdrawal not only triggers income tax on the tax-deferred funds that are withdrawn but also a 10 percent penalty on those funds. This checklist is for those of you who may need to tap into your account early and seek to avoid the 10 percent penalty, if possible.

There are several exceptions to the early withdrawal penalty rule. This checklist covers the exception known as "annuitizing" (taking what tax law calls "a series of substantially equal periodic payments") or simply abbreviated as "72(t)" (after the section of the tax law that allows this exception). I'll use the latter reference because it is shorter.

The 72(t) payment exception is a way to take penalty-free early distributions based on an IRS approved payment schedule. This checklist tells you what to consider before deciding whether to take the early withdrawal plunge, guides you through the ins and outs of the basic 72(t) payment rules so that you will execute the plunge safely, and shows you how to create the most-tax-efficient 72(t) payment schedule, one that will eat up the smallest amount of your IRA or plan assets.

What this checklist does *not* do is calculate your 72(t) payments for you. For that you will need a financial advisor with experience in

Ask Ed . . .

Q: Can I take 72(t) payments from my 401(k) plan?

A: Yes, but only if you are separated from service and the plan allows the 72(t) exception, which it does not have to. So, check with the plan custodian.

Q: Do I have to use my entire IRA for making the 72(t) payment calculation?

A: No. You can split your IRA into several IRAs and use only one to calculate your 72(t) payments, leaving your other IRA funds free of any 72(t) current commitment—and therefore able to be used in the future for other 72(t) payment plans if the need arises.

this area. He or she will use a computer program—such as "Pension & Roth IRA Analyzer" (Brentmark Software—www.brentmark.com)—for calculating the 72(t) payment schedule for you under applicable interest rates. Your advisor should provide printouts of your payment schedule for documentation purposes in the event the IRS ever questions you about how you came up with your payment amounts. So, be sure to ask for them before you leave.

What's In It for Me?

Although not advisable, there are some valid reasons for tapping into your account early. For example, let's say you are already retired but are not yet 59½, and you need funds to pay your everyday ex-

Ask Ed . . .

Q: If I am taking 72(t) payments and I die, do my beneficiaries have to keep the payments going?

A: No. Death gets you out of your 72(t) commitment—and with no penalty either. Ain't that great!

Q: What if the plan custodian issues a 1099-R form indicating that the 10 percent penalty applies even though I am taking 72(t) payments correctly? How will I explain this to the IRS and avoid the penalty?

A: This happens all the time. You can set things straight on your tax return by attaching Form 5329 and enter code 2 (distributions made as a part of a series of substantially equal periodic payments) showing that this exception applies to you. Better yet, make the IRA custodian aware you are taking 72(t) payments so that your 1099-R is issued correctly. But at least you have a backup plan if the custodian still messes up.

penses. Or you are doing some estate planning and need to fund some trusts. These reasons are exactly what this exception was created for.

What If I Don't?

Well, if you don't tap your funds early, there's no harm, no foul. A problem arises only if you tap them early and incorrectly. You'll probably get hit with the 10 percent penalty, and that would be a real waste of money, especially at a time that you need it most. Here's why:

The 72(t) payment exception is a way to take penalty-free early distributions based on an IRS-approved payment schedule. But you must *stick* like glue to that schedule, or else you won't qualify for the exception and will have to pay the piper. As if that isn't bad enough, here's the even worse part—the penalty is assessed *retroactively,* which means that you will owe the IRS the 10 percent penalty for all the back years since you began the 72(t) schedule, *plus interest*!

The bottom line is that this can get ugly, so if I still haven't talked you out of it by now, you must really need early access to your money, and should read on.

Ask Ed . . .

Q: If I am taking 72(t) distributions from an IRA, can I move that IRA to a different IRA custodian without breaking the 72(t) payment schedule?

A: Yes, as long as you continue the scheduled 72(t) payments from that account. Also, you cannot move the funds to an IRA that has existing funds in it; otherwise, you will have changed the balance and broken the 72(t) payment schedule. If you are going to transfer the funds to another IRA, it must be a new IRA with no other money in it.

Q: If I have four separate accounts—all of them IRAs, for example—can I use all four in one calculation for a 72(t) payment schedule and then take just one check from one of the accounts? Or, would there need to be four calculations, then a distribution from each of the four accounts separately?

A: You can add the four balances in the four IRAs, make one calculation based on the total, and take the 72(t) payments from any one or combination of those accounts. But if you use all four in making the one 72(t) calculation, you cannot contribute to those 72(t) accounts nor roll over funds from, say, a fifth IRA not used in the calculation into any of those four accounts. You can only transfer funds among the four 72(t) accounts.

Instructions

Use this checklist to determine (a) if you qualify for the 72(t) payment exception, (b) if it is right for you, and (c) how to go about it correctly. As mentioned earlier, there are other penalty-free exceptions (see this section Part 6) that you might consider as an alternative.

To qualify for the 72(t) payment exception, you must use one of the IRS-approved payment schedules and adhere to this schedule for five years or until you reach 59½, whichever is longer. You may find that you are too young or do not have enough in your IRA or company plan to generate a large enough payment. The IRS-approved 72(t) payments do not let you just empty your retirement savings. You can only take a portion, and it is based on your age. The younger you are, the longer your life expectancy and the lower your payments will be.

So first off, see if taking the 72(t) payments will be enough since they will be taken over time. Many people, especially younger people, find that even the best 72(t) payment method still does not produce the amount of income that they need, especially if they need a big lump sum. For example, if you need $50,000 and, based on your age, your 72(t) payments under the best method come out to only $1,000 a month (or $12,000 a year), that won't help you. If that is the case, the monthly or annual payments simply won't cut it for your cash needs. But if you need the payments on an ongoing basis—for retirement or living expenses as an example—then taking 72(t) payments may work out better for you.

Ask Ed . . .

Q: What if I begin taking 72(t) payments because I lost my job and needed the money, but later get a new job and no longer need the 72(t) payments? I know I cannot break the schedule without getting hit with the retroactive 10 percent penalty. But since I no longer need the money, can I stick to the schedule but roll the payments back into my account?

A: No. You cannot do that. Under the law, 72(t) payments are not eligible rollover distributions.

THE EARLY-DISTRIBUTION EXCEPTIONS—72(t) PAYMENTS CHECKLIST

MY NAME: ______________________ **DATE:** __________

MY ADVISOR'S NAME: ______________________ **PLAN #:** __________

Follow-ups should be added to the To Do Lists at the end of this checklist.

Once a 72(t) payment plan is established, it CANNOT be modified or changed except in the case of your death or disability.

1. Reasons why I might need to set up a 72(t) payment plan:

- Early retirement—my retirement funds are my only source of income __________
- For estate planning—I need to fund a trust, make gifts, buy life insurance, equalize assets in my estate __________
- Financial hardship __________

Comments: ______________________

2. Factors to consider before setting up a payment plan:

- What other sources of nonretirement funds are available to me? __________
- Can I afford to deplete my retirement savings now? __________
- How much do I have in my retirement account? __________
- Am I too young or too old to qualify? __________
- Have I really retired? __________
- Do I have a company plan? (If I separated from service in the year I was age 55 or later, my distributions are not subject to the 10 percent penalty.) __________
- Am I ready to make the commitment? __________

3. The Basic Rules

- I can start at any age. __________

  EXCEPTION: for a company plan I must be separated from service (if I separated from service at age 55 or later the 10 percent penalty does not apply to distributions from the plan). __________

- Distributions must continue for 5 full years (until the last day of the fifth year) or until age 59½ (the date I turn 59½, not the year), whichever is ***later.*** __________

- Payments cannot be modified by changing the amount of the payment, the balance in the plan account, or the calculation method. __________

  EXCEPTION: My death __________

  EXCEPTION: I become disabled __________

  EXCEPTION: My account balance is exhausted __________

  EXCEPTION: An allowed onetime only change from either the annuitized or amortized payment method to the minimum distribution method. (The IRS has approved three methods for calculating the 72(t) distributions: annuitization; amortization; minimum distribution.) __________

  Will I qualify for a onetime switch to the minimum distribution method? __________

  EXCEPTION: Divorce (if all or a part of your account is awarded to your ex-spouse). If only part is awarded, the 72(t) distributions can be adjusted proportionally (it is recommended that you get a Private Letter Ruling to do this). __________

- I can take no other distributions from the account, even if they qualify for a different penalty exception. __________

- No other contributions, rollovers, or deposits can be made to the account. __________

- The interest rate used cannot be more than 120 percent of the federal midterm rate for either of the 2 months preceding the month of the first distribution. __________

- Failure to satisfy any of the basic rules means disqualification of all payments made under the plan since inception. The 10 percent early distribution penalty will be applied to all taxable payments made to me prior to age 59½. __________

Comments: ____

____

____

____

____

____

4. Thoroughly analyze income and expenses—once a payment schedule is set up, it generally *cannot* be changed. __________

5. Determine the amount desired from the account. __________

Comments: ____

____

____

____

____

6. Calculate amount allowable using IRS-approved methods, allowable interest rate, and life-expectancy tables (software is a big help here; there are also calculators available on the Internet). __________

- Use the Single Life Table (Appendix I) to produce the largest possible 72(t) payment from the smallest amount of retirement funds. __________
- If the amount calculated is too large, split the account into two smaller accounts—one that will give me the desired distribution amount and one with the excess. __________

7. More than one account can be used in the calculation to produce the amount needed. Distributions can be made from any one of the accounts or across all the accounts as long as the required amount is distributed annually. Amounts can be transferred between these accounts. (Such transfers will probably result in 1099-R coding showing a taxable distribution).

- How many accounts will be used in the 72(t) calculation? __________

8. Decide on amount/payment method to use. __________

9. **Will I need a PLR to set up a customized payment schedule for inflation adjustments, etc.?** ________

Comments: ________

10. **If I must split the account to allow for a smaller distribution amount, transfer all necessary assets *before* taking the first withdrawal.** ________

11. **Instruct my plan provider, in writing, to set up the 72(t) schedule.** ________

- Distributions can be taken more frequently than annually. ________
- Distributions can be set up on a fiscal year rather than a calendar year. ________

12. **Maintain detailed records of all calculations and correspondence, in case of an IRS audit.** ________

13. **Look for modifications that could jeopardize my penalty exception.** ________

14. **I can convert my 72(t) payment account to a Roth IRA before the payment schedule is completed, but:**

- Distributions required under the 72(t) plan must continue from the Roth IRA until the payment schedule is completed. ________
- Distributions required under the plan cannot be converted. ________

15. **Follow up with my plan provider (custodian) to ensure that distributions are coded correctly on its tax-reporting system so that the 1099-R is issued correctly, showing an early distribution exception applies.** ________

16. **At year-end, double-check to be sure the total distribution has been made for the year (check fiscal-year schedules).** ________

Comments: ______________________________

____

____

____

____

____

Follow-Up

My To Do List | Date Completed

1 ______________________________

2 ______________________________

3 ______________________________

4 ______________________________

5 ______________________________

6 ______________________________

7 ______________________________

8 ______________________________

9 ______________________________

10 ______________________________

______________________________ ______________

My Signature | Date

Part 6

THE EARLY-DISTRIBUTION—OTHER EXCEPTIONS CHECKLIST

For account owners

Account Owner Alert!

The Pension Protection Act of 2006 created two new 10-percent penalty exceptions. The first is for reservists called to active duty and it creates an opportunity to file for a tax refund for closed tax years for the amount of the penalty that was paid. The exception applies to those who were on active duty for more than 179 days and took a distribution subject to the 10 percent early distribution penalty while they were on active duty after September 11, 2001. They are also being given an opportunity to repay the distribution they took. The repayment must go to an IRA and the reservist will not be able to take a deduction for the repayment. Funds for repayment could come from parents, grandparents, friends and any other interested party. The second exception to the penalty applies to public safety personnel who have separated from service at age 50 or older. Distributions from their plans will not be subject to the 10 percent early distribution penalty. Employees who qualify are policemen, firefighters, and emergency medical service workers who are covered by a governmental defined benefit pension plan offered by state or local governments.

What It Does

If you tap into your IRA or company plan funds early (before eligibility age 59½), you will have to pay a 10 percent penalty on any withdrawals. It is bad enough that most distributions from IRAs and other plans, even if not taken early, are subject to regular income tax, but adding a 10 percent penalty on top of that is criminal. After all, it is *your* money; why shouldn't you have penalty-free access to it whenever you wish?

Ask Ed . . .

Q: How does the IRS know that I qualify for an exception?

A: Every distribution from an IRA or company plan generates a 1099-R form that is sent to you and to the IRS. Your 1099-R will be coded to tell the IRS that the distribution qualifies for an exception to the 10 percent penalty. If it is coded incorrectly by the plan custodian (and that happens frequently), you will give the IRS the correct information by filing Form 5329 with your tax return claiming the exception that applies to you. (You can get Form 5329 and the instructions on the IRS website at www.irs.gov under "Forms and Publications.") The IRS usually accepts your word on the tax return, but of course they can audit you just to make sure, so you should keep all documentation (paid bills from schools, hospitals, or home purchases, for example) showing why you qualify for the exception you claimed and how you used the money.

But the government has decided that it is in your best interest to be discouraged from touching these funds until you reach 59½, which is probably good advice. But the enforcement of a 10 percent penalty only adds insult to injury. Still, that's the rule, and you are wise to pay heed to it before prematurely touching one red cent of your retirement account—unless you qualify for an exception to the penalty rule.

One of the more complicated exceptions is to take a series of substantially equal periodic payments—known as 72(t) payments—and because of those complexities, I have given this exception its own separate checklist (see this section, Part 5). All of the other exceptions to the early withdrawal penalty rule are covered here in this checklist, which will guide you through the maze, helping you to identify which exceptions apply to which plans, what you have to do to qualify, and the rules you must follow for each to ensure that you don't make a costly mistake.

What's In It for Me?

If you need to withdraw early, this checklist will help you find an exception that may apply to you and help you to avoid the 10 percent penalty. For example, if you have high medical bills and need to withdraw early from your IRA or company plan to pay for them, you may be able to es-

Ask Ed . . .

Q: If I am using the series of substantially equal periodic payments exception—72(t)—can I take extra payments if they qualify for other exceptions? For example can I take penalty-free payments from an IRA that I am taking 72(t) payments from, if they are used for medical or education purposes?

A: No. That will break the 72(t) payment plan even though the medical and education withdrawals are valid exceptions, but they must be used on their own against other (non-72(t) exception)

IRAs. As noted in the previous checklist on 72(t) payments (this section, Part 5), the only exceptions that can be used to modify a 72(t) payment plan without triggering the 10 percent penalty are death and disability.

cape the 10 percent penalty if you meet certain requirements—in this case, that the distribution is used to pay those medical bills in excess of 7.5 percent of your adjusted gross income (AGI).

The checklist also will tip you off to the major tax traps that can befall account owners who qualify for an exception but miss an important detail in the execution, which means that the transaction winds up costing them more money.

What If I Don't?

Again, I am not recommending here that if you qualify for an exception, withdrawing early is, as Martha Stewart might say, a "good thing." I believe quite the opposite. If you are strapped for cash, I'd even recommend taking out a home equity loan before tapping into your retirement account early; at least you will get a tax deduction on the loan interest rather than face a possible tax penalty on the cash withdrawal. But if you must withdraw early, and I guess you feel you must otherwise you wouldn't be reading these words in the first place—then what you risk by not using this checklist to structure your early withdrawal properly is the possibility of paying taxes and penalties (and more of both) that could have been easily avoided. The tax courts are full of such cases. Here's one of them:

A budding attorney attending law school withdrew money from his 401(k) plan to pay his tuition. The IRS assessed him the 10 percent penalty because tax law says that the education exception applies only to distributions from IRAs, not from company plans. So he hired himself as his lawyer and took the IRS to court to show it a thing or two, arguing that he could have rolled the funds from his 401(k) to his

IRA and taken the money from there penalty-free, so what's the difference? The court agreed that had he done this he would have been fine, but pointed out the one big difference: He hadn't. So, he wound up paying the 10 percent penalty (and losing his first case) because he did not know rule number one: If there is an exception available, make sure it applies to the plan you are going to withdraw from. (Rule number two is: Never act as your own lawyer.)

Even if you use the right exception, timing counts too. Funds distributed early must be taken in the same year as the expense to qualify for the exception. So, if you need the cash for education (like our budding attorney) or medical expenses, you must pay the school in the same year as the distribution or pay the medical bills in the same year as the distribution to beat the penalty.

For example, a woman withdrew $17,222.69 from her qualified plan in 2000 to pay for medical treatments that began in 2000. Most of these medical bills though were actually paid in 2001. She and her husband reported the $17,222.69 distribution on their 2000 joint tax return but did not pay the 10 percent early withdrawal penalty (neither of them had hit age 59½ yet). The IRS sent them a deficiency notice stating that they were liable for the 10 percent penalty on the $17,222.69 early withdrawal, or $1,722. They claimed that since they used the funds for medical expenses, they qualified for the medical expense exception, so they did not owe the $1,722. The IRS disagreed, and the next thing you knew, the couple landed in tax court where,

Ask Ed . . .

Q: Why do you have conversions to Roth IRAs listed as an exception on the checklist?

A: Because a conversion is really a rollover, and you also will notice on the checklist that rollovers are exempt from the 10 percent penalty.

surprise, surprise, they lost. Why? Because, as the IRS noted (and the court agreed), they had not read the fine print: The exception applies only to those distributions used for expenses (in this case medical) paid *in the same deductible year as the distribution is made.*

Instructions

Now you understand why it is so important to do this right, beginning with using the right exception for the right retirement account. There are exceptions that apply to distributions (a) from both IRAs *and* company plans, (b) from IRAs only; and (c) from company plans only. There have been many instances where early withdrawal taxpayers have lost out by claiming the wrong exception for the wrong plan, the most common of which is when a person withdraws funds early from a 401(k) plan either for education expenses or to purchase a home not realizing that neither of those exceptions applies to distributions from company plans. As you'll see in the checklist, the first-time homebuyer and the education exceptions only apply to distributions from IRAs.

Ask Ed . . .

Q: Is the $10,000 lifetime cap for the first-time homebuyer exception per person or per couple? In other words, could a couple withdraw $20,000 penalty-free?

A: The first-time homebuyer exception is per person; however, if each spouse has an individual IRA, they can each withdraw $10,000 from his or her own account penalty-free. One spouse cannot use any part of the other spouse's $10,000 lifetime amount. Both spouses must qualify as first-time homebuyers for this exception though (neither one having owned a house in the past 2 years) for even one spouse to be able to claim the exemption.

So, if you think you may have to withdraw any funds from your IRA or company plan before you hit the milestone age of 59½ (there is even an age 55 exception for company plans), go through this checklist first to find out whether there is an exception to the 10 percent early withdrawal penalty that applies to you. And if an exception does apply, make sure that you will qualify to get it by withdrawing from the right plan under the right rules in the right year.

THE EARLY-DISTRIBUTION—OTHER EXCEPTIONS CHECKLIST

MY NAME: ______________________ **DATE:** ________

MY ADVISOR'S NAME: ______________________ **PLAN #:** ________

Follow-ups should be added to the To Do Lists at the end of this checklist.

The 10 percent early-distribution penalty applies to all taxable distributions made before the attainment of age 59½ (for IRAs) or age 55 (for employer plans if separated from service at age 55 or older) unless one of the following exceptions applies. The penalty is 10 percent of the taxable amount distributed and is reported on Form 5329.

IRA exceptions, not employer exceptions, apply to SEP and SIMPLE IRAs.

1. Death (applies to all plans and IRAs) ________

2. Disability (applies to all plans and IRAs) ________

- Disability is defined as being unable to engage in any substantial gainful activity by reason of a medically determinable physical or mental impairment that can be expected to result in death or to be of long-continued and indefinite duration. ________
- There is no specific form required by IRS to prove disability. The retirement plan custodian may require some sort of proof. ________

Comments: ______________________

____

____

____

3. Medical expenses (applies to all plans and IRAs) ________

- Distribution must be for medical expenses in excess of 7.5 percent of my AGI and the expenses must be paid in the year of the distribution. ________
- The medical expenses must be deductible (even if I don't itemize) in the same year as the distribution. ________
- Medical expenses can be for me, for my spouse, or my dependent(s). ________
- Medical expenses include dental, prescription drug, and health insurance premiums. ________

- I do not have to itemize deductions to qualify for the exemption. ________

4. Series of substantially equal periodic payments (applies to all plans and IRAs) (see The Early Distributions—72(t) Payments Checklist, this section, Part 5). ________

5. IRS tax levy (applies to all plans and IRAs) ________

6. Rollover of eligible assets to another tax deferred account (applies to all plans and IRAs) ________

7. Active reservists (applies to IRAs, 401(k) and 403(b) plans) ________

- Must be called to active duty between September 11, 2001 and December 31, 2007 for more than 179 days. ________
- Took a distribution subject to the 10 percent penalty between the date of the call to duty and the end of the active duty period. ________
- Can file an amended tax return for the penalty amount. For closed tax years the amended return must be filed by August 16, 2007. ________
- Can pay back the amount withdrawn during the 2 years beginning on the day after active duty ends. The 2-year period will not end any earlier than August 16, 2008 (2 years after the signing of the legislation). The repayment goes to an IRA and does not affect IRA contribution limits. The reservist does not get a tax deduction for amounts repaid. ________

8. Health insurance (applies to IRAs only) ________

- To qualify I must be unemployed and have received unemployment compensation under either a federal or state unemployment compensation law for 12 consecutive weeks in either the current year or previous year. (Self-employed individuals do not qualify.) ________
- Distribution must be made in the year of or the year after unemployment. ________
- The distribution cannot exceed the amount paid (in the year of distribution) for health insurance for me, my spouse, or my dependents. ________
- The exception does not apply to distributions made after I have been reemployed for 60 days. ________

9. First-time homebuyer (applies to IRAs only) __________

- Exception applies if I am purchasing a first-time home for me or my spouse, or a child, grandchild, parent, or other ancestor of me and my spouse. "First-time" is defined as having had no ownership interest in a principal residence for the past 2 years. If married, my spouse must also qualify under the same definition. __________
- Distribution can be used to purchase, construct, or reconstruct a principal residence. __________
- Distribution can be used for reasonable financing, settlement, or closing costs of a principal residence. __________
- The principal residence can be a houseboat, house trailer, or stock held in a housing co-op. __________
- Distribution must be used within 120 days beginning the day it is received. __________
- Date of acquisition is the date on which a binding contract is entered into or the date on which construction commences. __________
- If distribution will fail to qualify for exception solely due to delays or cancellation of the acquisition of the primary residence, distribution may be rolled over to an IRA by the 120th day. (The one-per-year rollover rule does not apply.) __________
- There is a lifetime cap of $10,000 per IRA owner; more than one IRA owner's distribution can be used in the purchase of one primary residence. __________

Comments: ____

____

____

____

____

____

10. Higher-education expenses (applies to IRAs only) __________

- Exception applies to me and my spouse, our children and grandchildren. __________
- Expenses include postsecondary tuition, fees, books, supplies, and equipment. __________

- Distribution cannot exceed education expenses (less any financial aid) for the year and must be taken in the year of the expense. ________
- Room and board are qualified expenses only if the student is enrolled at an eligible institution on at least a half-time basis. The maximum allowable amount is the amount used in federal financial aid programs or, if greater, the actual amount charged by the institution for the student living in housing owned or operated by the school. ________

11. Conversions to a Roth (currently applies to IRAs only but beginning in 2008 will apply to employer plans also) ________

- IRA distributions that are converted to a Roth IRA are not subject to the early withdrawal penalty at the time of conversion (but may be subject to the penalty if withdrawn too early from the Roth—see this section, Part 11). ________

Comments: ________

12. QDRO—Qualified Domestic Relations Order (applies to employer plans only) (For explanation of QDRO, see the Divorce Checklist in this section, Part 4.) ________

13. Section 457 plans (applies to 457 plans only) ________

- Distributions from 457 plans are exempt from the penalty. Pretax amounts rolled into the 457 plan do not qualify for the exception. ________

14. Early distributions to public safety employees (applies to plans only) ________

- Effective August 17, 2006, for policemen, firefighters, and emergency medical service personnel employed by state or local governments. ________
- Must be separated from service at age 50 or later. ________
- Distribution must be made after separation from service. ________

Follow-Up

My To Do List	Date Completed
1	
2	
3	
4	
5	
6	
7	
8	
9	
10	

My Signature

Date

Part 7

THE TAX BREAKS FOR LUMP-SUM DISTRIBUTION CHECKLIST

For account owners

What It Does

Taking a lump-sum distribution means withdrawing all the assets from your retirement plan in one fell swoop—typically at retirement. If you participate in a 401(k), taking a lump-sum distribution could net you a couple of big tax breaks you may not have considered, or, perhaps, never even heard about: NUA (Net Unrealized Appreciation) on company stock in your plan, and 10-year averaging on your distribution. Not everyone with a 401(k) qualifies for these breaks, but if you do, either or both of them can make a big, big dent in your tax bill by helping you get funds out of your plan at bargain-basement tax rates, and maybe even for free.

These breaks do not apply to lump-sum distributions from 403(b) or 457 plans or from IRAs (including SEP and SIMPLE IRAs). And a triggering event must occur for 401(k) owners to qualify for a lump-sum distribution. For the lump-sum distribution NUA tax break, the triggering events are: (1) Separation from service (not for self-employed individuals); (2) Reaching age 59½; (3) Death; (4) Disability (for self-employed individuals only). Triggering events for 10-year averaging qualification are the same, plus these extras: (1) You must have participated in the plan for a minimum of 5 years; (2) You must have been born before 1936; (3) You cannot have elected 10-year averaging anytime since 1986.

Ask Ed . . .

Q: What if I am separated from service because my employer fires me? Can I still qualify for any of these lump-sum tax breaks?

A: Yes. Whether you were fired, quit, resigned, or retired, it does not matter. The tax code does not care how or why you left the company; even if you're the CEO and left in handcuffs, you still qualify.

The NUA tax break allows you to withdraw employer stock (stock of the company you work for) from your 401(k) as part of a lump-sum distribution and pay tax only on the original cost of the stock, not its appreciated value over your years of service. So, let's say you have $1,000,000 worth of company stock in your 401(k) and the original cost of that stock when purchased for your plan was $100,000. The NUA amount is $900,000 (the difference between the $1,000,000 value of the company stock at the date of the lump-sum distribution and the $100,000 original cost of the stock). That $900,000 is not taxed until you sell the stock, at which time you pay just long-term capital gains tax, no matter how long you've held the stock. The rule requiring you to hold stock for more than one year to receive long-term capital gains rates does not apply to NUA stock, so you can sell the stock one day after your lump-sum distribution and still pay only long-term capital gains tax (currently at 15 percent).

The 10-year-averaging tax break applies to fewer and fewer people each year because of its additional requirement rules, such as being born before 1936. But if you do qualify, it means you get to pay tax on

Ask Ed . . .

Q: Can I use the NUA break if I leave the company when I am only 45 years old?

A: Yes, if you take a lump-sum distribution (withdraw all the funds in your 401(k) in 1 calendar year) after separating from service. There is one hitch here though. Because you separated from service before reaching age 55, you are subject to the 10 percent early withdrawal penalty. That's the bad news. The good news is that the penalty only applies to the amount that is taxable, which is the cost of the stock in the plan. You can still withdraw all of the NUA tax- and penalty-free.

your lump-sum distribution as if you were taking the entire withdrawal over a ten-year period rather than all at once, thereby lowering the overall tax you must pay.

Furthermore, if you were born before 1936 and part of your lump-sum distribution is from pre-1974 plan participation, you can elect (on IRS Form 4972) to pay a flat 20 percent capital gains rate on that portion. You may also choose *not* to elect capital gain treatment where averaging produces a lower tax.

Ask Ed . . .

Q: Can I use 10-year averaging if I leave the company when I am only 45 years old?

A: No. To qualify for 10-year averaging on your 401(k) distribution, you must have been born before 1936. If you are 45 years old now, then you cannot have been born before 1936, at least not without backdating your birth certificate.

As with everything else in the tax code, the devil is in the details, so this checklist takes you through all the things you must know in order to secure these potentially huge lump-sum distribution tax breaks.

You also will require the cooperation of the people in the Benefits or Human Resources Department of the company where you work to provide you with the key contact and tax-reporting information on your 401(k) that you will need to keep track of now and to retrace your steps later.

A Word to the Wise

Another little-known fact is that both the NUA and 10-year-averaging tax breaks carry over to your beneficiaries. This means that if you are in a 401(k) and qualify for either or both of these tax breaks, then so do your beneficiaries if they inherit your 401(k) plan and take a qualifying lump-sum distribution. So, be sure to point this out to them, and refer them (if you haven't already) to the Tax Breaks for Beneficiaries' Checklist, Section III, Part 5.

What's In It for Me?

You won't know until you run the numbers, but there is the potential for huge tax savings here depending on the amount of company stock in your 401(k). For example, if you have company stock in your plan, the longer you worked for your company, the more likely it is that your stock has appreciated in value. The greater the appreciation in the value of your company stock, the greater your NUA tax break.

Once you get the numbers for NUA and/or 10-year averaging, contact your tax advisor to determine what the tax benefit for you will be and whether either strategy is right for you in terms of your overall tax-planning goals. Remember that with either break, you will have to pay some tax up front (whereas with an IRA rollover you will have to pay no tax but irrevocably lose both tax breaks). The idea is to see how much less that tax can be.

Ask Ed . . .

Q: If I separate from service, do I have to take the lump-sum distribution in the year I left the company or in the year after to qualify for the tax breaks?

A: Once you are separated from service, you can take your lump-sum distribution then or in any subsequent year—as long as you take no partial distributions after your separation from service. Whenever you take it, you must take it all in one calendar year. For example, let's say you separate from service in 2007. You take a lump-sum distribution of your entire 401(k) plan balance in 2011. As long as you take no distributions in 2007 through 2010, then your 2011 lump-sum distribution qualifies for the NUA and 10-year-averaging tax breaks.

What If I Don't?

If you would have qualified for these tax breaks but didn't know about them, or, in taking them, make a misstep along the way, you will probably wind up paying more tax on your lump-sum distribution than you would have had to. Or, you might sell shares of company stock in your 401(k) while your funds are still in there and negate the possibility of NUA tax savings on that portion.

In some cases, these tax breaks cannot be recouped if a mistake is made. For example, if your 401(k) plan balance contains company stock with substantial appreciation, and you roll all or part of that balance into an IRA, that is an irrevocable election and will cost you *and* your beneficiaries the NUA tax break forever.

Ask Ed . . .

Q: How does the IRS know that I am taking advantage of these tax breaks?

A: You report 10-year averaging by filling out and attaching Form 4972 (Tax on Lump-Sum Distributions) to your tax return. If you use the NUA tax break, your employer reports the NUA amount in Box 6 on the 1099-R issued for your distribution. You simply report the cost of the shares withdrawn as income from a pension distribution on your Form 1040 tax return, just as you would any other pension distribution. When you sell the NUA shares, you report that gain as a long-term capital gain on Schedule D with your other stock and property sales. Your beneficiaries will do the same if they take a qualifying lump-sum distribution or inherit the NUA on the stock you withdrew, so be sure to tell them.

Instructions

Knowing about NUA and 10-year averaging is not enough. You must take the distribution *exactly* according to the tax laws. The reason the government is giving a tax break here is because you have agreed to withdraw *all* of your funds from the 401(k) plan instead of keeping them there, tax-deferred.

With 10-year averaging, you must withdraw everything and pay the tax now, so you get a tax break by paying the tax up front. None of the funds withdrawn from the plan can be rolled over, so the tax shelter ends. You need to project the tax before you choose 10-year averaging because in some cases, especially as the lump-sum distribution increases, it may not benefit you to pay the tax up front. You need to know that ahead of time so that you do not go into shock at tax time wondering what the heck happened to your retirement savings.

Using the NUA break is a bit different. You still have to withdraw everything from your 401(k) plan, but you have the option of rolling all or any part of the distribution over to an IRA to retain the tax shelter. Of course if you roll *everything* over to an IRA, there will be no NUA break. But you can roll some of the company stock over to an IRA if you wish and transfer the rest to a taxable account and use the amount of the NUA tax break that is right for you. As with 10-year averaging, you need to project your tax bill in order to make that decision and avoid any nasty surprises at tax time.

THE TAX BREAKS FOR LUMP-SUM DISTRIBUTION CHECKLIST

MY NAME: ____________________ **DATE:** __________

MY ADVISOR'S NAME: ____________________ **PLAN #:** __________

Follow-ups should be added to the To Do lists at the end of this checklist.

1. Reasons to do a lump-sum distribution (LSD):

- I need to spend some or all of this money right away or soon after the distribution. __________
- I qualify for tax breaks on the distribution (10-year averaging, Net Unrealized Appreciation [NUA], or pre-1974 capital gains break at 20 percent). __________
- My tax bracket is lower now than it will be in retirement. __________
- I need liquid funds for estate planning (equalizing estates or to buy insurance). __________

Comments: ____________________

2. To qualify as a lump-sum distribution:

- My entire account balance must be distributed to me all in the same tax year. __________
- The distribution must occur after a triggering event, such as: __________
  —Separation from service (does not apply to a self-employed individual) __________
  —Attainment of age 59½ __________
  —Death __________
  —Disability (only if I am self-employed) __________

Comments: ____________________

3. When was the last triggering event and when will the next triggering event be? If you have taken distributions from the plan after your last triggering event, including RMDs, you cannot do an LSD until you have a new triggering event. ______

4. What is my age in the year of the LSD? ______

- If I separate from service in the year I am 55 or older, the 10 percent penalty does not apply to the LSD. ______
- Otherwise, if I am under 59½, there will be a 10 percent penalty on the taxable amount of the LSD. ______

5. Do I have more than one employer-sponsored company plan? If so, all may have to be considered one plan for LSD purposes. ______

6. What are the assets in the plan(s)? ______

- Company stock. If so, what is the *total* amount? ______
- What is the basis amount (the cost to the plan) of the company stock? ______

7. Where will the cash come from to pay the tax on my LSD? ______

Comments: ______

______

______

______

______

8. I must start the distribution process early in the year to ensure that the distribution is completed in one taxable year. ______

9. Keeping track of the process:

- Contact person and phone number ______
- Date contacted ______
- Result of contact ______

10. I must advise my CPA or tax preparer of the LSD and seek his/her advice on the tax benefits. ______

Comments: ______________________________

____

____

____

____

11. I can elect to pay ordinary income tax on the entire LSD (but this is not generally recommended). ______

12. Tell beneficiaries who will be inheriting my employer plan(s) that all my LSD options are passed on to them. ______

13. NUA can be combined with 10-year averaging if none of the LSD is going to be rolled over. ______

- This option works best with distributions under $125,000 (produces a lower tax). ______
- I must elect to include NUA amount in income. ______
- I must use 10-year averaging to calculate taxes. ______

Comments: ______________________________

____

____

____

____

Net Unrealized Appreciation (NUA)

14. NUA eligibility requirements, rules and regulations:

- I can only use NUA if I have a qualified plan—(401(k), ESOP plans, etc.—that holds stock or bonds of the company for which I work. (I should only consider NUA when the company stock in the plan has low basis. In order to determine the basis, find out from the company, which must keep track of it.) ______
- Employer stock must be distributed in kind (actual shares of stock) to qualify. Stock sold in the plan or rolled over is not eligible. ______
- NUA on stock distributed in LSD is not taxed at the time of the distribution. It is taxed when the stock is sold. ______
- Only the cost of the stock to the plan is subject to income tax. ______

- The tax is paid at ordinary income tax rates. ____________
- The stock must be transferred to a taxable account. (I do not have to take all of the company stock; I can take just part of it, transferring the balance to a tax-deferred account where it will not qualify for the NUA tax break.) ____________
- The tax on the NUA is paid at long-term capital gains rates. ____________
- I can roll my other plan assets to an IRA or another plan if I want to and still be eligible for NUA on my company stock. ____________

Comments: ____

____

____

____

____

15. How to calculate NUA and its cost (be sure to include the value of the employer-contributed shares and after-tax shares)

- Determine the market value for the company stock. (it should be on the plan statement). ____________
- Determine the cost to the plan of the company stock. (It should be on the plan statement.) ____________

  If the company tracks basis share by share, I may have to calculate the cost to the plan by adding up the cost of the shares I want to use the NUA election on (I can elect to use specific shares if I want). ____________
- Subtract the cost from the market value to determine the NUA amount. ____________
- Calculate the tax cost of the LSD on the basis amount. ____________
- If applicable, calculate the amount of the 10 percent early distribution penalty on the basis amount. ____________

Comments: ____

____

____

____

____

16. The process:

- Do a direct rollover of noncompany stock assets (or non-NUA assets if I am not using NUA on all of the company stock) to another tax-deferred account first. __________
- Then have the company stock distributed to a taxable, non-IRA account. (20 percent withholding will not apply to this transfer.) __________
- I must withdraw all plan assets, leaving a zero balance as of 12/31 of the year of withdrawal. __________
- If there is a balance left in the plan account as of year-end, I cannot elect to use NUA. __________
- Stock dividends deposited in my plan account after year-end are not an issue. __________

Comments: ____

____

____

____

____

17. If I have inherited the company stock from someone who took an LSD, the following NUA issues apply:

- There is no step up in basis on NUA; I will owe long-term capital gains tax on the remaining NUA amount. __________
- Growth after the date of distribution will receive a step up. __________
- Make sure the correct basis amount was used in the taxable account (from the 1099-R issued for the year of the distribution, the total distribution amount minus the NUA amount in Box 6). __________

18. The Income in Respect of a Decedent (IRD) tax deduction is also available, in addition to NUA, if the estate was subject to federal estate tax. (See The IRD Checklist in Section III, Part 6.) __________

Comments: ____

____

____

____

10-Year Averaging

19. 10-year averaging eligibility requirements, rules, and regulations:

- I must withdraw my entire plan balance in a lump sum. ______
- I must have been born before 1936 or become the account owner as the result of inheriting it from someone born before 1936. ______
- I must have been in the plan for at least 5 years (does not apply if beneficiary is taking an LSD). ______
- I cannot have previously elected 10-year averaging after 1986 (it is a onetime election). ______
- I cannot roll over any of the plan balance. ______

Comments: ______

20. 10-year-averaging distributions are reported on Form 4972, and they bypass AMT. ______

21. The tax on lump-sum distributions under $70,000 is reduced by the Minimum Distribution Allowance calculated on Form 4972. ______

Comments: ______

Capital Gains Treatment

22. 20 percent capital gains treatment requirements, rules, and regulations:

- I must have been born before 1936. ______
- Part of the lump-sum distribution must be from pre-1974 plan participation. ______

23. I can elect to pay a flat 20 percent capital gains rate on the pre-1974 portion. (The rate stays at 20 percent based on rates in effect in 1986 and does not change.) I should not elect capital gains treatment if 10-year averaging produces a lower tax. ______

Comments: ____

____

____

____

____

24. To recap, I must make sure that:

- I have taken no distributions in the years since my LSD triggering event, or I will not qualify for an LSD. ______
- My entire plan balance is distributed to me by 12/31 of the year of withdrawal. ______
- I do not transfer the company stock I want to qualify for NUA to another tax-deferred account. ______
- I transfer my non-NUA assets to an IRA or other tax-deferred account if I do not cash them out. ______
- I do not sell the company stock in the plan if I want to use it for NUA. ______
- The 1099-R issued by the plan is correct (NUA should be shown in Box 6). ______
- I keep copies of all documentation, company plan statements, correspondence, calculations, etc. ______
- I keep track of the NUA basis. ______
- The correct basis amount (the amount I paid tax on) is used in the after-tax account holding the shares of company stock. ______
- I do not roll over any assets to another tax-deferred account if I want to use 10-year averaging or receive capital gains treatment. ______
- I file Form 4972 with my tax return if using 10-year averaging or want capital gains treatment. ______
- I advise my beneficiaries that there is NUA in my estate. ______

Comments: ______

______

______

______

______

______

Follow-Up

My To Do List	Date Completed
1	
2	
3	
4	
5	
6	
7	
8	
9	
10	

My Signature ______ Date ______

Part 8

THE INCAPACITY CHECKLIST

What It Does

This checklist is for those of you who are or may become unable for a number of reasons to make legal and financial decisions on your own behalf or that of your family. It is also for you if you are considering naming a beneficiary for your retirement assets who is incapacitated.

Incapacity is a topic that is not much discussed in the financial-planning media, but I receive questions on it regularly, such as "How do I leave my IRA to a disabled child?" or "What if I become disabled? Who will look after the retirement funds I need to live on and take my required distributions for me?" These are the type of items on the minds of account owners like yourself that this special issue checklist will address.

For our purposes, the term "incapacity" means not just physically or mentally incapacitated but also legally incapacitated—for example, a minor child (a grandchild, for instance). The minor child may be physically and mentally okay, but at 2 years old is hardly in a position to make legal decisions and tax elections now or for a good many years. You don't want to leave your planning decisions in limbo for that long, and to make plans now you need to know all your planning choices—for example, (1) should you leave the account to a special needs trust for the child's benefit or (2) leave it to a Uniform Gifts to Minors Account (UGMA) or Uniform Transfers to Minors Account (UTMA)? These are all viable options covered by this checklist.

It also will address many other need-to-plan-in-advance items such as creating a power of attorney that contains specific provisions that grant the person you appoint (and only that person) the power to make the financial and legal decisions you want. For example, will you want your attorney-in-fact (the person to whom you grant this power) to be able to change the beneficiary on your account? Probably not, but that might happen if you do not address such specifics ahead of time. Of course, to actually set up your power of attorney, trust for a minor child, and so on, you will need the professional services of an experienced lawyer or advisor in these fields. This checklist will not make you one.

Ask Ed . . .

Q: How will I know if my bank will accept my power of attorney with its specific provisions?

A: You'll have to show it to the bank and get the bank's acceptance in writing, or punt accordingly if the bank insists you use its own power of attorney form. That's why it is so important to take care of this while you are still healthy and able to, as you may have to decide to move your account to a bank that is more flexible and reasonable in terms of your desired provisions (see the "My Custodial Agreement Checklist," Section II, Part 2).

What's In It For Me?

Here again, peace of mind is the key benefit. If you become incapacitated or have named a beneficiary who is, you will know that the funds you are relying on to take care of you (or that your beneficiary is relying on) will be looked after properly under your terms and conditions by the people you have appointed to do so. You will be assured that your IRA or plan custodian allows the power of attorney or the trust you have set up because you have addressed that point ahead of time so there will be no surprises later on. As with postdeath planning, planning ahead here also means not leaving it to chance that your family will be able to fix things up after the fact if you do nothing now. There is no guarantee they will be able to do so, let alone in accordance with your known wishes.

You want to address the incapacity issue now and set things right the first time to save yourself and your family thousands of dollars in legal expenses from not having to go to court to determine what you should or would have wanted done.

Ask Ed . . .

Q: I have a disabled child and want to set up a special needs trust to inherit my IRA for him. What will be the effect of the annual Required Minimum Distributions the trust must take?

A: If your child is getting any type of government benefits due to disability, the amounts the trust distributes to your child are not only taxable but will have to go right back to the government program your child is benefiting from. Usually, the special needs trust will pay only for extra items like amenities that the government program does not provide. The rest of the RMDs should remain in the trust. This accumulation could quickly cause a loss of assets to taxes in excess of 40 percent if there are state trust taxes to pay in addition to the 35 percent the IRS receives. Therefore, an IRA or other plan is not the best asset to leave to a special needs trust. I would look to leave other assets to the trust for your disabled child and leave the IRA or plan asset to other beneficiaries.

What If I Don't?

You will not only be leaving your fate but the fate of your retirement money—and your family—up to chance. There are laws governing what must happen if the owner of a retirement account becomes incapable of making decisions about that account and there is no plan in place or documents available clarifying his or her specific intentions on these matters.

Even if you have a spouse or other family member who can take care of you, remember that your IRA or other plan is an *individual* account, not a *joint* account. That means even your spouse will have no say over what decisions to make about your money or what distributions to take for your benefit should you become incapacitated and have not specified those arrangements. It will be up to the courts to decide. And not only will the courts be less sensitive to your desires or concerned about them in making its decision, they also will be more costly.

Instructions

Intent is all-important not only in postdeath planning but with incapacity planning, too. You will use this checklist to make sure your intent is always clear so that no questions will arise later about choices that you may no longer be able to clarify. This can help to keep the biggest asset you own and will need—your retirement account—out of court, or at least dramatically smooth the proceedings if court involvement does come up for some reason.

For example, let's say that in the event you become incapacitated and must have care, you want other resources (long-term-care insurance, perhaps) to cover those costs so that the balance in your retirement account can go entirely to your grandchild. But a minor cannot legally hold assets (including an IRA or other plan) in his or her name. So, if you leave your IRA to a minor, your plan custodian will not let the minor act for him or herself. And a parent might not automatically be allowed to act for the minor either. Instead, the custodian might require a "guardianship of the property" for the minor, and a parent may have to go to court and ask to be named the "guardian of the property," which normally is not an extensive process. But if your overall intent is for your grandchild to get your retirement funds free and clear, it would be better if you named a custodian for your grandchild *now* under your state's Uniform Gift/Transfers to Minors Act (UGMA/UTMA) so that your intent is explicit and bulletproof.

This checklist will take you through the various items you need to consider in deciding upon and clarifying your intent, but for the specifics on naming a beneficiary, the ins and outs of custodial agreements, and setting up trusts, please refer to their respective checklists (The Naming a Trust-As-Beneficiary Checklist in Part 2 of this section and The Account Owner's Care Solution in Section II).

Ask Ed . . .

Q: I want my grandchild, a minor, to inherit my IRA and the guardian I name to be approved by the court or the plan custodian. How do I set up the IRA to accomplish this?

A: You should contact the plan custodian to determine its specific requirements. Generally, the plan custodian will ask to see evidence of the guardian's legal authority before opening the inherited IRA account. If the guardian is a parent (your son or daughter, for example), a birth certificate probably will be sufficient. A parent is usually considered to be the natural guardian, unless there is some objection. For an individual other than a parent, a record of a court-ordered guardianship is generally required. Alternatively, a written opinion of counsel, attesting to the legality of the guardianship in a last will and testament, should suffice.

THE INCAPACITY CHECKLIST

MY NAME: ______________________ **DATE:** __________

MY ADVISOR'S NAME: ______________________ **PLAN #:** __________

Follow-ups should be added to the To Do Lists at the end of this checklist.

1. What is incapacity?

- Mental incapacity—where I or my beneficiary is unable to make financial decisions. __________
- Physical incapacity—where my or my beneficiary's physical limitations render us unable to make financial decisions. __________
- Legal incapacity—where my beneficiary is a minor and not able to make financial decisions. __________
- Fiscal incapacity—where my beneficiary is not able to make sound financial decisions or is in financial difficulties. __________

Comments: ____

2. Planning for incapacity:

- In the event that I or my beneficiary should become incapacitated, I will seek the assistance of a qualified attorney for Medicaid assistance. The rules are complicated and differ from state to state. (A Roth IRA may be treated very differently than a traditional IRA under Medicaid rules.) __________
- IRS has granted a Private Letter Ruling (PLR 200620025) allowing the transfer of retirement assets after my death to a special needs trust (set up as a grantor trust) for the benefit of a disabled beneficiary. This strategy may provide some protection in very limited situations. __________

3. Types of powers of attorney (POA): (A legal document that gives another person the authority to handle my financial affairs; I should consult an attorney before executing one.)

- General POA—ceases to be effective when I become incapacitated. ____________
- Springing POA—the power is granted today but does not become effective until a specific event "springs" it. ____________
- Durable POA—I grant the power when I sign it and that power does not end until my death or until I revoke it. ____________

4. Power of attorney issues:

- Who should have my POA? ____________
- Who are my current beneficiaries? ____________
- Could there be any sources of conflict between my POA holder and my beneficiaries? ____________
- Will my plan custodian accept a POA? ____________
- Can I use my own POA or must I use one provided by the plan custodian? ____________

5. Consider whether or not the following powers should be granted to my attorney-in-fact and included in my POA for my retirement plans:

- The power to make contributions. ____________
- The power to request that required distributions be made. ____________
- The power to take distributions other than required distributions. ____________
- The ability to do rollover transactions. ____________
- The power to change my beneficiary, or a limited power to change beneficiaries. ____________
- The power to manage my retirement plan investments. ____________
- The power to sign all necessary paperwork with respect to retirement plan transactions. (There may be a delay in processing transactions initiated by the person holding a POA for another person while the plan custodian verifies the power and the identity of the holder.) ____________

6. Review my POA periodically to be sure that it is up-to-date:

- Is the person holding the power still alive and able to act for me? ____________

- Have state laws changed? __________
- Does my plan custodian still accept my POA? __________

7. I might want to set up a trusteed IRA (a trust set up during my lifetime that names a trustee to handle retirement account transactions if I become incapacitated) **instead of using a POA: A trusteed IRA is effective both while I'm alive and after my death.** __________

- Check with my plan custodian to be sure it will accept a trusteed IRA. __________

Comments: ____

____

____

____

____

8. Things to consider before naming a plan beneficiary who is incapacitated:

- Does he or she have a guardian to act for him or her? __________
  - —If yes, the guardian is (name and contact information): __________
  - —If no, court proceedings may be necessary to establish a guardian. __________
  - —Have I named a successor guardian? __________
- Will I need to set up a trust for my plan beneficiary? (Setting up a trust requires the services of an attorney specializing in that type of trust and who is also familiar with IRA trust and distribution rules.) __________
- If so, which type of trust? __________
  - —Special needs trust—for disabled beneficiaries. __________
  - —Spendthrift trust—for beneficiaries who have financial difficulties. __________
  - —Trust for minor beneficiaries—to force the stretch option by extending distributions over a minor's life. __________
  - —A trust can also provide a level of creditor protection for my plan beneficiary, depending on state law. __________

—I should set up a trust for my disabled beneficiary so that he or she will not inherit my retirement plan assets directly if eligible for government assistance programs in order to avoid tax and program repayment issues. __________

9. If I wish, I can arrange to have two different people be the trustee of the trust and the guardian for my minor or disabled beneficiary: The former can take care of the assets; the latter can take care of my beneficiary. __________

10. If I name a minor as my plan beneficiary, at what age do I want him or her to have access to my retirement funds? __________

- Leaving the plan directly to the minor or through an UGMA (Uniform Gifts to Minors Act) or UTMA (Uniform Transfers to Minors Act) means the minor has access to my retirement funds at the age of majority (18 or 21 depending on state law). __________
- Leaving the plan to a trust means I can control the minor's access to funds through the terms of the trust. __________

11. Life insurance is a much better asset than my retirement plan for a beneficiary who is receiving government assistance: (1) When it is properly purchased and owned it comes into the special needs trust estate- and income-tax-free and any remaining funds at the death of the special needs beneficiary can go to my contingent or successor beneficiaries. (2) Plan distributions can be used to purchase the life insurance. __________

Comments: ____

____

____

____

____

Follow-Up

My To Do List	Date Completed
1	
2	
3	

4 ______________________________

5 ______________________________

6 ______________________________

7 ______________________________

8 ______________________________

9 ______________________________

10 ______________________________

______________________ ______________

My Signature Date

Part 9

THE SAME SEX AND UNMARRIED COUPLE CHECKLIST

For account owners and beneficiaries

What It Does

Regardless of whether you have lived together for years without tying the knot in a common law situation or a same sex partnership, as far as the tax laws are concerned, you're *single.* With that in mind there are serious issues you need to be aware of and serious decisions for you to make when it comes to retirement account planning for you and your significant other.

Our tax laws offer numerous built-in legal protections for spouses, but none of them apply to you as an unmarried partner. For example, spouses can leave each other unlimited amounts of IRA or plan money estate-tax-free, but you cannot. If you leave your partner an IRA or plan money that, combined with your other assets, exceeds the current federal estate tax exemption, then your estate will be subject to federal estate tax. Also, married couples can make unlimited gifts to each other, but unmarried partners cannot; they are stuck with the annual and lifetime gift tax limits—but at least they are not shut out of these, which means all is not lost for unmarried couples. In fact, there are some advantages to being unmarried (no, I'm *not* trying to be funny) but not single.

For example, there is no marriage penalty. I don't mean there is no penalty for being married (that's a personal issue). I mean the *tax penalty* married couples face when they file a joint tax return. Often, married couples would pay less tax if they could file as two single people. They don't have that option, but as an unmarried couple, *you do.* Roth conversions have a huge marriage penalty built in because you cannot convert to a Roth IRA if your income exceeds $100,000—a limit that is the same for singles as well as married couples who file a joint tax return. This means 2 single people (as in an unmarried couple situation) can each earn $100,000, effectively raising the limit to $200,000 ($100,000 on each tax return). Unmarried couples will continue to enjoy this advantage until 2010, when the law removes the limitation, thus taking even that advantage away from you.

So, here's the bottom line: Our tax laws do not favor unmarried couples the way they do married couples. This makes careful and considered retirement account planning arguably even more critical for unmarried couples who want to be able to provide for each other. This checklist will take you through the essential points you will need to understand in order to accomplish that.

Ask Ed . . .

Q: If I name my partner to inherit my IRA, how will the payout period be determined for her as my beneficiary?

A: The payout will be based on the same rules as for any nonspouse beneficiary. There is no spousal rollover because your partner is not legally a spouse, so distributions will have to begin in the year after your death and be taken over your partner's life expectancy based on his or her age the year after your death (see Section III and Appendix I—The Single Life Expectancy Table).

What's In It for Me?

If your intentions are to leave property (such as your retirement assets) to each other, and to name each other as decision-makers during times of incapacity, disability, or as your beneficiary after your death, this checklist will save you from lots of legal misery that would otherwise probably come your way. It will help to protect you and your partner legally where little or no legal protection would otherwise exist.

Ask Ed . . .

Q: My partner and I are unmarried but live together. If I withdraw from my IRA before reaching age 59½, but I use the funds to pay medical bills for my partner, am I exempt from the 10 percent early withdrawal penalty?

A: Not unless your partner is also your dependent. If your partner is not your dependent, you will have to pay the 10 percent penalty. The same rule applies to early withdrawals for other exceptions, such as education expenses and buying a first home.

What If I Don't?

Unmarried couples who leave assets to each other inherit under the same rules that apply to any nonspouse beneficiary (see The Nonspouse Beneficiary's Checklist in Part 1 of Section III). But unlike a nonspouse beneficiary who is a family member and might just inherit anyway under intestacy, if there was no beneficiary form or will, an unmarried partner would not gain any benefit in intestacy and would probably lose out even to a distant blood relative of the deceased. That alone is why planning for unmarried couples who want to provide for each other is so much more critical than for married couples. Your retirement funds might not go to your partner, and you might not inherit your partner's retirement assets. You might not even be involved in the distribution of your partner's property after death or involved in any decisions if you are not the named executor or trustee.

For example, when a spouse has funds in a 401(k) plan and that spouse dies, the beneficiary is automatically the surviving spouse—unless he or she waives that right. But if a partner in an unmarried couple situation has funds in a 401(k), these funds will go to whoever is named as the plan beneficiary. So, if you have failed to specifically name your partner, who knows who will inherit your retirement savings? If it goes to your estate, even that is no guarantee your partner will get it, if your will does not clearly name a beneficiary. There is a good chance that either the government or your relatives, however remote, will have a better claim on your property than your partner. Estate planning, which includes retirement beneficiary planning, is *essential* for unmarried couples, as the law is not with you on any of this.

Ask Ed . . .

Q: If my longtime companion and I split up, how much of my company plan is he entitled to?

A: None of it, since he is not your spouse. He has no legal right to any of your property if you are not legally married. If you feel your ex-partner is entitled to some of your retirement plan funds, you can keep him as your primary or contingent beneficiary on your beneficiary form. Of course, you will have to die before he can collect, so I hope the split was amicable.

Instructions

Make sure you and your partner take action to ensure protection of your retirement assets by following the essential points of this checklist. Among them: Be sure to make out an IRA or other plan beneficiary form, specifically naming who you want as your primary and contingent beneficiary (see Section II for details), and then keeping your beneficiary form current.

You will also need to be sure that any children you may have are well protected by naming each other as their legal guardian in your respective wills (if that is what you wish) and including your children's names in all documents. If you do not name each other as their legal guardian, the court may not necessarily appoint you, although even in unmarried couple situations, any parent has a better standing to be appointed legal guardian than someone else. But it is still much easier to avoid the courts in the first place by having this spelled out.

Ask Ed . . .

Q: Is a same sex couple married in a state that allows gay marriage treated by the IRS as a married couple?

A: Not under current federal tax rules, where even a same sex married couple that is legally married is not considered married insofar as the IRS is concerned. This may change over time, but not as of this writing.

THE SAME SEX AND UNMARRIED COUPLE CHECKLIST

MY NAME: ______________________ DATE: __________

MY ADVISOR'S NAME: ______________________ PLAN #: __________

Follow-ups should be added to the To Do lists at the end of this checklist.

1. As an unmarried partner, I cannot do the following:

- Be accepted as legally married under federal law (currently) even if my union is recognized by the laws of my state. __________
- Claim the unlimited marital deduction at my partner's death. __________
- Make unlimited financial gifts to my partner for tax purposes. __________
- File a joint tax return. __________
- Claim a right of election (the legal right to inherit a portion of a spouse's property) __________

Comments: ______________________

____

____

____

____

2. As an unmarried partner, I am able to do the following:

- Avoid the marriage penalty by having to file a separate tax return. __________
- Receive a better deal on Roth conversion eligibility since the $100,000 income cap applies to each unmarried partner individually (this limitation is eliminated in 2010). __________

Comments: ______________________

____

____

____

3. Retirement account planning for unmarried couples:

- If I want my partner to receive my plan benefits, I must complete a beneficiary form for each account I own (see My Beneficiary Form Checklist in Section II, Part 1 for details). __________
- When inheriting, my partner and I will be treated as each other's nonspouse beneficiaries (see the Nonspouse Beneficiary's Checklist in Section III, Part 1 for details). __________
- As an account owner, I must use the Uniform Lifetime Table (see Appendix II) in determining RMDs, even if my partner is more than 10 years younger than I am (see the RMD Calculations Checklist in Section II, Part 5 for explanation and details). __________

Comments: ____

____

____

____

____

4. As an unmarried partner, I should make sure the following are part of my estate plan and review them on a regular basis:

- Contingent beneficiaries for all my accounts, keeping in mind the effect a disclaimer (see the Disclaimer Planning Checklist in this section, Part 3) would have. __________
- Clearly stated custody issues for my children (especially guardianship for a minor child) who inherit my retirement plan or these issues may be contested (see the Incapacity Checklist in this section, Part 8). __________
- My children are named in all documents and thus well protected. __________
- A simultaneous death clause in my will, in case my partner and I die together. __________
- Choose a trustee (if I set up a trust), an executor of my estate, name a power of attorney, and so on. __________

Comments: ______

5. **Problems I want to avoid:**

- The possibility of any of my bequests being contested by family members after my death. ______
- Dying intestate—blood relatives will have better standing if I do not clearly name my choices for beneficiaries, guardians, or personal representatives. ______

6. **Share my wishes with family members by making a video record of me stating them.** ______

Comments: ______

Follow-Up

My To Do List	Date Completed
1	
2	
3	
4	
5	
6	
7	
8	
9	
10	

My Signature ______ Date ______

Part 10

THE ALTERNATIVE INVESTMENTS AND PROHIBITED TRANSACTIONS CHECKLIST

For account owners

A Word to the Wise

Terry: *"You was my brother, Charlie, you shoulda looked out for me a little bit. You shoulda taken care of me just a little bit so I wouldn't have to take them dives for the short-end money."*

Charlie: *"Oh I had some bets down for you. You saw some money."*

Terry: *"You don't understand. I coulda had class. I coulda been a contender. I coulda been somebody, instead of a bum, which is what I am, let's face it."*

Your retirement account "coulda been a contender" too, or at least the investments in your plan could have, and that is the big issue here. Remember, like Charlie in that memorable exchange from the movie *On the Waterfront,* you have an obligation to watch over your retirement savings and to make prudent decisions so that you don't lose your money and turn your account into a "bum."

What It Does

"I don't need no stinkin' stocks and bonds in my IRA. Gimme the good stuff!" Yes, the grass is always greener (and so is the cash) in someone else's retirement account. At least that is what many account owners seem to think. They see others making a fortune in real estate and other business investments and they want a piece of that sweet action. But the only money they have to invest in these "sure things" is their retirement savings—so those are the funds they want to use to make their killing. Then, when they strike it rich, they tell themselves, all of the profits will be tax-free from being in a retirement account! Sounds like a plan that's too good to be true! And it just may be. But if you do decide to go the alternative investment route, such as real estate, with your retirement account choices, this checklist will keep you safe and straight on course.

You can put your retirement plan contributions in pretty much any investment you want, except for life insurance and collectibles. But most people stick with what the typical plan custodian (bank, broker, mutual fund, or insurance company) offers, which may be a wide

Ask Ed . . .

Q: If I use a self-directed IRA custodian, will that guarantee that I won't make any mistakes?

A: A self-directed IRA custodian will inform you of the rules and not let you invest your IRA funds in property that is not appropriate for your IRA, but they are not the police and cannot monitor your every move. If you use the property improperly for your own purposes or some other family member does, the custodian is not likely to know or be able to help you out of the bind.

range of investment options but are usually limited to the major investment categories of stocks, bonds, funds, and Certificates of Deposit (CDs). If you want anything with more pizzazz—real estate, a small business, a start-up company, mortgages, equipment-leasing, or other nontraditional retirement plan investment choices—you will have to do it yourself with a self-directed IRA (SDIRA) offered by a bank, broker, fund, insurance, or other company (such as PENSCO Trust Company in San Francisco) that specializes in SDIRAs.

Ask Ed . . .

Q: If I am contemplating a nontraditional IRA investment, would the opinion of an attorney be helpful in determining if it's a prohibited transaction?

A: Not really. The only opinion that counts is the opinion of the US Department of Labor, which issues the Prohibited Transaction Exemption rulings (PTEs). You can ask them for a ruling in advance to see if they bless your IRA or plan transaction, but this process can take a year or more and be very expensive. By the time you receive an opinion, your investment deal will probably be long gone.

If you are thinking about unconventional or even exotic investments for your plan funds, you have to be careful because the tax rules are rigid and designed mostly to ensure that you don't cheat the government out of its cut of your tax-deferred funds.

But secondarily, the rules are there to make sure you don't do anything foolish by mistake that might cause you to cheat *yourself* out of your retirement savings. This checklist will help you to structure the alternative investment in your account properly so that you do not miss an essential detail that might derail things before they get started and do damage to your account.

Ask Ed . . .

Q: What if I lend my IRA funds to a family member but receive a fair market interest rate, or even charge a higher interest rate to make sure I am dealing the same as I would with a stranger?

A: Dealing with family members when it comes to your IRA is a prohibited transaction because you are considered to be self-dealing.

What's In It for Me?

The bottom line is that making alternative investments in your IRA is usually not the problem. It is what the IRS says you can and cannot do in making them that is the problem. The prohibitions mainly involve what is called "self-dealing," which can be defined as using the funds in your account for your benefit not that of the account. I know this sounds like splitting hairs, but the IRS looks at your retirement ac-

Ask Ed . . .

Q: You say that if an IRA transaction is prohibited, the entire IRA balance becomes subject to tax and penalty. What if I used only *part* of my IRA funds for the investment and the transaction turned out to be a prohibited transaction? Is my entire IRA still subject to tax or just the part I invested?

A: Your entire IRA is subject to tax and penalty even if you only used a small percentage of it. But a way to avoid this potential nightmare is to first split your IRA into two IRAs. The tax and penalty would then apply only to the IRA making the investment. Your other one is spared.

count (and insists that you look at it too) as a *separate entity* from you. This means that even though it is your savings account, you cannot just treat it as another pocket to dip into for cash you may need to make any old investment. If you do, your entire account may become taxable due to a prohibited transaction penalty, and you could end up taking such a hit that your nest egg is depleted.

The crux of the matter is this: Prohibited transactions are there to monitor alternative IRA investing—and that is why this checklist is so important to review before investing in a choice piece of real estate you've seen that tickles your fancy more than traditional mutual fund investing. Of course, even if you are able to steer clear of all the potential traps involved in alternative investing and prohibited transactions, you should still follow the main precept of wise investing, which is to put money only into what you *know and understand;* otherwise, there is a real chance that you could still lose out big-time.

Ask Ed . . .

Q: If I am allowed to invest in the stock of businesses like Microsoft, General Electric or other big, listed companies, can I invest my IRA funds in the stock of my own business too?

A: The answer is no precisely because it is your business and, therefore, you exercise control over all business decisions. That is considered "self-dealing," whereas even though you may own Microsoft stock, Bill Gates does not have to call YOU whenever he wants to make a decision about Microsoft operations. The fact that your business may be a better investment for your IRA is meaningless as far as the self-dealing rules are concerned—unless you brought in someone else (unrelated to you) to run your business for you. Then you might qualify to invest your IRA in your own business.

What If I Don't?

The big benefit of using plan funds for an alternative investment is that the gain (or income) is not taxed until you take a distribution from the SDIRA. But wait . . . there's a catch (surprise! surprise!); some income inside the SDIRA *is* taxed if you invest in certain businesses. Not only is the income taxed, but since your SDIRA is technically speaking a trust, the tax you pay will be at *trust tax rates,* which are the highest rates in the land. This can easily erode profits inside your plan and is just one trap you could fall into if you blast ahead without going over this checklist.

Ask Ed . . .

Q: If I have real estate in my IRA and I sell it at a huge profit, is there any way to get any of those profits out of the IRA at capital gains rates?

A: No. All distributions from IRAs are taxable at ordinary income tax rates. The only way you can beat the tax on real estate or any business profits in an IRA is if the IRA is a Roth IRA (see this section, Part 11). Roth IRA funds are already taxed money so that is the best type of IRA money to use for alternative IRA investments like real estate and businesses. The distributions from a Roth IRA will generally be tax-free, which is much better than any capital gains rates, since you cannot beat zero percent!

Another potential trap is debt financing. You cannot loan money to your account to make investments, but your account can borrow from the accounts of others. If your IRA does borrow, you cannot personally guarantee the loan since that is the same as loaning money to your IRA, which is a prohibited transaction. Who would make a loan to your IRA without a guarantee that you will pay them back, you may be asking. Believe it or not, many individuals and banks will. It is becoming a booming business to target the growing balances in IRAs and the number of people looking at nontraditional investments such as real estate for loan opportunities. These lenders are called "nonrecourse lenders," which means they will loan your IRA money to buy property with just the property as their collateral and no personal guarantee from you. They generally will only lend you an amount up to a certain percentage of the property's value so that if your IRA cannot repay the loan, they can just take the property in foreclosure. If you are able to arrange the nonrecourse financing for property you buy in your IRA, you could still lose the property and your life savings at the same time if you do not know what you are doing. And if you

Ask Ed . . .

Q: Why do you focus on the rules for making nontraditional investments in IRAs? Don't they apply to 401(k)s or other company plans?

A: Yes, most of these rules apply to company plans as well. In fact, qualified plans like a 401(k) allow a broader range of options than an IRA, at least as far as prohibited investments are concerned. For example, you can invest in life insurance in a company plan, even though that is prohibited in an IRA. And with a 401(k) certain debt-financed real-estate-related income taxes that you could end up paying in your SDIRA do not apply. But the reason I reference IRAs mostly is that most 401(k)s will never let you do self-directed investing within the plan. They just don't want the liability or the administrative headaches of allowing thousands of employees to start putting their 401(k) funds into real estate and all kinds of other nontraditional investments. They feel it could easily get out of control, in addition to which many employees may not be sophisticated enough as investors to steer clear of the many tax traps with these investments.

make money, some of that money will be subject to income tax now because it comes from a debt-financed asset.

Instructions

Before you even consider making any type of IRA or plan investment other than stocks, bonds, mutual funds, or CDs, consult this checklist to see if there is a chance it could be deemed a prohibited transaction. If you are still unsure, this tells you something too, and you should perhaps not engage in the transaction.

The penalty for engaging in a prohibited transaction with your IRA funds is so severe that you should always err on the side of caution. Measure your nontraditional investment selection against each point in this checklist to see if it will stand up to the Ed Slott test: (1) Is the investment for you, and (2) Can you make the investment without violating the self-dealing rules?

Ask Ed . . .

Q: What if my IRA owns an interest in an apartment building and I pay some of the maintenance bills personally, but am reimbursed by my IRA? Is that a prohibited transaction?

A: Yes. Paying bills for an investment owned by your IRA is the same as loaning money to your IRA, and loaning money to your IRA is a prohibited transaction.

Also, as you reflect on this checklist, consider the long-term impact on your beneficiaries of having the types of nontraditional investments you are thinking about. If you die holding these types of nontraditional investments, you will want to make sure your beneficiaries know what to do about taking RMDs after they inherit. Which then begs the question, Will they understand these types of investments as well as you do—e.g., what should be sold and for what price? Think this through as you go over the checklist, then have a conversation with your family.

After that, go over everything again with your accountant or financial advisor, or plan custodian, as one final precaution that everything you are doing is okay—before you take the big step and actually do it.

A Word to the Wise

The Right Way to Reduce Risk Investing IRAs in Nontraditional Assets

- Establish separate IRAs for each nonstandard asset.
- Assemble a team of professional experts and use them.
- Only buy assets from unrelated third parties.
- Don't use the asset for personal use, and that includes allowing family members use of the asset.
- Check the scenario with your IRA custodian.
- If you are unsure if it is a prohibited transaction, ask the Department of Labor (DOL) for approval before doing the transaction.
- Don't try to use your professional expertise to benefit your IRA asset (buy a piece of land and use your architectural firm to draw up the plans for the building to go on the land).
- Don't rely on the "expertise" of family members.

THE ALTERNATIVE INVESTMENTS AND PROHIBITED TRANSACTIONS CHECKLIST

MY NAME: ______________________ **DATE:** __________

MY ADVISOR'S NAME: ______________________ **PLAN #:** __________

Follow-ups should be added to the To Do lists at the end of this checklist

WARNING: Are you aware of the risks of making nontraditional IRA investments? Violation of the rules could result in the disqualification of your IRA, leaving your entire account balance subject to income tax (and a 10 percent penalty if you are under age 59½). Generally you will need a self-directed IRA custodian to hold your IRA.

1. What types of transactions are prohibited?

- Borrowing from or lending money to my account. __________
- Pledging my account as security. __________
- Buying, selling, or leasing any property to or from my account. __________
- Buying property for personal use with funds from my account. __________
- Investing in my own business or in a business wherein I or any other prohibited participant have a majority interest. __________
- Receiving compensation for managing my account. __________
- Disguised transactions—doing business with an LLC or multiple entities in which I, or other prohibited participants, have a majority interest (this includes the purchase of insurance through other entities). __________

2. What types of investments are prohibited?

- Collectibles (art, rugs, antiques, gems, stamps, alcoholic beverages, etc.). (Exceptions are made for some coins and metals.) __________
- Owning life insurance in my account. __________
- Funds used to purchase prohibited investments are considered to be distributed and taxable to me in the year the investment was purchased. The 10 percent early-distribution penalty will apply if I am under the age of 59½. __________

3. Who is considered a prohibited participant?

- Myself. __________
- A beneficiary of my account. __________

- My fiduciary (anyone who exercises or has discretionary authority, control, or responsibility in managing or administering my account or in disposing of its assets; or who provides investment advice to me on the account for a fee or has any authority or responsibility to do so. ________
- Members of my family (spouse, parents, lineal descendant, and any spouse of a lineal descendant). ________

4. My IRA assets must be kept separate from my personal assets, and: ________

- No prohibited participants can work for my IRA investment. ________
- No prohibited participants can do maintenance, repairs, or remodeling on property owned by my IRA. ________
- No prohibited participants can use their personal funds to pay bills due on investments in my IRA, even if my IRA reimburses them. ________
- No prohibited participants can use any property in the IRA for any personal use, not even to store unused personal property. ________
- No prohibited participant can receive any personal benefit from my IRA investments. ________

5. Tax benefits such as capital gains, step up in basis, depreciation, and losses cannot be taken advantage of for investments inside my IRA. ________

6. Financing inside my IRA will be more difficult because:

- I must use nonrecourse loans. ________
- I cannot lend money to my IRA or personally guarantee a loan for it. ________
- Debt-financed income may be subject to Unrelated Debt Financed Income (UDFI) taxes. ________

7. I understand that all of the preceding rules and warnings apply to the investment of my IRA funds in any business owned by my IRA, any other prohibited participant (including myself), or any other person or entity if the IRA investment could be construed to be a conflict of interest or provide a benefit to me. ________

Comments: ________________________________

____

____

____

____

8. If the proposed nontraditional investment triggers a tax on my IRA's income:

- Unrelated Business Income Tax (UBIT) is assessed on income earned by a business owned by the IRA, e.g. a pizza parlor. ________
- UBIT is calculated at trust tax rates. ________
- Exceptions to UBIT include investment income, royalties, rent from real and personal property (rent from personal property cannot exceed 50 percent), gains on the sale of property—except for business inventory). ________
- The first $1,000 of income is exempt from UBIT. ________
- If my investment is debt-financed, income in the IRA attributable to the debt-financed portion of the investment is subject to Unrelated Debt Financed Income (UDFI) tax. ________
- Both taxes are reported on Form 990-T, which is signed by the self-directed IRA custodian, and the tax is paid from IRA funds. (Note: The payment of the tax is an expense of the IRA and is not considered a distribution subject to income tax.) ________

9. To avoid disqualification, I will: ________

- Assemble a team of professional advisors for their expertise in investment selection. ________
- Choose a self-directed IRA custodian to hold my IRA and check my investment scenario. ________
- Ask the Department of Labor for approval before going ahead with the transaction if I am unsure whether it is prohibited. ________
- Not use my professional expertise or resources (or those of other disqualified participants) to benefit my IRA. ________
- Consider using a Roth IRA for the investment (if the transaction is disqualified, there is generally no tax effect; if it works, earnings will be income-tax-free). ________

10. Make sure my named beneficiaries are capable of managing this IRA if they were to inherit it. ____________

11. Make sure I fully understand this investment and invest only in what I know. ____________

Comments: ____________

____

____

____

____

12. If buying real estate in a self-directed IRA:

- Have I evaluated the benefits of purchasing the real estate outside of the IRA assuming I have the ability to do so? (REMINDER: The following tax benefits are not available when real estate is purchased in the IRA. Capital gains tax rates, step up in basis, depreciation and other related deductions, and losses.) ____________
- Do I have enough cash in the IRA to purchase the property and pay all the annual expenses on it for as long as I own it? ____________
- Have I found a nonrecourse lender to work with me if I must borrow? ____________
- Have all payments to purchase the real estate come from my IRA (including the initial deposit) and do all documents show the title of my IRA account as the property owner? ____________

Comments: ____________

____

____

____

____

13. Will I need to establish separate self-directed IRAs for each nontraditional investment? ____________

14. I understand that annual fair market valuations will be required for my investment (this may require the help of an expert). ____________

15. I should periodically review the prohibited transactions and prohibited participant rules to ensure that I am not violating them with the nontraditional investment in my IRA. ____________

16. I understand that required distributions will begin at age 70½ or upon my death. If there is no liquidity in the IRA or no other IRAs from which to make the distribution, then distributions of shares of the investment will have to be made to me or to my beneficiaries. Thus, a valuation of the asset will have to be established as of the prior year-end to calculate the correct RMD, and a valuation of the distributed share will have to be established as of the distribution date to ensure that I have taken the correct RMD amount. ____________

Comments: ____

____

____

____

____

Follow-Up

My To Do List	Date Completed
1 ______________________________	
2 ______________________________	
3 ______________________________	
4 ______________________________	
5 ______________________________	
6 ______________________________	
7 ______________________________	
8 ______________________________	
9 ______________________________	
10 ______________________________	

____________________________ ____________

My Signature Date

Part 11

THE ROTH IRA CONVERSION CHECKLIST

For account owners

What It Does

Here's a quick Roth IRA conversion fact sheet:

- To "convert" means to roll your traditional IRA to a Roth IRA. (Beginning in 2008 you will be able to roll employer plan funds to a Roth IRA)
- Traditional IRAs include SEP and SIMPLE IRAs and those funds can also be converted to Roth IRAs.
- There is no need to have earned income, or any income to be able to convert.
- There is no limit on the amount of traditional IRA or plan funds that can be converted as long as you qualify to convert to a Roth IRA.
- You cannot convert if your modified adjusted gross income (MAGI) exceeds $100,000, or if you file married separate. The Tax Increase Prevention and Reconciliation Act (TIPRA) eliminates these requirements beginning in 2010.

- You pay ordinary income tax on the amount you convert to a Roth IRA.
- You can undo a Roth conversion for any reason whatsoever, up to October 15 of the year following the year of the Roth conversion. If you convert in 2007, you have until October 15, 2008, to change your mind and undo part or all of the 2007 Roth IRA conversion.
- Contributions and converted amounts can be withdrawn at any time.
- Withdrawals are income-tax-free forever to you and/or your named beneficiaries if the withdrawal is qualified: You have held the account for a minimum of 5 years (the 5-year period begins with the establishment of the Roth IRA), and, in addition, have met any *one* of the following conditions: (1) You are at least 59½ (withdrawals of converted amounts before age 59½ within the 5-year exclusion period for that conversion will be subject to a 10 percent penalty on the amount withdrawn); (2) Death; (3) Disability; (4) You withdraw as a first-time homebuyer (maximum lifetime cap of $10,000 per IRA owner).

These are the facts, and they are all well and good. But here's the question: *Should* you convert your traditional IRA to a Roth IRA or roll over your plan funds to a traditional IRA so that you can convert to a Roth IRA, which the tax laws currently require you to do if you have a 401(k) or other employer-sponsored plan (as of 2008 you will be able to roll your employer funds to a Roth)? The answers to these questions are what you will find as you go through this checklist. And if you can and do convert to a Roth IRA, you should continue making contributions afterward, if you qualify. See the following fact sheet to keep your Roth happy and healthy.

I am a big fan of the Roth IRA. They are great for account owners because earnings and distributions are tax-free, and they are great for named inheritors who will get to receive an income-tax-free inheritance. If the value of your estate could be large enough to be subject to estate tax, your inheritors will reap another benefit from your hav-

A Quick Fact Sheet

Roth IRA Contributions

- You contribute already taxed funds (after-tax funds) to a Roth IRA.
- You receive no tax deduction for your Roth IRA contribution.
- You can continue to contribute to a Roth IRA after age 70½.
- Qualified withdrawals are income-tax free (a withdrawal made after the account has been established for 5 years and the Roth owner is over the age of 59½ or qualifies for the first-time homebuyer exception).
- You can also have and contribute to a spousal Roth IRA, based on your income even if your spouse has no income.
- Withdrawals of your contribution or converted amounts are always income-tax free.
- Withdrawals of converted amounts may be subject to the 10 percent early distribution penalty if the 5-year exclusion period has not been met and the Roth owner is under age 59½ at the time of the withdrawal.
- Withdrawals of earnings may be taxed and subject to the 10 percent early distribution penalty if it is not a qualified withdrawal.
- There are no required minimum distributions for Roth IRA owners.
- Roth IRA designated beneficiaries can stretch (extend distributions) over their lifetimes the same as traditional IRA beneficiaries.

ing converted because the income tax you will have paid on the conversion will reduce the overall size of your estate. All that being said, I would never tell you to go full speed ahead and convert to a Roth IRA without having first examined for yourself the tax costs and benefits, the pros and the cons, of doing so. This checklist will guide you through that process so you can make your own determination and be able to follow through properly if your decision is yes.

Ask Ed . . .

Q: You mentioned MAGI. What the heck is that?

A: MAGI (modified adjusted gross income) is a totally made-up term that appears absolutely nowhere on your tax return. It's put in the tax code to drive you insane, and it works. But for current (but ending in 2010) Roth IRA conversion eligibility you must know what your MAGI is. You figure this by starting with your adjusted gross income (AGI), which does appear on your return at the bottom of page one, and involves adding back the following deductions that are applicable to you: IRA contributions; student loan interest payments; tuition and fee payments; foreign-earned income and housing exclusions or deductions; qualified savings bond interest exclusions (from Form 8815); and exclusions of employer-provided adoption benefits (shown on Form 8839). You then subtract required distributions and the amount of the conversion subject to income tax to find your MAGI for Roth IRA conversion eligibility, which currently stands at a $100,000 limit for all taxpayers, except those filing married separate, who are *not permitted* to convert to a Roth IRA. But again, all such roadblocks will disappear for Roth IRA converters in 2010.

What's In It for Me?

A big benefit of converting to a Roth IRA is that a Roth comes with one of the few built-in second chances permitted by the tax code. It's called "recharacterization." And it means this: If the funds you convert grow in the Roth IRA, you can keep them, but if your investments tank, you get to undo the conversion and remove any tax you would have owed on the value that no longer exists. You have until October 15 of the year following the year of the conversion to change your mind (for any reason at all). It's like getting to bet on a horse after the race is over. What a deal!

Also, a Roth conversion is not an all-or-nothing proposition. If you wish, you can convert just a portion of your traditional IRA should you just want to dip your toes in the Roth IRA waters.

Ask Ed . . .

Q: A change to the tax code in 2005 allows RMDs to be excluded from MAGI for Roth IRA conversion purposes. Does this new RMD provision allow RMDs to be excluded for other tax provisions, like taxation of social security?

A: No. It only allows you to exclude RMDs for purposes of Roth conversion eligibility, and that's it. Your RMDs still count as income—that is, as part of your adjusted gross income—for all other tax provisions, so no extra break here.

Some will say that converting to a Roth does not pay if you will be in a lower tax bracket when you are ready to withdraw from your traditional IRA. That can be true—sometimes. But even so, you don't know what future tax rates will be when the time comes to have to start paying the piper on your deferred account earnings. At least a Roth IRA takes the uncertainty out of future tax rates since you cannot beat their now-and-forever zero percent tax rate on withdrawals.

With this checklist, you will know once and for all if a Roth IRA conversion is right for you *at this time*. And if not, you will have the checklist available to go back to for future reconsideration should events in your life occur that may change your situation or rationale.

What If I Don't?

As noted earlier, the checklist points out some of the reasons why a Roth IRA conversion may not be right for you at this time. For example it does not pay to convert to a Roth IRA if you will be withdrawing early (before age 59½), as this could subject your converted funds

Ask Ed . . .

Q: Can I convert an RMD from a traditional IRA to a Roth IRA? After all, I've already paid the tax, so this should be okay, right?

A: Wrong! You cannot convert any funds from your traditional IRA to a Roth IRA until you take your RMD even if your MAGI does not exceed the $100,000 income limitation, and you qualify to convert. A Roth conversion is a rollover and an RMD cannot be rolled over (it says so in IRS Regulation § 1.408A-4). Once you satisfy your RMD, then any amount remaining in your IRA can be converted as long as your MAGI (which now does not include your RMD) does not exceed $100,000 and you are not married filing separately.

and earnings to the same 10 percent penalty you would get hit with by withdrawing early from a traditional IRA or other plan. Likewise, it would not be worthwhile to convert if you do not intend to hold on to the Roth long-term (i.e., at least the minimum five-year holding period to avoid paying a penalty, but better yet at least ten years to give your funds in the account a chance to bloom tax-free).

It also does not pay to convert if you don't have the money to pay the tax on the conversion, or you may need to tap into your traditional IRA to pay the tax. After all, you don't want to go broke converting. Furthermore, a Roth IRA conversion may not be for you if you are older; you may not have the years left to recoup the tax you will have to pay now for the conversion.

If you are in need of a tax deduction now, you are better off contributing to your traditional IRA or company plan rather than converting to a Roth. But if that is all that's holding you back from converting, I would rethink this short-term strategy and look long term instead. A deduction might save you in taxes now, but you'll pay for it later when the IRS becomes a partner on your tax-deferred IRA or other distributions for the rest of your life. You'll miss out on what I believe is the

Ask Ed . . .

Q: I won't know if I will qualify for a Roth IRA conversion until after the end of the year, and by then it will be too late to convert for the past year, so what do I do?

A: Convert anyway. It pays to do the conversion even if you are not sure if you will qualify. One of the great features of the Roth conversion is that you can always undo (recharacterize) it for any reason and you have up to October 15 of the year following the year you convert to do so. Also, if it is early in the year, you can plan to keep your income under the 100,000-dollar limitation (if that is the problem) by doing things like not taking capital gains or increasing your plan contributions.

greatest opportunity in the tax code to build a tax-free retirement savings account for yourself, then pass it on to your children and grandchildren. So don't be intimidated by the thought of conversion. This checklist is easy to navigate; use it so that you don't miss out.

Ask Ed . . .

Q: Can my beneficiaries stretch my Roth IRA over their lifetimes the same way they can with an inherited traditional IRA?

A: Yes, the distributions rules are the same, but even better, those distributions will generally be tax-free. I say "generally" tax-free because they could be taxable to your beneficiaries if you had not held the Roth for the five-year holding period before you died and your beneficiaries started withdrawing. But even in that case, only the earnings withdrawn before the five-year period is up are taxable; after that all distributions taken by your heirs are tax-free forever.

Instructions

If there is any magic at all to building retirement wealth (and building it fast), the magic lies in keeping your money away from the government for the longest possible amount of time, preferably forever, which is what Roth IRAs are all about. So go over each point in the checklist, which addresses all the benefits and the costs of converting to a Roth IRA, as you answer *for yourself* the following question: "Why on earth would I voluntarily pay tax on my retirement funds before I have to?"

Your answer may be, "I wouldn't." If so, then you can move on and, perhaps, come back to revisit that answer another day.

Or, your answer could be, "Sure I'll have to pay tax up front, but in the overall scheme of things it will be a relatively small amount compared to the tax-free windfall I and my family could benefit from long term."

Don't make your decision in a vacuum. Review this checklist of advantages and disadvantages of a Roth IRA conversion with your spouse if you have one, and your children, too, if they are to be your beneficia-

Ask Ed . . .

Q: What if I do not know my RMD amount yet, but want to convert to a Roth?

A: You need to calculate your RMD and withdraw it before you can convert any amounts to a Roth IRA. Your RMD amount is based on the prior year's December 31 balance in your account. Your plan custodian (bank, broker, fund company, or other financial institution holding your account) must provide you with the RMD calculation for your account if you request it, so request it, then you'll know. Or calculate it yourself (see "My RMD Calculations Checklist" Section II, Part 5) at the beginning of the year you are thinking about converting.

ries. For that matter, go over this checklist with your own parents; they may still be young enough to gain from a Roth IRA conversion if they qualify, not only for your benefit, but theirs, too. Remember to tell them that the tax laws will change in 2010 to make anyone eligible to convert thereafter, and with special tax payment deals too; so if they will be reaching age 59½ by then, or if you will, converting now (if currently eligible) and getting that 5-year clock rolling for tax-free distributions should factor into everyone's thinking.

Ask Ed . . .

Q: If I am not eligible to make a Roth IRA conversion now due to the income limit, but would like to convert someday when able, what can I do?

A: It may seem counterintuitive, but if you haven't already, you start stuffing all you can into your traditional IRA (or SEP or SIMPLE IRA) or company plan right now, as you will be able to convert everything in 2010, regardless of income. So, the more you have in your traditional IRA (deductible or nondeductible) or other plan, the more that can be converted. And for conversions done in 2010, you will be permitted to spread the tax bite over 2 years instead of having to pay taxes on the conversion all at once. The tax-free earnings in the Roth during that time could cover a chunk of the tax bill, or you can start on the way now to accumulating the funds that will be needed to pay the income taxes on the conversion.

THE ROTH IRA CONVERSION CHECKLIST

MY NAME: ______________________ DATE: __________

MY ADVISOR'S NAME: ______________________ PLAN #: __________

Follow-ups should be added to the To Do lists at the end of this checklist.

1. Reasons to convert to a Roth IRA:

- Eligible withdrawals from a Roth IRA are tax-free to me and to my account's named beneficiaries. __________
- I will have no required minimum distributions (RMDs). __________
- I can continue to make Roth IRA contributions even after I am age 70½ if I am still working (have earned income). __________
- I can leave an income-tax-free legacy to my children and grandchildren who can stretch tax-free distributions over their own life expectancies. __________
- A Roth IRA makes a better trust beneficiary because qualified distributions are income-tax free. __________
- If I have a taxable estate, the income tax paid on the amount converted reduces the value of my total estate that will be subject to estate tax. __________
- Paying the tax now takes the uncertainty out of future tax rates that go with a tax-deferred account. __________
- Using Roth funds for an alternative (nontraditional) investment will lessen the impact if the transaction is prohibited since there are no income taxes on Roth distributions. (See the Alternative Investments and Prohibited Transactions Checklist in this section, Part 10.) __________
- I can do a partial conversion in any year that I qualify and do not have to convert everything at one time. __________

Comments: ______________________

____

____

____

2. Disadvantages of converting to a Roth IRA:

- I will have to pay income tax on the amount I convert at my tax rate for the year (possibly pushing me into a higher tax bracket). __________
- I do not receive a tax deduction for contributions. __________

- I could be subject to a 10 percent early distribution penalty if I withdraw before age 59½. (The same is true of a tax-deferred account.) ____________
- I don't have the money to pay the income tax on the conversion unless I tap into my traditional IRA or other plan funds to pay the income tax. ____________
- I am older and need my traditional IRA or other plan funds to live on and/or I do not wish to leave my beneficiaries an income-tax-free legacy. ____________
- I need the tax deduction now and don't want to pay the income tax. ____________
- I know for sure that I will be in a much lower tax bracket when I am eligible to start taking my traditional IRA or other plan distributions. ____________
- The increased income can affect the taxability of my social security income, my income tax deductions, exemptions, and the ability to use tax credits. ____________

Comments: ____

____

____

____

3. Distributions are income-tax free if I meet the following Roth distribution requirements:

- I have held the account for 5 years (the 5-year period begins on the first day of the first year a Roth account is established). ____________
- And, I have reached the age of 59½, or the payment is because of death, disability, or a first-time home purchase ($10,000 lifetime maximum per IRA owner). ____________

4. Distributions from Roth IRAs come first from annual contributions, then converted amounts—taxable amounts, then nontaxable, and lastly from earnings. If a distribution is not qualified, taxes and penalties depend on the 5-year exclusion periods that apply to the type of Roth IRA funds distributed (contributions, conversions, earnings). ____________

5. Distributions of annual Roth IRA contributions can be withdrawn at any time for any reason tax- and penalty-free. ____________

6. If I have an immediate need for cash from the Roth and have met the 5-year exclusion period for conversions, withdrawals of converted funds will be tax- and penalty-free even if taken before I am 59½. ____________

Comments: ____

____

____

____

____

7. I understand that in order to convert any employer plan funds to a Roth IRA, I must first roll those funds to a traditional IRA, then convert them to the Roth. (This requirement is eliminated as of 2008.) ____________

8. I must have $100,000 or less in modified adjusted gross income (MAGI) to do a conversion. (See IRS Publication 590 for the latest version of the MAGI formula.) This requirement is eliminated in 2010. ____________

- The amount converted is not counted in the $100,000 MAGI limit. ____________

9. I cannot do a Roth IRA conversion if I am married, filing separately. (This requirement is eliminated in 2010). ____________

10. If I am 70½ or older, I must take my RMD from my traditional IRA for the year before doing a conversion, and cannot convert the RMD amount. ____________

11. If I put off (or have to wait to become eligible) converting to a Roth IRA, for conversions done in 2010 only, the tax can be paid ratably in 2011 and 2012. ____________

12. The pro rata rule applies to funds I convert from a traditional IRA that contains both pretax and after-tax amounts. I cannot convert the after-tax amounts only, even if they are in a separate IRA. (See the RMD Calculations Checklist in Section II, Part 5.) ____________

13. I understand there is a 5-year exclusion period for each conversion (if I do 5 conversions over 5 years, I have 5 different exclusion periods), and that: ____________

Converted funds withdrawn before the 5-year exclusion period ends are subject to the 10 percent early distribution penalty if I am under the age of 59½ at the time of the distribution. ________

I must keep track of each 5-year holding period, as follows: ________

________________ ________
Date of Conversion Amount

________________ ________
Date of Conversion Amount

Comments: ________________

____

____

____

____

14. Recharacterization allows me to undo my Roth IRA conversion for any reason, and I have until October 15 of the year after the conversion to do so. To recharacterize I must:

- Notify both the Roth IRA custodian and the traditional IRA custodian that I am recharacterizing. ________
- Transfer the amount I wish to recharacterize, plus or minus earnings or losses, to the traditional IRA via a trustee-to-trustee (direct) transfer. ________
- Amend my tax return to get a refund of the income taxes paid on the recharacterized amount if I recharacterize after filing. ________
- Conversions that fail because I don't meet the eligibility requirements should be recharacterized by the October 15 deadline. And if I miss the deadline: ________

—The amount converted becomes an excess contribution subject to annual penalties as long as it remains in the Roth IRA. ________

—I will need an IRS Private Letter Ruling allowing an extension of time for doing the recharacterization. ________

15. I can do a partial recharacterization and do not have to recharacterize the entire converted amount, but I cannot choose to recharacterize only assets that have lost value unless they are in a separate Roth IRA account I have established for that purpose. ____________

16. I should consider making all current conversions to a new Roth IRA account until the time to recharacterize expires. ____________

Comments: ____

____

____

____

17. If I am not eligible to do a Roth IRA conversion now, but will qualify in 2010 when the tax law changes to allow anyone to do a Roth IRA conversion of IRA or other plan funds, I should prepare now by:

- Maximizing contributions to my current retirement plan in order to make the most of the conversion opportunity in 2010. ____________
- Consider making nondeductible IRA and employer plan contributions to maximize the amount available for conversion to a Roth IRA in 2010. ____________
- Start accumulating the funds that will be necessary to pay the taxes on the conversion. ____________

Comments: ____

____

____

____

____

Follow-Up

My To Do List	Date Completed
1	
2	
3	

4 ____________________

5 ____________________

6 ____________________

7 ____________________

8 ____________________

9 ____________________

10 ____________________

My Signature

Date

Section V

THE FOLLOW-UP CARE SOLUTION

If you have reached this section, it means you have looked under the hood of your owned or inherited retirement account and checked upward of 250 items to determine how healthy it is and how long and fruitful a life it potentially has. Now you fully understand what I meant in my introduction about most people being financial daredevils when it comes to the care of their retirement accounts. Even the rare few of you who may have looked under the hood from time to time really had no idea just how *many* moving parts should be checked, did you? But now that you have completed my diagnostic, you have a greater appreciation of just how much money you can lose and how much planning can be derailed by just one neglected or mistakenly executed item or transaction. And you are at last almost free of daredevil-itis.

"*Almost?*" you ask. "What *else* could there possibly be left to check?"

Good question, and this section, which in effect serves as the safety net for your safety net, will provide the answer. It is designed to make sure that the route you have mapped for your money will remain free of ruts that might otherwise become huge potholes if not quickly paved along the way. This assurance comes from follow-up, a process involving two more moving parts.

Since many aspects of retirement account care and distribution planning are based on a calendar-year schedule, it is important to take a final look under the hood of your account as the books close each year by doing an annual year-end checkup. That's the first part.

You also will need the specialized help of a tax attorney and/or financial and legal professional to draw up key documents and execute key transactions for you. You want them to do so correctly, the first time. That means being sure the advisors you use are experienced in these matters and well up to the task, which is where the last moving part of my care solution comes in—the Advisor Checkup Tool.

Part 1

MY YEAR-END CHECKLIST

For account owners and beneficiaries

Ask Ed . . .

Q: You say this year-end checkup is for beneficiaries too? How so?

A: If you are or will be a plan beneficiary, you will know from going through the various checklists in Section III that there are many timely decisions that have to be made and requirements that have to be met by year-end or even earlier in order to inherit properly (retain the stretch option, for example). Also, beneficiaries of inherited accounts are subject to taking Required Minimum Distributions too and the same 50 percent penalty applies if they miss one or take a wrong amount. This goes equally for Roth IRA beneficiaries. They have to take RMDs from their inherited Roth IRAs by year-end, even though the distributions are tax-free.

What It Does

So how do you follow up on your retirement savings? You can't call your money and ask it how it's doing (though I know many people who do talk to their money all the time. No comment). You follow up by, among other things, making sure that each one of your key retirement account transactions is checked and that you have taken care of all your To Do's.

As you should know by now, whenever you move IRA or other plan money, or take distributions, bad things can happen, and it only takes one mistake, or one bungled keystroke by a data entry person at a financial institution to end a retirement account by causing it to be taxed and stripped of its sheltered status.

There is one sure thing about IRA and plan distribution mistakes; eventually they get found out. Every time money is distributed from a retirement account, a Form 1099-R is generated by your plan custodian, and copies go to you and almost everywhere else, including, of course, to the IRS. So if a mistake is made by you, your plan custodian, your advisor, or anyone else, it will get picked up, often too late for you to do anything about it except pay through the nose.

The most common mistake is missing a Required Minimum Distribution, which will trigger an immediate 50 percent penalty on the

Ask Ed . . .

Q: I notice you include Roth conversions on your year-end checklist. Can't those be undone even after the end of the year in the event of a mistake or change of mind? So, what's the problem?

A: Yes, Roth conversions can be reversed (technical term: recharacterized) up to October 15 of the year after the conversion. The reason Roth conversions are on this checklist is to remind you to get them done by year-end if you decide to convert. You don't have until April 15 to do a conversion for the previous year.

amount that should have been withdrawn. But there are others. And this checklist will help you identify all those potential problem areas—the timely maneuvers you must make—and remind you to take one more look before year-end to make sure you have taken care of them.

What's in It for Me?

You'll avoid a potential mess, as well as save your money and lots of time by eliminating years of paperwork, letter writing to the IRS, complaining to your advisors, begging the government for mercy, and beseeching your attorney for a discount, none of which are productive activities. I know this is true because I receive e-mails daily from people all across the country who are in that boat. They have made a costly error (or it was made by their financial advisor, bank, or broker from not following instructions properly or knowing the rules) and they are desperate to find a way out and turn things around when, in most cases, it is already much too late. You will be very glad this isn't you.

What If I Don't?

Maybe you are an eternal optimist, which is great for your health, but not for your retirement savings. You will be flirting with Murphy's Law, which says that anything that can go wrong, will, and usually at the worst possible time.

Imagine deciding to roll your 401(k) balance of, say, $400,000 to your IRA during the year, instructing your plan custodian accordingly, believing it was done, only to find out too late that the funds never made it into an IRA but ended up in a regular taxable account, due to a clerical coding error. That would mean your having to pay tax on $400,000—plus a $40,000 (10 percent) penalty if you were younger than 59½ at the time (or under age 55 depending on which rule applies to you). Could you get this fixed? Possibly—in fact, probably—but not without an IRS Private Letter Ruling, a process that is expensive and offers no guarantees. You have the best chance of correcting a fund transfer or plan distribution mistake, for example, in the year it is made.

That's why this final check up before year-end is so important. Otherwise, you could not only be flirting with Murphy's Law, but also playing Russian roulette.

Ask Ed . . .

Q: I just inherited my husband's IRA and plan to roll it over to my own IRA. Must I do the rollover before year-end?

A: No. There is no deadline for a spousal rollover, but you still should do it as soon as possible because your RMD will likely be lower if you take ownership rather than remain a beneficiary (see Section III, Part 2). Also, if you were to die suddenly before doing the rollover, your beneficiaries might not get the stretch option. Remember, procrastination is a thief, and not just of time.

Instructions

When I say year-end follow-up, I don't mean the literal last day of the year. I mean during the year, perhaps even close to the end, but never really *the* end. It is almost impossible to get anything done in the last week of the year, let alone the last day, when everyone is overwhelmed scurrying about trying to get things done at the last minute so they can get out the door for the holidays. It is in the heat of battle when mistakes are sure to occur. And the last week of any year is a battle in almost all businesses, I can assure you.

For example, I once got a call from a broker on the last business day of the year (Friday, December 30, 2005). He told me he had mistakenly taken a $120,000 distribution for his mother from her retirement account for the year rather than her actual RMD amount, which was about a tenth of that figure. When he asked his firm to correct his mistake by undoing the distribution and putting the funds back in, the firm refused because it was New Year's and not only the books but also the doors were closing. I told him he could go for a PLR on his mother's behalf, claiming his own negligence as the reason, and he would probably get it. But in the meantime, what would Mom say about messing up her IRA? How about, "Gimme back those presents and take this lump of coal, sonny."

Here's a recommendation: Plan to do your year-end checkup *before Thanksgiving.* To me, Thanksgiving signals the end of the year. Most people really don't do much from Thanksgiving until New Year's anyway (unless, of course, you are in a holiday-related business, in which case it is even more unlikely that you will have time to address IRA distribution and other retirement-planning issues, so my Thanksgiving rule applies even more so to you). It's November, and so you will still get to see another statement in time to correct any mistakes or even make planning improvements before the year ends. But if you wait until December, you won't see a statement until, well, January, when year-end has already passed, and it may be either too late to fix a problem or require lots of work and cooperation on the part of your plan custodian to reopen last year's books to make a change just for you. You might need the Jaws of Life.

A Word to the Wise

Instead of thinking of this as your year-end planning checklist, think of it as your "year-round planning checklist." Year-round is even better than before-Thanksgiving planning. It is always the best way to follow up on your plan decisions and transactions, required or otherwise. For example, whenever you move IRA or plan money, that distribution should show up on your next month's statement. So, it makes sense to follow up that month to see if the funds actually made it to the right place in the right amount. If you use this checklist as a reminder from month to month, almost any problem can be fixed or strategy improved upon. It is the passage of time that solidifies most errors, turning them into stone.

MY YEAR-END CHECKLIST

MY NAME: ______________________ DATE: __________

MY ADVISOR'S NAME: ______________________ PLAN #: __________

Follow-ups should be added to the To Do lists at the end of this checklist.

Before Year-end

1. Have I (the owner or beneficiary) satisfied all my required distributions for the year? __________

- RMDs __________
- RMDs from inherited Roth IRAs __________
- Year-of-death RMDs from inherited accounts __________
- 72(t) early distribution payments __________

____

Comments: ______________________

____

____

____

____

2. For Roth IRA conversions in the current year, company plan funds must be rolled over to a traditional IRA and all funds must leave my traditional IRA before year-end. __________

3. Lump-sum distributions from company plans must be completed in order to qualify for 10-year averaging and NUA treatment. __________

4. Check to see that all employer stock qualifying for NUA treatment has been transferred to a non-tax-deferred account. __________

5. Check to see that all 60-day rollovers were completed on time. __________

6. If I want to split an inherited account, I must do so by year-end (12/31) if the account owner died the previous year. __________

7. Check plan beneficiary forms and update them if necessary. __________

Comments: ____________________

____

____

____

____

After Year-end

8. Check the 1099-R issued by the plan for accuracy. ________

9. Make sure all checks issued by the plan at year-end are received and deposited in the appropriate accounts. ________

10. Check year-end statement for accuracy: ________

- Are all deposits/contributions for the year recorded correctly? ________
- Are all distributions for the year recorded correctly? ________

Comments: ____________________

____

____

11. IRA deadlines to meet in the upcoming year:

- 9/30—Beneficiary determination date ________
- 10/15—Roth recharacterization deadline ________
- 10/31—Trust documentation deadline ________
- Pending 60-day rollover deadlines ________

Comments: ____________________

____

____

____

Follow-Up

My To Do List	Date Completed
1	
2	
3	
4	

5 ______________________________

6 ______________________________

7 ______________________________

8 ______________________________

9 ______________________________

10 ______________________________

______________________________ ______________

My Signature Date

Part 2

MY ADVISOR CHECKUP TOOL

A Dirty Little Secret

This last piece of the retirement distribution-planning puzzle is not a checklist, but rather a lengthy word to the wise, and a tool.

The checklists in this book are to educate you so that:

1. You will become keenly aware of all the issues involved in the proper care and maintenance of your retirement account.
2. You will have a written record of all your choices and decisions, deadlines and reminders, which you can quickly put your hands on, update, and share with your family (who will need this information at some point).

But any truly comprehensive care system cannot be a total do-it-yourself kit. Even a car junkie needs a hotshot mechanic from time to time.

So it is with your retirement savings account, which, as I noted in the introduction, is unlike any other type of asset you own because it is loaded with built-in taxes, complex distribution rules and rigid deadlines that demand specialized attention at some point to ensure proper execution, the first time. This is why I have stressed throughout this book, and am offering as a final word to the wise to you here, that after you have gone through these checklists on your own, you should work with a financial advisor to execute your wishes. Not just any old financial advisor, either. You need—and your savings deserve—a financial advisor trained specifically in the IRA and retirement plan distribution issues you have just reviewed.

But here's a dirty little secret: Most financial advisors are not that experienced in this area. In fact, about 1 percent are specifically trained and equipped for such hazardous duty—and I am likely being generous with that figure. This means that more than 99 percent of all the financial advisors in this country are not prepared or lack the expertise to work with you and your family on the care of your retirement accounts. And that sad statistic is not entirely the fault of the advisors either—because here is another dirty little secret: The banks, brokerage firms, and other financial companies they work for do not prepare or encourage them to develop this expertise. Why not? Because most of these institutions are stuck in just one mode—the investing mode. This means they are so focused on that single area that they are virtually ignoring the really big elephant in the room—the 76 million baby boomers coming up on retirement who need to know (and need to know *now*) how to set up their accumulations and tap into them in the most tax-advantaged way possible.

You see, the job of a financial advisor is not just to make you money (which is certainly important) but also to help you *keep* it. This rounding out of expertise is what truly transforms a reasonably fair or good financial advisor into a great one—indeed, into an *expert* financial advisor. And an expert financial advisor is what you should have now that you've got your retirement planning road map in hand.

What to Do

So, how do you know if your financial advisor is an expert, and, if not, how do you find one that is?

Here's a test. Show this book to your current financial advisor after you have gone through the checklists. If the advisor looks as surprised as you did when you first opened this book at the volume of moving parts under the hood that must be checked, you should feel a red flag rising. And if the advisor becomes outraged when you share some of my observations in this chapter, consider that red flag flying high and look for assistance elsewhere.

If word of mouth or the phone book fails you, here's another checkup tool you can use. It's called "Ed Slott's Elite IRA Advisor Group" and you can find it on my website (www.irahelp.com) by clicking the line Looking for an Advisor Who Knows IRAs? It is my mission to create more competent financial advisors for consumers to use and to educate consumers to expect—indeed demand—a higher level of expertise from the financial advisors they work with. In an effort to accomplish both goals, Ed Slott's Elite IRA Advisor Group is a listing of all the financial advisors across the country I have trained personally.

To become members of this elite group of not just competent but *top-notch* financial advisors, they must first attend my intensive two-day workshop (I refer to it as Basic Training) in retirement account distribution planning. I then give each of them more advanced training year-round where I teach them how to apply the same system of checklists used in this book to better serve their clients and keep them up to date in their education and expertise with my books and articles, my workshops, streaming video on my website, my newsletter, and other alerts. When each Elite Group advisor has completed two years of advanced training, he or she becomes a member of my "Master Elite" group, also listed on the site, where you can review each member by state or, using a zip code search feature, narrow the names down to those closest to your home or business.

I created this registry (the only one of its kind) specifically to help people like you connect with a financial advisor who will know where you are coming from and know how to get you where you want your road map to take you because they are schooled in the same system. Is this the only way to find a competent advisor? Probably not. But it will definitely help to narrow your search.

Can you expect to pay more for the services of an expert financial advisor? Yes, just as you would for the services of any other type of professional with specialized skills and training. But it won't cost a fortune, certainly not in the long run, especially when you consider the cost you would otherwise be paying in grief, time, energy, *and* money undoing the damage a less expensive nonexpert financial advisor can cause.

You Need an Estate-planning Attorney with Special Expertise, Too!

In addition to an expert financial advisor, you likely will also need an estate-planning attorney to craft many of the legal documents referred to throughout this book—a will, trust, powers of attorney, living will, health care proxies, and so on. Here again, just any old estate-planning attorney won't do. When a good portion of your assets consists of your retirement account, you need an estate-planning attorney with the know-how to incorporate that account with all its separate rules and regulations into your *overall* estate plan. Many estate-planning attorneys are not familiar with these rules and, for example, may set up a will or create a trust to handle retirement assets the same way they would any other piece of property. In fact, though most estate-planning attorneys won't admit it, deep down they *hope* you will spend every dime of your retirement savings before you die so that they don't have to deal with it in your estate after you're gone.

The financial advisors I train are always asking me for the name of an attorney who can prepare a trust to inherit an IRA (what I call an "IRA trust") because it is so hard to find one. If you want to see whether your estate-planning attorney is up on this, a good way of telling is to review the checklist in Section IV on naming a trust a beneficiary and ask if he or she is familiar with the many—or *any*—of the points that must be addressed in this one area alone. If not, then you'll know you must look elsewhere to find an attorney that has this specialized knowledge.

You can start by again going to my website and this time clicking the line "Looking for an Attorney Who Knows IRAs?" where all the estate-planning attorneys I have personally trained are listed, also by state. (In creating this listing I want to acknowledge The American Academy of Estate Planning Attorneys, the first attorney group to undergo this specialized training from me.)

If you have taken a lifetime to build your retirement savings and taken time out of your life to go through this book, address all the points it covers that apply to you and your beneficiaries, and create a care plan for yourself, you need a financial advisor and estate-planning attorney capable of carrying out that plan correctly and protecting what you have built. This advisor checkup tool will help achieve that goal.

One last point. If you go to my website to seek the name of financial advisors and estate planning attorneys, you will notice the disclaimer and legal warning. You should read and carefully consider the information in that disclaimer before contacting these professionals.

Appendix I

SINGLE LIFE EXPECTANCY TABLE

To be used for calculating postdeath required distributions to beneficiaries **(from the April 2002 Final Regulations)**

AGE OF IRA OR PLAN BENEFICIARY	LIFE EXPECTANCY (IN YEARS)	AGE OF IRA OR PLAN BENEFICIARY	LIFE EXPECTANCY (IN YEARS)	AGE OF IRA OR PLAN BENEFICIARY	LIFE EXPECTANCY (IN YEARS)
0	82.4				
1	81.6	21	62.1	41	42.7
2	80.6	22	61.1	42	41.7
3	79.7	23	60.1	43	40.7
4	78.7	24	59.1	44	39.8
5	77.7	25	58.2	45	38.8
6	76.7	26	57.2	46	37.9
7	75.8	27	56.2	47	37.0
8	74.8	28	55.3	48	36.0
9	73.8	29	54.3	49	35.1
10	72.8	30	53.3	50	34.2
11	71.8	31	52.4	51	33.3
12	70.8	32	51.4	52	32.3
13	69.9	33	50.4	53	31.4
14	68.9	34	49.4	54	30.5
15	67.9	35	48.5	55	29.6
16	66.9	36	47.5	56	28.7
17	66.0	37	46.5	57	27.9
18	65.0	38	45.6	58	27.0
19	64.0	39	44.6	59	26.1
20	63.0	40	43.6	60	25.2

61	24.4	81	9.7	101	2.7
62	23.5	82	9.1	102	2.5
63	22.7	83	8.6	103	2.3
64	21.8	84	8.1	104	2.1
65	21.0	85	7.6	105	1.9
66	20.2	86	7.1	106	1.7
67	19.4	87	6.7	107	1.5
68	18.6	88	6.3	108	1.4
69	17.8	89	5.9	109	1.2
70	17.0	90	5.5	110	1.1
71	16.3	91	5.2	111+	1.0
72	15.5	92	4.9		
73	14.8	93	4.6		
74	14.1	94	4.3		
75	13.4	95	4.1		
76	12.7	96	3.8		
77	12.1	97	3.6		
78	11.4	98	3.4		
79	10.8	99	3.1		
80	10.2	100	2.9		

Appendix II

UNIFORM LIFE EXPECTANCY TABLE

(For use by all IRA owners and plan participants except those whose named beneficiary for the entire year is a spouse more than 10 years younger than the owner)

AGE OF IRA OWNER OR PLAN PARTICIPANT	LIFE EXPECTANCY (IN YEARS)	AGE OF IRA OWNER OR PLAN PARTICIPANT	LIFE EXPECTANCY (IN YEARS)
70	27.4	93	9.6
71	26.5	94	9.1
72	25.6	95	8.6
73	24.7	96	8.1
74	23.8	97	7.6
75	22.9	98	7.1
76	22.0	99	6.7
77	21.2	100	6.3
78	20.3	101	5.9
79	19.5	102	5.5
80	18.7	103	5.2
81	17.9	104	4.9
82	17.1	105	4.5
83	16.3	106	4.2
84	15.5	107	3.9
85	14.8	108	3.7
86	14.1	109	3.4
87	13.4	110	3.1
88	12.7	111	2.9
89	12.0	112	2.6
90	11.4	113	2.4
91	10.8	114	2.1
92	10.2	115+	1.9

Appendix III

JOINT LIFE EXPECTANCY TABLE

(For use by owners whose spouses are more than 10 years younger)

AGES	0	1	2	3	4	5	6	7	8	9
0	90.0	89.5	89.0	88.6	88.2	87.8	87.4	87.1	86.8	86.5
1	89.5	89.0	88.5	88.1	87.6	87.2	86.8	86.5	86.1	85.8
2	89.0	88.5	88.0	87.5	87.1	86.6	86.2	85.8	85.5	85.1
3	88.6	88.1	87.5	87.0	86.5	86.1	85.6	85.2	84.8	84.5
4	88.2	87.6	87.1	86.5	86.0	85.5	85.1	84.6	84.2	83.8
5	87.8	87.2	86.6	86.1	85.5	85.0	84.5	84.1	83.6	83.2
6	87.4	86.8	86.2	85.6	85.1	84.5	84.0	83.5	83.1	82.6
7	87.1	86.5	85.8	85.2	84.6	84.1	83.5	83.0	82.5	82.1
8	86.8	86.1	85.5	84.8	84.2	83.6	83.1	82.5	82.0	81.6
9	86.5	85.8	85.1	84.5	83.8	83.2	82.6	82.1	81.6	81.0
10	86.2	85.5	84.8	84.1	83.5	82.8	82.2	81.6	81.1	80.6
11	85.9	85.2	84.5	83.8	83.1	82.5	81.8	81.2	80.7	80.1
12	85.7	84.9	84.2	83.5	82.8	82.1	81.5	80.8	80.2	79.7
13	85.4	84.7	84.0	83.2	82.5	81.8	81.1	80.5	79.9	79.2
14	85.2	84.5	83.7	83.0	82.2	81.5	80.8	80.1	79.5	78.9
15	85.0	84.3	83.5	82.7	82.0	81.2	80.5	79.8	79.1	78.5
16	84.9	84.1	83.3	82.5	81.7	81.0	80.2	79.5	78.8	78.1
17	84.7	83.9	83.1	82.3	81.5	80.7	80.0	79.2	78.5	77.8
18	84.5	83.7	82.9	82.1	81.3	80.5	79.7	79.0	78.2	77.5
19	84.4	83.6	82.7	81.9	81.1	80.3	79.5	78.7	78.0	77.3
20	84.3	83.4	82.6	81.8	80.9	80.1	79.3	78.5	77.7	77.0
21	84.1	83.3	82.4	81.6	80.8	79.9	79.1	78.3	77.5	76.8
22	84.0	83.2	82.3	81.5	80.6	79.8	78.9	78.1	77.3	76.5
23	83.9	83.1	82.2	81.3	80.5	79.6	78.8	77.9	77.1	76.3
24	83.8	83.0	82.1	81.2	80.3	79.5	78.6	77.8	76.9	76.1
25	83.7	82.9	82.0	81.1	80.2	79.3	78.5	77.6	76.8	75.9
26	83.6	82.8	81.9	81.0	80.1	79.2	78.3	77.5	76.6	75.8

AGES	0	1	2	3	4	5	6	7	8	9
27	83.6	82.7	81.8	80.9	80.0	79.1	78.2	77.4	76.5	75.6
28	83.5	82.6	81.7	80.8	79.9	79.0	78.1	77.2	76.4	75.5
29	83.4	82.6	81.6	80.7	79.8	78.9	78.0	77.1	76.2	75.4
30	83.4	82.5	81.6	80.7	79.7	78.8	77.9	77.0	76.1	75.2
31	83.3	82.4	81.5	80.6	79.7	78.8	77.8	76.9	76.0	75.1
32	83.3	82.4	81.5	80.5	79.6	78.7	77.8	76.8	75.9	75.0
33	83.2	82.3	81.4	80.5	79.5	78.6	77.7	76.8	75.9	74.9
34	83.2	82.3	81.3	80.4	79.5	78.5	77.6	76.7	75.8	74.9
35	83.1	82.2	81.3	80.4	79.4	78.5	77.6	76.6	75.7	74.8
36	83.1	82.2	81.3	80.3	79.4	78.4	77.5	76.6	75.6	74.7
37	83.0	82.2	81.2	80.3	79.3	78.4	77.4	76.5	75.6	74.6
38	83.0	82.1	81.2	80.2	79.3	78.3	77.4	76.4	75.5	74.6
39	83.0	82.1	81.1	80.2	79.2	78.3	77.3	76.4	75.5	74.5
40	82.9	82.1	81.1	80.2	79.2	78.3	77.3	76.4	75.4	74.5
41	82.9	82.0	81.1	80.1	79.2	78.2	77.3	76.3	75.4	74.4
42	82.9	82.0	81.1	80.1	79.1	78.2	77.2	76.3	75.3	74.4
43	82.9	82.0	81.0	80.1	79.1	78.2	77.2	76.2	75.3	74.3
44	82.8	81.9	81.0	80.0	79.1	78.1	77.2	76.2	75.2	74.3
45	82.8	81.9	81.0	80.0	79.1	78.1	77.1	76.2	75.2	74.3
46	82.8	81.9	81.0	80.0	79.0	78.1	77.1	76.1	75.2	74.2
47	82.8	81.9	80.9	80.0	79.0	78.0	77.1	76.1	75.2	74.2
48	82.8	81.9	80.9	80.0	79.0	78.0	77.1	76.1	75.1	74.2
49	82.7	81.8	80.9	79.9	79.0	78.0	77.0	76.1	75.1	74.1
50	82.7	81.8	80.9	79.9	79.0	78.0	77.0	76.0	75.1	74.1
51	82.7	81.8	80.9	79.9	78.9	78.0	77.0	76.0	75.1	74.1
52	82.7	81.8	80.9	79.9	78.9	78.0	77.0	76.0	75.0	74.1
53	82.7	81.8	80.8	79.9	78.9	77.9	77.0	76.0	75.0	74.0
54	82.7	81.8	80.8	79.9	78.9	77.9	76.9	76.0	75.0	74.0
55	82.6	81.8	80.8	79.8	78.9	77.9	76.9	76.0	75.0	74.0
56	82.6	81.7	80.8	79.8	78.9	77.9	76.9	75.9	75.0	74.0
57	82.6	81.7	80.8	79.8	78.9	77.9	76.9	75.9	75.0	74.0
58	82.6	81.7	80.8	79.8	78.8	77.9	76.9	75.9	74.9	74.0
59	82.6	81.7	80.8	79.8	78.8	77.9	76.9	75.9	74.9	74.0
60	82.6	81.7	80.8	79.8	78.8	77.8	76.9	75.9	74.9	73.9
61	82.6	81.7	80.8	79.8	78.8	77.8	76.9	75.9	74.9	73.9
62	82.6	81.7	80.7	79.8	78.8	77.8	76.9	75.9	74.9	73.9
63	82.6	81.7	80.7	79.8	78.8	77.8	76.8	75.9	74.9	73.9
64	82.5	81.7	80.7	79.8	78.8	77.8	76.8	75.9	74.9	73.9
65	82.5	81.7	80.7	79.8	78.8	77.8	76.8	75.8	74.9	73.9
66	82.5	81.7	80.7	79.7	78.8	77.8	76.8	75.8	74.9	73.9
67	82.5	81.7	80.7	79.7	78.8	77.8	76.8	75.8	74.9	73.9
68	82.5	81.6	80.7	79.7	78.8	77.8	76.8	75.8	74.8	73.9

AGES	0	1	2	3	4	5	6	7	8	9
69	82.5	81.6	80.7	79.7	78.8	77.8	76.8	75.8	74.8	73.9
70	82.5	81.6	80.7	79.7	78.8	77.8	76.8	75.8	74.8	73.9
71	82.5	81.6	80.7	79.7	78.7	77.8	76.8	75.8	74.8	73.8
72	82.5	81.6	80.7	79.7	78.7	77.8	76.8	75.8	74.8	73.8
73	82.5	81.6	80.7	79.7	78.7	77.8	76.8	75.8	74.8	73.8
74	82.5	81.6	80.7	79.7	78.7	77.8	76.8	75.8	74.8	73.8
75	82.5	81.6	80.7	79.7	78.7	77.8	76.8	75.8	74.8	73.8
76	82.5	81.6	80.7	79.7	78.7	77.8	76.8	75.8	74.8	73.8
77	82.5	81.6	80.7	79.7	78.7	77.7	76.8	75.8	74.8	73.8
78	82.5	81.6	80.7	79.7	78.7	77.7	76.8	75.8	74.8	73.8
79	82.5	81.6	80.7	79.7	78.7	77.7	76.8	75.8	74.8	73.8
80	82.5	81.6	80.7	79.7	78.7	77.7	76.8	75.8	74.8	73.8
81	82.4	81.6	80.7	79.7	78.7	77.7	76.8	75.8	74.8	73.8
82	82.4	81.6	80.7	79.7	78.7	77.7	76.8	75.8	74.8	73.8
83	82.4	81.6	80.7	79.7	78.7	77.7	76.8	75.8	74.8	73.8
84	82.4	81.6	80.7	79.7	78.7	77.7	76.8	75.8	74.8	73.8
85	82.4	81.6	80.6	79.7	78.7	77.7	76.8	75.8	74.8	73.8
86	82.4	81.6	80.6	79.7	78.7	77.7	76.7	75.8	74.8	73.8
87	82.4	81.6	80.6	79.7	78.7	77.7	76.7	75.8	74.8	73.8
88	82.4	81.6	80.6	79.7	78.7	77.7	76.7	75.8	74.8	73.8
89	82.4	81.6	80.6	79.7	78.7	77.7	76.7	75.8	74.8	73.8
90	82.4	81.6	80.6	79.7	78.7	77.7	76.7	75.8	74.8	73.8
91	82.4	81.6	80.6	79.7	78.7	77.7	76.7	75.8	74.8	73.8
92	82.4	81.6	80.6	79.7	78.7	77.7	76.7	75.8	74.8	73.8
93	82.4	81.6	80.6	79.7	78.7	77.7	76.7	75.8	74.8	73.8
94	82.4	81.6	80.6	79.7	78.7	77.7	76.7	75.8	74.8	73.8
95	82.4	81.6	80.6	79.7	78.7	77.7	76.7	75.8	74.8	73.8
96	82.4	81.6	80.6	79.7	78.7	77.7	76.7	75.8	74.8	73.8
97	82.4	81.6	80.6	79.7	78.7	77.7	76.7	75.8	74.8	73.8
98	82.4	81.6	80.6	79.7	78.7	77.7	76.7	75.8	74.8	73.8
99	82.4	81.6	80.6	79.7	78.7	77.7	76.7	75.8	74.8	73.8
100	82.4	81.6	80.6	79.7	78.7	77.7	76.7	75.8	74.8	73.8
101	82.4	81.6	80.6	79.7	78.7	77.7	76.7	75.8	74.8	73.8
102	82.4	81.6	80.6	79.7	78.7	77.7	76.7	75.8	74.8	73.8
103	82.4	81.6	80.6	79.7	78.7	77.7	76.7	75.8	74.8	73.8
104	82.4	81.6	80.6	79.7	78.7	77.7	76.7	75.8	74.8	73.8
105	82.4	81.6	80.6	79.7	78.7	77.7	76.7	75.8	74.8	73.8
106	82.4	81.6	80.6	79.7	78.7	77.7	76.7	75.8	74.8	73.8
107	82.4	81.6	80.6	79.7	78.7	77.7	76.7	75.8	74.8	73.8
108	82.4	81.6	80.6	79.7	78.7	77.7	76.7	75.8	74.8	73.8
109	82.4	81.6	80.6	79.7	78.7	77.7	76.7	75.8	74.8	73.8
110	82.4	81.6	80.6	79.7	78.7	77.7	76.7	75.8	74.8	73.8

AGES	0	1	2	3	4	5	6	7	8	9
111	82.4	81.6	80.6	79.7	78.7	77.7	76.7	75.8	74.8	73.8
112	82.4	81.6	80.6	79.7	78.7	77.7	76.7	75.8	74.8	73.8
113	82.4	81.6	80.6	79.7	78.7	77.7	76.7	75.8	74.8	73.8
114	82.4	81.6	80.6	79.7	78.7	77.7	76.7	75.8	74.8	73.8
115+	82.4	81.6	80.6	79.7	78.7	77.7	76.7	75.8	74.8	73.8

AGES	10	11	12	13	14	15	16	17	18	19
10	80.0	79.6	79.1	78.7	78.2	77.9	77.5	77.2	76.8	76.5
11	79.6	79.0	78.6	78.1	77.7	77.3	76.9	76.5	76.2	75.8
12	79.1	78.6	78.1	77.6	77.1	76.7	76.3	75.9	75.5	75.2
13	78.7	78.1	77.6	77.1	76.6	76.1	75.7	75.3	74.9	74.5
14	78.2	77.7	77.1	76.6	76.1	75.6	75.1	74.7	74.3	73.9
15	77.9	77.3	76.7	76.1	75.6	75.1	74.6	74.1	73.7	73.3
16	77.5	76.9	76.3	75.7	75.1	74.6	74.1	73.6	73.1	72.7
17	77.2	76.5	75.9	75.3	74.7	74.1	73.6	73.1	72.6	72.1
18	76.8	76.2	75.5	74.9	74.3	73.7	73.1	72.6	72.1	71.6
19	76.5	75.8	75.2	74.5	73.9	73.3	72.7	72.1	71.6	71.1
20	76.3	75.5	74.8	74.2	73.5	72.9	72.3	71.7	71.1	70.6
21	76.0	75.3	74.5	73.8	73.2	72.5	71.9	71.3	70.7	70.1
22	75.8	75.0	74.3	73.5	72.9	72.2	71.5	70.9	70.3	69.7
23	75.5	74.8	74.0	73.3	72.6	71.9	71.2	70.5	69.9	69.3
24	75.3	74.5	73.8	73.0	72.3	71.6	70.9	70.2	69.5	68.9
25	75.1	74.3	73.5	72.8	72.0	71.3	70.6	69.9	69.2	68.5
26	75.0	74.1	73.3	72.5	71.8	71.0	70.3	69.6	68.9	68.2
27	74.8	74.0	73.1	72.3	71.6	70.8	70.0	69.3	68.6	67.9
28	74.6	73.8	73.0	72.2	71.3	70.6	69.8	69.0	68.3	67.6
29	74.5	73.6	72.8	72.0	71.2	70.4	69.6	68.8	68.0	67.3
30	74.4	73.5	72.7	71.8	71.0	70.2	69.4	68.6	67.8	67.1
31	74.3	73.4	72.5	71.7	70.8	70.0	69.2	68.4	67.6	66.8
32	74.1	73.3	72.4	71.5	70.7	69.8	69.0	68.2	67.4	66.6
33	74.0	73.2	72.3	71.4	70.5	69.7	68.8	68.0	67.2	66.4
34	73.9	73.0	72.2	71.3	70.4	69.5	68.7	67.8	67.0	66.2
35	73.9	73.0	72.1	71.2	70.3	69.4	68.5	67.7	66.8	66.0
36	73.8	72.9	72.0	71.1	70.2	69.3	68.4	67.6	66.7	65.9
37	73.7	72.8	71.9	71.0	70.1	69.2	68.3	67.4	66.6	65.7
38	73.6	72.7	71.8	70.9	70.0	69.1	68.2	67.3	66.4	65.6
39	73.6	72.7	71.7	70.8	69.9	69.0	68.1	67.2	66.3	65.4
40	73.5	72.6	71.7	70.7	69.8	68.9	68.0	67.1	66.2	65.3
41	73.5	72.5	71.6	70.7	69.7	68.8	67.9	67.0	66.1	65.2
42	73.4	72.5	71.5	70.6	69.7	68.8	67.8	66.9	66.0	65.1
43	73.4	72.4	71.5	70.6	69.6	68.7	67.8	66.8	65.9	65.0
44	73.3	72.4	71.4	70.5	69.6	68.6	67.7	66.8	65.9	64.9
45	73.3	72.3	71.4	70.5	69.5	68.6	67.6	66.7	65.8	64.9

AGES	10	11	12	13	14	15	16	17	18	19
46	73.3	72.3	71.4	70.4	69.5	68.5	67.6	66.6	65.7	64.8
47	73.2	72.3	71.3	70.4	69.4	68.5	67.5	66.6	65.7	64.7
48	73.2	72.2	71.3	70.3	69.4	68.4	67.5	66.5	65.6	64.7
49	73.2	72.2	71.2	70.3	69.3	68.4	67.4	66.5	65.6	64.6
50	73.1	72.2	71.2	70.3	69.3	68.4	67.4	66.5	65.5	64.6
51	73.1	72.2	71.2	70.2	69.3	68.3	67.4	66.4	65.5	64.5
52	73.1	72.1	71.2	70.2	69.2	68.3	67.3	66.4	65.4	64.5
53	73.1	72.1	71.1	70.2	69.2	68.3	67.3	66.3	65.4	64.4
54	73.1	72.1	71.1	70.2	69.2	68.2	67.3	66.3	65.4	64.4
55	73.0	72.1	71.1	70.1	69.2	68.2	67.2	66.3	65.3	64.4
56	73.0	72.1	71.1	70.1	69.1	68.2	67.2	66.3	65.3	64.3
57	73.0	72.0	71.1	70.1	69.1	68.2	67.2	66.2	65.3	64.3
58	73.0	72.0	71.0	70.1	69.1	68.1	67.2	66.2	65.2	64.3
59	73.0	72.0	71.0	70.1	69.1	68.1	67.2	66.2	65.2	64.3
60	73.0	72.0	71.0	70.0	69.1	68.1	67.1	66.2	65.2	64.2
61	73.0	72.0	71.0	70.0	69.1	68.1	67.1	66.2	65.2	64.2
62	72.9	72.0	71.0	70.0	69.0	68.1	67.1	66.1	65.2	64.2
63	72.9	72.0	71.0	70.0	69.0	68.1	67.1	66.1	65.2	64.2
64	72.9	71.9	71.0	70.0	69.0	68.0	67.1	66.1	65.1	64.2
65	72.9	71.9	71.0	70.0	69.0	68.0	67.1	66.1	65.1	64.2
66	72.9	71.9	70.9	70.0	69.0	68.0	67.1	66.1	65.1	64.1
67	72.9	71.9	70.9	70.0	69.0	68.0	67.0	66.1	65.1	64.1
68	72.9	71.9	70.9	70.0	69.0	68.0	67.0	66.1	65.1	64.1
69	72.9	71.9	70.9	69.9	69.0	68.0	67.0	66.1	65.1	64.1
70	72.9	71.9	70.9	69.9	69.0	68.0	67.0	66.0	65.1	64.1
71	72.9	71.9	70.9	69.9	69.0	68.0	67.0	66.0	65.1	64.1
72	72.9	71.9	70.9	69.9	69.0	68.0	67.0	66.0	65.1	64.1
73	72.9	71.9	70.9	69.9	68.9	68.0	67.0	66.0	65.0	64.1
74	72.9	71.9	70.9	69.9	68.9	68.0	67.0	66.0	65.0	64.1
75	72.8	71.9	70.9	69.9	68.9	68.0	67.0	66.0	65.0	64.1
76	72.8	71.9	70.9	69.9	68.9	68.0	67.0	66.0	65.0	64.1
77	72.8	71.9	70.9	69.9	68.9	68.0	67.0	66.0	65.0	64.1
78	72.8	71.9	70.9	69.9	68.9	67.9	67.0	66.0	65.0	64.0
79	72.8	71.9	70.9	69.9	68.9	67.9	67.0	66.0	65.0	64.0
80	72.8	71.9	70.9	69.9	68.9	67.9	67.0	66.0	65.0	64.0
81	72.8	71.8	70.9	69.9	68.9	67.9	67.0	66.0	65.0	64.0
82	72.8	71.8	70.9	69.9	68.9	67.9	67.0	66.0	65.0	64.0
83	72.8	71.8	70.9	69.9	68.9	67.9	67.0	66.0	65.0	64.0
84	72.8	71.8	70.9	69.9	68.9	67.9	67.0	66.0	65.0	64.0
85	72.8	71.8	70.9	69.9	68.9	67.9	66.9	66.0	65.0	64.0
86	72.8	71.8	70.9	69.9	68.9	67.9	66.9	66.0	65.0	64.0
87	72.8	71.8	70.9	69.9	68.9	67.9	66.9	66.0	65.0	64.0

AGES	10	11	12	13	14	15	16	17	18	19
88	72.8	71.8	70.9	69.9	68.9	67.9	66.9	66.0	65.0	64.0
89	72.8	71.8	70.9	69.9	68.9	67.9	66.9	66.0	65.0	64.0
90	72.8	71.8	70.9	69.9	68.9	67.9	66.9	66.0	65.0	64.0
91	72.8	71.8	70.9	69.9	68.9	67.9	66.9	66.0	65.0	64.0
92	72.8	71.8	70.9	69.9	68.9	67.9	66.9	66.0	65.0	64.0
93	72.8	71.8	70.9	69.9	68.9	67.9	66.9	66.0	65.0	64.0
94	72.8	71.8	70.8	69.9	68.9	67.9	66.9	66.0	65.0	64.0
95	72.8	71.8	70.8	69.9	68.9	67.9	66.9	66.0	65.0	64.0
96	72.8	71.8	70.8	69.9	68.9	67.9	66.9	66.0	65.0	64.0
97	72.8	71.8	70.8	69.9	68.9	67.9	66.9	66.0	65.0	64.0
98	72.8	71.8	70.8	69.9	68.9	67.9	66.9	66.0	65.0	64.0
99	72.8	71.8	70.8	69.9	68.9	67.9	66.9	66.0	65.0	64.0
100	72.8	71.8	70.8	69.9	68.9	67.9	66.9	66.0	65.0	64.0
101	72.8	71.8	70.8	69.9	68.9	67.9	66.9	66.0	65.0	64.0
102	72.8	71.8	70.8	69.9	68.9	67.9	66.9	66.0	65.0	64.0
103	72.8	71.8	70.8	69.9	68.9	67.9	66.9	66.0	65.0	64.0
104	72.8	71.8	70.8	69.9	68.9	67.9	66.9	66.0	65.0	64.0
105	72.8	71.8	70.8	69.9	68.9	67.9	66.9	66.0	65.0	64.0
106	72.8	71.8	70.8	69.9	68.9	67.9	66.9	66.0	65.0	64.0
107	72.8	71.8	70.8	69.9	68.9	67.9	66.9	66.0	65.0	64.0
108	72.8	71.8	70.8	69.9	68.9	67.9	66.9	66.0	65.0	64.0
109	72.8	71.8	70.8	69.9	68.9	67.9	66.9	66.0	65.0	64.0
110	72.8	71.8	70.8	69.9	68.9	67.9	66.9	66.0	65.0	64.0
111	72.8	71.8	70.8	69.9	68.9	67.9	66.9	66.0	65.0	64.0
112	72.8	71.8	70.8	69.9	68.9	67.9	66.9	66.0	65.0	64.0
113	72.8	71.8	70.8	69.9	68.9	67.9	66.9	66.0	65.0	64.0
114	72.8	71.8	70.8	69.9	68.9	67.9	66.9	66.0	65.0	64.0
115+	72.8	71.8	70.8	69.9	68.9	67.9	66.9	66.0	65.0	64.0

AGES	20	21	22	23	24	25	26	27	28	29
20	70.1	69.6	69.1	68.7	68.3	67.9	67.5	67.2	66.9	66.6
21	69.6	69.1	68.6	68.2	67.7	67.3	66.9	66.6	66.2	65.9
22	69.1	68.6	68.1	67.6	67.2	66.7	66.3	65.9	65.6	65.2
23	68.7	68.2	67.6	67.1	66.6	66.2	65.7	65.3	64.9	64.6
24	68.3	67.7	67.2	66.6	66.1	65.6	65.2	64.7	64.3	63.9
25	67.9	67.3	66.7	66.2	65.6	65.1	64.6	64.2	63.7	63.3
26	67.5	66.9	66.3	65.7	65.2	64.6	64.1	63.6	63.2	62.8
27	67.2	66.6	65.9	65.3	64.7	64.2	63.6	63.1	62.7	62.2
28	66.9	66.2	65.6	64.9	64.3	63.7	63.2	62.7	62.1	61.7
29	66.6	65.9	65.2	64.6	63.9	63.3	62.8	62.2	61.7	61.2
30	66.3	65.6	64.9	64.2	63.6	62.9	62.3	61.8	61.2	60.7
31	66.1	65.3	64.6	63.9	63.2	62.6	62.0	61.4	60.8	60.2
32	65.8	65.1	64.3	63.6	62.9	62.2	61.6	61.0	60.4	59.8

AGES	20	21	22	23	24	25	26	27	28	29
33	65.6	64.8	64.1	63.3	62.6	61.9	61.3	60.6	60.0	59.4
34	65.4	64.6	63.8	63.1	62.3	61.6	60.9	60.3	59.6	59.0
35	65.2	64.4	63.6	62.8	62.1	61.4	60.6	59.9	59.3	58.6
36	65.0	64.2	63.4	62.6	61.9	61.1	60.4	59.6	59.0	58.3
37	64.9	64.0	63.2	62.4	61.6	60.9	60.1	59.4	58.7	58.0
38	64.7	63.9	63.0	62.2	61.4	60.6	59.9	59.1	58.4	57.7
39	64.6	63.7	62.9	62.1	61.2	60.4	59.6	58.9	58.1	57.4
40	64.4	63.6	62.7	61.9	61.1	60.2	59.4	58.7	57.9	57.1
41	64.3	63.5	62.6	61.7	60.9	60.1	59.3	58.5	57.7	56.9
42	64.2	63.3	62.5	61.6	60.8	59.9	59.1	58.3	57.5	56.7
43	64.1	63.2	62.4	61.5	60.6	59.8	58.9	58.1	57.3	56.5
44	64.0	63.1	62.2	61.4	60.5	59.6	58.8	57.9	57.1	56.3
45	64.0	63.0	62.2	61.3	60.4	59.5	58.6	57.8	56.9	56.1
46	63.9	63.0	62.1	61.2	60.3	59.4	58.5	57.7	56.8	56.0
47	63.8	62.9	62.0	61.1	60.2	59.3	58.4	57.5	56.7	55.8
48	63.7	62.8	61.9	61.0	60.1	59.2	58.3	57.4	56.5	55.7
49	63.7	62.8	61.8	60.9	60.0	59.1	58.2	57.3	56.4	55.6
50	63.6	62.7	61.8	60.8	59.9	59.0	58.1	57.2	56.3	55.4
51	63.6	62.6	61.7	60.8	59.9	58.9	58.0	57.1	56.2	55.3
52	63.5	62.6	61.7	60.7	59.8	58.9	58.0	57.1	56.1	55.2
53	63.5	62.5	61.6	60.7	59.7	58.8	57.9	57.0	56.1	55.2
54	63.5	62.5	61.6	60.6	59.7	58.8	57.8	56.9	56.0	55.1
55	63.4	62.5	61.5	60.6	59.6	58.7	57.8	56.8	55.9	55.0
56	63.4	62.4	61.5	60.5	59.6	58.7	57.7	56.8	55.9	54.9
57	63.4	62.4	61.5	60.5	59.6	58.6	57.7	56.7	55.8	54.9
58	63.3	62.4	61.4	60.5	59.5	58.6	57.6	56.7	55.8	54.8
59	63.3	62.3	61.4	60.4	59.5	58.5	57.6	56.7	55.7	54.8
60	63.3	62.3	61.4	60.4	59.5	58.5	57.6	56.6	55.7	54.7
61	63.3	62.3	61.3	60.4	59.4	58.5	57.5	56.6	55.6	54.7
62	63.2	62.3	61.3	60.4	59.4	58.4	57.5	56.5	55.6	54.7
63	63.2	62.3	61.3	60.3	59.4	58.4	57.5	56.5	55.6	54.6
64	63.2	62.2	61.3	60.3	59.4	58.4	57.4	56.5	55.5	54.6
65	63.2	62.2	61.3	60.3	59.3	58.4	57.4	56.5	55.5	54.6
66	63.2	62.2	61.2	60.3	59.3	58.4	57.4	56.4	55.5	54.5
67	63.2	62.2	61.2	60.3	59.3	58.3	57.4	56.4	55.5	54.5
68	63.1	62.2	61.2	60.2	59.3	58.3	57.4	56.4	55.4	54.5
69	63.1	62.2	61.2	60.2	59.3	58.3	57.3	56.4	55.4	54.5
70	63.1	62.2	61.2	60.2	59.3	58.3	57.3	56.4	55.4	54.4
71	63.1	62.1	61.2	60.2	59.2	58.3	57.3	56.4	55.4	54.4
72	63.1	62.1	61.2	60.2	59.2	58.3	57.3	56.3	55.4	54.4
73	63.1	62.1	61.2	60.2	59.2	58.3	57.3	56.3	55.4	54.4
74	63.1	62.1	61.2	60.2	59.2	58.2	57.3	56.3	55.4	54.4

AGES	20	21	22	23	24	25	26	27	28	29
75	63.1	62.1	61.1	60.2	59.2	58.2	57.3	56.3	55.3	54.4
76	63.1	62.1	61.1	60.2	59.2	58.2	57.3	56.3	55.3	54.4
77	63.1	62.1	61.1	60.2	59.2	58.2	57.3	56.3	55.3	54.4
78	63.1	62.1	61.1	60.2	59.2	58.2	57.3	56.3	55.3	54.4
79	63.1	62.1	61.1	60.2	59.2	58.2	57.2	56.3	55.3	54.3
80	63.1	62.1	61.1	60.1	59.2	58.2	57.2	56.3	55.3	54.3
81	63.1	62.1	61.1	60.1	59.2	58.2	57.2	56.3	55.3	54.3
82	63.1	62.1	61.1	60.1	59.2	58.2	57.2	56.3	55.3	54.3
83	63.1	62.1	61.1	60.1	59.2	58.2	57.2	56.3	55.3	54.3
84	63.0	62.1	61.1	60.1	59.2	58.2	57.2	56.3	55.3	54.3
85	63.0	62.1	61.1	60.1	59.2	58.2	57.2	56.3	55.3	54.3
86	63.0	62.1	61.1	60.1	59.2	58.2	57.2	56.2	55.3	54.3
87	63.0	62.1	61.1	60.1	59.2	58.2	57.2	56.2	55.3	54.3
88	63.0	62.1	61.1	60.1	59.2	58.2	57.2	56.2	55.3	54.3
89	63.0	62.1	61.1	60.1	59.1	58.2	57.2	56.2	55.3	54.3
90	63.0	62.1	61.1	60.1	59.1	58.2	57.2	56.2	55.3	54.3
91	63.0	62.1	61.1	60.1	59.1	58.2	57.2	56.2	55.3	54.3
92	63.0	62.1	61.1	60.1	59.1	58.2	57.2	56.2	55.3	54.3
93	63.0	62.1	61.1	60.1	59.1	58.2	57.2	56.2	55.3	54.3
94	63.0	62.1	61.1	60.1	59.1	58.2	57.2	56.2	55.3	54.3
95	63.0	62.1	61.1	60.1	59.1	58.2	57.2	56.2	55.3	54.3
96	63.0	62.1	61.1	60.1	59.1	58.2	57.2	56.2	55.3	54.3
97	63.0	62.1	61.1	60.1	59.1	58.2	57.2	56.2	55.3	54.3
98	63.0	62.1	61.1	60.1	59.1	58.2	57.2	56.2	55.3	54.3
99	63.0	62.1	61.1	60.1	59.1	58.2	57.2	56.2	55.3	54.3
100	63.0	62.1	61.1	60.1	59.1	58.2	57.2	56.2	55.3	54.3
101	63.0	62.1	61.1	60.1	59.1	58.2	57.2	56.2	55.3	54.3
102	63.0	62.1	61.1	60.1	59.1	58.2	57.2	56.2	55.3	54.3
103	63.0	62.1	61.1	60.1	59.1	58.2	57.2	56.2	55.3	54.3
104	63.0	62.1	61.1	60.1	59.1	58.2	57.2	56.2	55.3	54.3
105	63.0	62.1	61.1	60.1	59.1	58.2	57.2	56.2	55.3	54.3
106	63.0	62.1	61.1	60.1	59.1	58.2	57.2	56.2	55.3	54.3
107	63.0	62.1	61.1	60.1	59.1	58.2	57.2	56.2	55.3	54.3
108	63.0	62.1	61.1	60.1	59.1	58.2	57.2	56.2	55.3	54.3
109	63.0	62.1	61.1	60.1	59.1	58.2	57.2	56.2	55.3	54.3
110	63.0	62.1	61.1	60.1	59.1	58.2	57.2	56.2	55.3	54.3
111	63.0	62.1	61.1	60.1	59.1	58.2	57.2	56.2	55.3	54.3
112	63.0	62.1	61.1	60.1	59.1	58.2	57.2	56.2	55.3	54.3
113	63.0	62.1	61.1	60.1	59.1	58.2	57.2	56.2	55.3	54.3
114	63.0	62.1	61.1	60.1	59.1	58.2	57.2	56.2	55.3	54.3
115+	63.0	62.1	61.1	60.1	59.1	58.2	57.2	56.2	55.3	54.3

AGES	30	31	32	33	34	35	36	37	38	39
30	60.2	59.7	59.2	58.8	58.4	58.0	57.6	57.3	57.0	56.7
31	59.7	59.2	58.7	58.2	57.8	57.4	57.0	56.6	56.3	56.0
32	59.2	58.7	58.2	57.7	57.2	56.8	56.4	56.0	55.6	55.3
33	58.8	58.2	57.7	57.2	56.7	56.2	55.8	55.4	55.0	54.7
34	58.4	57.8	57.2	56.7	56.2	55.7	55.3	54.8	54.4	54.0
35	58.0	57.4	56.8	56.2	55.7	55.2	54.7	54.3	53.8	53.4
36	57.6	57.0	56.4	55.8	55.3	54.7	54.2	53.7	53.3	52.8
37	57.3	56.6	56.0	55.4	54.8	54.3	53.7	53.2	52.7	52.3
38	57.0	56.3	55.6	55.0	54.4	53.8	53.3	52.7	52.2	51.7
39	56.7	56.0	55.3	54.7	54.0	53.4	52.8	52.3	51.7	51.2
40	56.4	55.7	55.0	54.3	53.7	53.0	52.4	51.8	51.3	50.8
41	56.1	55.4	54.7	54.0	53.3	52.7	52.0	51.4	50.9	50.3
42	55.9	55.2	54.4	53.7	53.0	52.3	51.7	51.1	50.4	49.9
43	55.7	54.9	54.2	53.4	52.7	52.0	51.3	50.7	50.1	49.5
44	55.5	54.7	53.9	53.2	52.4	51.7	51.0	50.4	49.7	49.1
45	55.3	54.5	53.7	52.9	52.2	51.5	50.7	50.0	49.4	48.7
46	55.1	54.3	53.5	52.7	52.0	51.2	50.5	49.8	49.1	48.4
47	55.0	54.1	53.3	52.5	51.7	51.0	50.2	49.5	48.8	48.1
48	54.8	54.0	53.2	52.3	51.5	50.8	50.0	49.2	48.5	47.8
49	54.7	53.8	53.0	52.2	51.4	50.6	49.8	49.0	48.2	47.5
50	54.6	53.7	52.9	52.0	51.2	50.4	49.6	48.8	48.0	47.3
51	54.5	53.6	52.7	51.9	51.0	50.2	49.4	48.6	47.8	47.0
52	54.4	53.5	52.6	51.7	50.9	50.0	49.2	48.4	47.6	46.8
53	54.3	53.4	52.5	51.6	50.8	49.9	49.1	48.2	47.4	46.6
54	54.2	53.3	52.4	51.5	50.6	49.8	48.9	48.1	47.2	46.4
55	54.1	53.2	52.3	51.4	50.5	49.7	48.8	47.9	47.1	46.3
56	54.0	53.1	52.2	51.3	50.4	49.5	48.7	47.8	47.0	46.1
57	54.0	53.0	52.1	51.2	50.3	49.4	48.6	47.7	46.8	46.0
58	53.9	53.0	52.1	51.2	50.3	49.4	48.5	47.6	46.7	45.8
59	53.8	52.9	52.0	51.1	50.2	49.3	48.4	47.5	46.6	45.7
60	53.8	52.9	51.9	51.0	50.1	49.2	48.3	47.4	46.5	45.6
61	53.8	52.8	51.9	51.0	50.0	49.1	48.2	47.3	46.4	45.5
62	53.7	52.8	51.8	50.9	50.0	49.1	48.1	47.2	46.3	45.4
63	53.7	52.7	51.8	50.9	49.9	49.0	48.1	47.2	46.3	45.3
64	53.6	52.7	51.8	50.8	49.9	48.9	48.0	47.1	46.2	45.3
65	53.6	52.7	51.7	50.8	49.8	48.9	48.0	47.0	46.1	45.2
66	53.6	52.6	51.7	50.7	49.8	48.9	47.9	47.0	46.1	45.1
67	53.6	52.6	51.7	50.7	49.8	48.8	47.9	46.9	46.0	45.1
68	53.5	52.6	51.6	50.7	49.7	48.8	47.8	46.9	46.0	45.0
69	53.5	52.6	51.6	50.6	49.7	48.7	47.8	46.9	45.9	45.0
70	53.5	52.5	51.6	50.6	49.7	48.7	47.8	46.8	45.9	44.9

AGES	30	31	32	33	34	35	36	37	38	39
71	53.5	52.5	51.6	50.6	49.6	48.7	47.7	46.8	45.9	44.9
72	53.5	52.5	51.5	50.6	49.6	48.7	47.7	46.8	45.8	44.9
73	53.4	52.5	51.5	50.6	49.6	48.6	47.7	46.7	45.8	44.8
74	53.4	52.5	51.5	50.5	49.6	48.6	47.7	46.7	45.8	44.8
75	53.4	52.5	51.5	50.5	49.6	48.6	47.7	46.7	45.7	44.8
76	53.4	52.4	51.5	50.5	49.6	48.6	47.6	46.7	45.7	44.8
77	53.4	52.4	51.5	50.5	49.5	48.6	47.6	46.7	45.7	44.8
78	53.4	52.4	51.5	50.5	49.5	48.6	47.6	46.6	45.7	44.7
79	53.4	52.4	51.5	50.5	49.5	48.6	47.6	46.6	45.7	44.7
80	53.4	52.4	51.4	50.5	49.5	48.5	47.6	46.6	45.7	44.7
81	53.4	52.4	51.4	50.5	49.5	48.5	47.6	46.6	45.7	44.7
82	53.4	52.4	51.4	50.5	49.5	48.5	47.6	46.6	45.6	44.7
83	53.4	52.4	51.4	50.5	49.5	48.5	47.6	46.6	45.6	44.7
84	53.4	52.4	51.4	50.5	49.5	48.5	47.6	46.6	45.6	44.7
85	53.3	52.4	51.4	50.4	49.5	48.5	47.5	46.6	45.6	44.7
86	53.3	52.4	51.4	50.4	49.5	48.5	47.5	46.6	45.6	44.6
87	53.3	52.4	51.4	50.4	49.5	48.5	47.5	46.6	45.6	44.6
88	53.3	52.4	51.4	50.4	49.5	48.5	47.5	46.6	45.6	44.6
89	53.3	52.4	51.4	50.4	49.5	48.5	47.5	46.6	45.6	44.6
90	53.3	52.4	51.4	50.4	49.5	48.5	47.5	46.6	45.6	44.6
91	53.3	52.4	51.4	50.4	49.5	48.5	47.5	46.6	45.6	44.6
92	53.3	52.4	51.4	50.4	49.5	48.5	47.5	46.6	45.6	44.6
93	53.3	52.4	51.4	50.4	49.5	48.5	47.5	46.6	45.6	44.6
94	53.3	52.4	51.4	50.4	49.5	48.5	47.5	46.6	45.6	44.6
95	53.3	52.4	51.4	50.4	49.5	48.5	47.5	46.5	45.6	44.6
96	53.3	52.4	51.4	50.4	49.5	48.5	47.5	46.5	45.6	44.6
97	53.3	52.4	51.4	50.4	49.5	48.5	47.5	46.5	45.6	44.6
98	53.3	52.4	51.4	50.4	49.5	48.5	47.5	46.5	45.6	44.6
99	53.3	52.4	51.4	50.4	49.5	48.5	47.5	46.5	45.6	44.6
100	53.3	52.4	51.4	50.4	49.5	48.5	47.5	46.5	45.6	44.6
101	53.3	52.4	51.4	50.4	49.5	48.5	47.5	46.5	45.6	44.6
102	53.3	52.4	51.4	50.4	49.5	48.5	47.5	46.5	45.6	44.6
103	53.3	52.4	51.4	50.4	49.5	48.5	47.5	46.5	45.6	44.6
104	53.3	52.4	51.4	50.4	49.5	48.5	47.5	46.5	45.6	44.6
105	53.3	52.4	51.4	50.4	49.4	48.5	47.5	46.5	45.6	44.6
106	53.3	52.4	51.4	50.4	49.4	48.5	47.5	46.5	45.6	44.6
107	53.3	52.4	51.4	50.4	49.4	48.5	47.5	46.5	45.6	44.6
108	53.3	52.4	51.4	50.4	49.4	48.5	47.5	46.5	45.6	44.6
109	53.3	52.4	51.4	50.4	49.4	48.5	47.5	46.5	45.6	44.6
110	53.3	52.4	51.4	50.4	49.4	48.5	47.5	46.5	45.6	44.6
111	53.3	52.4	51.4	50.4	49.4	48.5	47.5	46.5	45.6	44.6
112	53.3	52.4	51.4	50.4	49.4	48.5	47.5	46.5	45.6	44.6

AGES	30	31	32	33	34	35	36	37	38	39
113	53.3	52.4	51.4	50.4	49.4	48.5	47.5	46.5	45.6	44.6
114	53.3	52.4	51.4	50.4	49.4	48.5	47.5	46.5	45.6	44.6
115+	53.3	52.4	51.4	50.4	49.4	48.5	47.5	46.5	45.6	44.6
AGES	**40**	**41**	**42**	**43**	**44**	**45**	**46**	**47**	**48**	**49**
40	50.2	49.8	49.3	48.9	48.5	48.1	47.7	47.4	47.1	46.8
41	49.8	49.3	48.8	48.3	47.9	47.5	47.1	46.7	46.4	46.1
42	49.3	48.8	48.3	47.8	47.3	46.9	46.5	46.1	45.8	45.4
43	48.9	48.3	47.8	47.3	46.8	46.3	45.9	45.5	45.1	44.8
44	48.5	47.9	47.3	46.8	46.3	45.8	45.4	44.9	44.5	44.2
45	48.1	47.5	46.9	46.3	45.8	45.3	44.8	44.4	44.0	43.6
46	47.7	47.1	46.5	45.9	45.4	44.8	44.3	43.9	43.4	43.0
47	47.4	46.7	46.1	45.5	44.9	44.4	43.9	43.4	42.9	42.4
48	47.1	46.4	45.8	45.1	44.5	44.0	43.4	42.9	42.4	41.9
49	46.8	46.1	45.4	44.8	44.2	43.6	43.0	42.4	41.9	41.4
50	46.5	45.8	45.1	44.4	43.8	43.2	42.6	42.0	41.5	40.9
51	46.3	45.5	44.8	44.1	43.5	42.8	42.2	41.6	41.0	40.5
52	46.0	45.3	44.6	43.8	43.2	42.5	41.8	41.2	40.6	40.1
53	45.8	45.1	44.3	43.6	42.9	42.2	41.5	40.9	40.3	39.7
54	45.6	44.8	44.1	43.3	42.6	41.9	41.2	40.5	39.9	39.3
55	45.5	44.7	43.9	43.1	42.4	41.6	40.9	40.2	39.6	38.9
56	45.3	44.5	43.7	42.9	42.1	41.4	40.7	40.0	39.3	38.6
57	45.1	44.3	43.5	42.7	41.9	41.2	40.4	39.7	39.0	38.3
58	45.0	44.2	43.3	42.5	41.7	40.9	40.2	39.4	38.7	38.0
59	44.9	44.0	43.2	42.4	41.5	40.7	40.0	39.2	38.5	37.8
60	44.7	43.9	43.0	42.2	41.4	40.6	39.8	39.0	38.2	37.5
61	44.6	43.8	42.9	42.1	41.2	40.4	39.6	38.8	38.0	37.3
62	44.5	43.7	42.8	41.9	41.1	40.3	39.4	38.6	37.8	37.1
63	44.5	43.6	42.7	41.8	41.0	40.1	39.3	38.5	37.7	36.9
64	44.4	43.5	42.6	41.7	40.8	40.0	39.2	38.3	37.5	36.7
65	44.3	43.4	42.5	41.6	40.7	39.9	39.0	38.2	37.4	36.6
66	44.2	43.3	42.4	41.5	40.6	39.8	38.9	38.1	37.2	36.4
67	44.2	43.3	42.3	41.4	40.6	39.7	38.8	38.0	37.1	36.3
68	44.1	43.2	42.3	41.4	40.5	39.6	38.7	37.9	37.0	36.2
69	44.1	43.1	42.2	41.3	40.4	39.5	38.6	37.8	36.9	36.0
70	44.0	43.1	42.2	41.3	40.3	39.4	38.6	37.7	36.8	35.9
71	44.0	43.0	42.1	41.2	40.3	39.4	38.5	37.6	36.7	35.9
72	43.9	43.0	42.1	41.1	40.2	39.3	38.4	37.5	36.6	35.8
73	43.9	43.0	42.0	41.1	40.2	39.3	38.4	37.5	36.6	35.7
74	43.9	42.9	42.0	41.1	40.1	39.2	38.3	37.4	36.5	35.6
75	43.8	42.9	42.0	41.0	40.1	39.2	38.3	37.4	36.5	35.6
76	43.8	42.9	41.9	41.0	40.1	39.1	38.2	37.3	36.4	35.5
77	43.8	42.9	41.9	41.0	40.0	39.1	38.2	37.3	36.4	35.5

AGES	40	41	42	43	44	45	46	47	48	49
78	43.8	42.8	41.9	40.9	40.0	39.1	38.2	37.2	36.3	35.4
79	43.8	42.8	41.9	40.9	40.0	39.1	38.1	37.2	36.3	35.4
80	43.7	42.8	41.8	40.9	40.0	39.0	38.1	37.2	36.3	35.4
81	43.7	42.8	41.8	40.9	39.9	39.0	38.1	37.2	36.2	35.3
82	43.7	42.8	41.8	40.9	39.9	39.0	38.1	37.1	36.2	35.3
83	43.7	42.8	41.8	40.9	39.9	39.0	38.0	37.1	36.2	35.3
84	43.7	42.7	41.8	40.8	39.9	39.0	38.0	37.1	36.2	35.3
85	43.7	42.7	41.8	40.8	39.9	38.9	38.0	37.1	36.2	35.2
86	43.7	42.7	41.8	40.8	39.9	38.9	38.0	37.1	36.1	35.2
87	43.7	42.7	41.8	40.8	39.9	38.9	38.0	37.0	36.1	35.2
88	43.7	42.7	41.8	40.8	39.9	38.9	38.0	37.0	36.1	35.2
89	43.7	42.7	41.7	40.8	39.8	38.9	38.0	37.0	36.1	35.2
90	43.7	42.7	41.7	40.8	39.8	38.9	38.0	37.0	36.1	35.2
91	43.7	42.7	41.7	40.8	39.8	38.9	37.9	37.0	36.1	35.2
92	43.7	42.7	41.7	40.8	39.8	38.9	37.9	37.0	36.1	35.1
93	43.7	42.7	41.7	40.8	39.8	38.9	37.9	37.0	36.1	35.1
94	43.7	42.7	41.7	40.8	39.8	38.9	37.9	37.0	36.1	35.1
95	43.6	42.7	41.7	40.8	39.8	38.9	37.9	37.0	36.1	35.1
96	43.6	42.7	41.7	40.8	39.8	38.9	37.9	37.0	36.1	35.1
97	43.6	42.7	41.7	40.8	39.8	38.9	37.9	37.0	36.1	35.1
98	43.6	42.7	41.7	40.8	39.8	38.9	37.9	37.0	36.0	35.1
99	43.6	42.7	41.7	40.8	39.8	38.9	37.9	37.0	36.0	35.1
100	43.6	42.7	41.7	40.8	39.8	38.9	37.9	37.0	36.0	35.1
101	43.6	42.7	41.7	40.8	39.8	38.9	37.9	37.0	36.0	35.1
102	43.6	42.7	41.7	40.8	39.8	38.9	37.9	37.0	36.0	35.1
103	43.6	42.7	41.7	40.8	39.8	38.9	37.9	37.0	36.0	35.1
104	43.6	42.7	41.7	40.8	39.8	38.8	37.9	37.0	36.0	35.1
105	43.6	42.7	41.7	40.8	39.8	38.8	37.9	37.0	36.0	35.1
106	43.6	42.7	41.7	40.8	39.8	38.8	37.9	37.0	36.0	35.1
107	43.6	42.7	41.7	40.8	39.8	38.8	37.9	37.0	36.0	35.1
108	43.6	42.7	41.7	40.8	39.8	38.8	37.9	37.0	36.0	35.1
109	43.6	42.7	41.7	40.7	39.8	38.8	37.9	37.0	36.0	35.1
110	43.6	42.7	41.7	40.7	39.8	38.8	37.9	37.0	36.0	35.1
111	43.6	42.7	41.7	40.7	39.8	38.8	37.9	37.0	36.0	35.1
112	43.6	42.7	41.7	40.7	39.8	38.8	37.9	37.0	36.0	35.1
113	43.6	42.7	41.7	40.7	39.8	38.8	37.9	37.0	36.0	35.1
114	43.6	42.7	41.7	40.7	39.8	38.8	37.9	37.0	36.0	35.1
115+	43.6	42.7	41.7	40.7	39.8	38.8	37.9	37.0	36.0	35.1
AGES	**50**	**51**	**52**	**53**	**54**	**55**	**56**	**57**	**58**	**59**
50	40.4	40.0	39.5	39.1	38.7	38.3	38.0	37.6	37.3	37.1
51	40.0	39.5	39.0	38.5	38.1	37.7	37.4	37.0	36.7	36.4
52	39.5	39.0	38.5	38.0	37.6	37.2	36.8	36.4	36.0	35.7

AGES	50	51	52	53	54	55	56	57	58	59
53	39.1	38.5	38.0	37.5	37.1	36.6	36.2	35.8	35.4	35.1
54	38.7	38.1	37.6	37.1	36.6	36.1	35.7	35.2	34.8	34.5
55	38.3	37.7	37.2	36.6	36.1	35.6	35.1	34.7	34.3	33.9
56	38.0	37.4	36.8	36.2	35.7	35.1	34.7	34.2	33.7	33.3
57	37.6	37.0	36.4	35.8	35.2	34.7	34.2	33.7	33.2	32.8
58	37.3	36.7	36.0	35.4	34.8	34.3	33.7	33.2	32.8	32.3
59	37.1	36.4	35.7	35.1	34.5	33.9	33.3	32.8	32.3	31.8
60	36.8	36.1	35.4	34.8	34.1	33.5	32.9	32.4	31.9	31.3
61	36.6	35.8	35.1	34.5	33.8	33.2	32.6	32.0	31.4	30.9
62	36.3	35.6	34.9	34.2	33.5	32.9	32.2	31.6	31.1	30.5
63	36.1	35.4	34.6	33.9	33.2	32.6	31.9	31.3	30.7	30.1
64	35.9	35.2	34.4	33.7	33.0	32.3	31.6	31.0	30.4	29.8
65	35.8	35.0	34.2	33.5	32.7	32.0	31.4	30.7	30.0	29.4
66	35.6	34.8	34.0	33.3	32.5	31.8	31.1	30.4	29.8	29.1
67	35.5	34.7	33.9	33.1	32.3	31.6	30.9	30.2	29.5	28.8
68	35.3	34.5	33.7	32.9	32.1	31.4	30.7	29.9	29.2	28.6
69	35.2	34.4	33.6	32.8	32.0	31.2	30.5	29.7	29.0	28.3
70	35.1	34.3	33.4	32.6	31.8	31.1	30.3	29.5	28.8	28.1
71	35.0	34.2	33.3	32.5	31.7	30.9	30.1	29.4	28.6	27.9
72	34.9	34.1	33.2	32.4	31.6	30.8	30.0	29.2	28.4	27.7
73	34.8	34.0	33.1	32.3	31.5	30.6	29.8	29.1	28.3	27.5
74	34.8	33.9	33.0	32.2	31.4	30.5	29.7	28.9	28.1	27.4
75	34.7	33.8	33.0	32.1	31.3	30.4	29.6	28.8	28.0	27.2
76	34.6	33.8	32.9	32.0	31.2	30.3	29.5	28.7	27.9	27.1
77	34.6	33.7	32.8	32.0	31.1	30.3	29.4	28.6	27.8	27.0
78	34.5	33.6	32.8	31.9	31.0	30.2	29.3	28.5	27.7	26.9
79	34.5	33.6	32.7	31.8	31.0	30.1	29.3	28.4	27.6	26.8
80	34.5	33.6	32.7	31.8	30.9	30.1	29.2	28.4	27.5	26.7
81	34.4	33.5	32.6	31.8	30.9	30.0	29.2	28.3	27.5	26.6
82	34.4	33.5	32.6	31.7	30.8	30.0	29.1	28.3	27.4	26.6
83	34.4	33.5	32.6	31.7	30.8	29.9	29.1	28.2	27.4	26.5
84	34.3	33.4	32.5	31.7	30.8	29.9	29.0	28.2	27.3	26.5
85	34.3	33.4	32.5	31.6	30.7	29.9	29.0	28.1	27.3	26.4
86	34.3	33.4	32.5	31.6	30.7	29.8	29.0	28.1	27.2	26.4
87	34.3	33.4	32.5	31.6	30.7	29.8	28.9	28.1	27.2	26.4
88	34.3	33.4	32.5	31.6	30.7	29.8	28.9	28.0	27.2	26.3
89	34.3	33.3	32.4	31.5	30.7	29.8	28.9	28.0	27.2	26.3
90	34.2	33.3	32.4	31.5	30.6	29.8	28.9	28.0	27.1	26.3
91	34.2	33.3	32.4	31.5	30.6	29.7	28.9	28.0	27.1	26.3
92	34.2	33.3	32.4	31.5	30.6	29.7	28.8	28.0	27.1	26.2
93	34.2	33.3	32.4	31.5	30.6	29.7	28.8	28.0	27.1	26.2
94	34.2	33.3	32.4	31.5	30.6	29.7	28.8	27.9	27.1	26.2

AGES	50	51	52	53	54	55	56	57	58	59
95	34.2	33.3	32.4	31.5	30.6	29.7	28.8	27.9	27.1	26.2
96	34.2	33.3	32.4	31.5	30.6	29.7	28.8	27.9	27.0	26.2
97	34.2	33.3	32.4	31.5	30.6	29.7	28.8	27.9	27.0	26.2
98	34.2	33.3	32.4	31.5	30.6	29.7	28.8	27.9	27.0	26.2
99	34.2	33.3	32.4	31.5	30.6	29.7	28.8	27.9	27.0	26.2
100	34.2	33.3	32.4	31.5	30.6	29.7	28.8	27.9	27.0	26.1
101	34.2	33.3	32.4	31.5	30.6	29.7	28.8	27.9	27.0	26.1
102	34.2	33.3	32.4	31.4	30.5	29.7	28.8	27.9	27.0	26.1
103	34.2	33.3	32.4	31.4	30.5	29.7	28.8	27.9	27.0	26.1
104	34.2	33.3	32.4	31.4	30.5	29.6	28.8	27.9	27.0	26.1
105	34.2	33.3	32.3	31.4	30.5	29.6	28.8	27.9	27.0	26.1
106	34.2	33.3	32.3	31.4	30.5	29.6	28.8	27.9	27.0	26.1
107	34.2	33.3	32.3	31.4	30.5	29.6	28.8	27.9	27.0	26.1
108	34.2	33.3	32.3	31.4	30.5	29.6	28.8	27.9	27.0	26.1
109	34.2	33.3	32.3	31.4	30.5	29.6	28.7	27.9	27.0	26.1
110	34.2	33.3	32.3	31.4	30.5	29.6	28.7	27.9	27.0	26.1
111	34.2	33.3	32.3	31.4	30.5	29.6	28.7	27.9	27.0	26.1
112	34.2	33.3	32.3	31.4	30.5	29.6	28.7	27.9	27.0	26.1
113	34.2	33.3	32.3	31.4	30.5	29.6	28.7	27.9	27.0	26.1
114	34.2	33.3	32.3	31.4	30.5	29.6	28.7	27.9	27.0	26.1
115+	34.2	33.3	32.3	31.4	30.5	29.6	28.7	27.9	27.0	26.1

AGES	60	61	62	63	64	65	66	67	68	69
60	30.9	30.4	30.0	29.6	29.2	28.8	28.5	28.2	27.9	27.6
61	30.4	29.9	29.5	29.0	28.6	28.3	27.9	27.6	27.3	27.0
62	30.0	29.5	29.0	28.5	28.1	27.7	27.3	27.0	26.7	26.4
63	29.6	29.0	28.5	28.1	27.6	27.2	26.8	26.4	26.1	25.7
64	29.2	28.6	28.1	27.6	27.1	26.7	26.3	25.9	25.5	25.2
65	28.8	28.3	27.7	27.2	26.7	26.2	25.8	25.4	25.0	24.6
66	28.5	27.9	27.3	26.8	26.3	25.8	25.3	24.9	24.5	24.1
67	28.2	27.6	27.0	26.4	25.9	25.4	24.9	24.4	24.0	23.6
68	27.9	27.3	26.7	26.1	25.5	25.0	24.5	24.0	23.5	23.1
69	27.6	27.0	26.4	25.7	25.2	24.6	24.1	23.6	23.1	22.6
70	27.4	26.7	26.1	25.4	24.8	24.3	23.7	23.2	22.7	22.2
71	27.2	26.5	25.8	25.2	24.5	23.9	23.4	22.8	22.3	21.8
72	27.0	26.3	25.6	24.9	24.3	23.7	23.1	22.5	22.0	21.4
73	26.8	26.1	25.4	24.7	24.0	23.4	22.8	22.2	21.6	21.1
74	26.6	25.9	25.2	24.5	23.8	23.1	22.5	21.9	21.3	20.8
75	26.5	25.7	25.0	24.3	23.6	22.9	22.3	21.6	21.0	20.5
76	26.3	25.6	24.8	24.1	23.4	22.7	22.0	21.4	20.8	20.2
77	26.2	25.4	24.7	23.9	23.2	22.5	21.8	21.2	20.6	19.9
78	26.1	25.3	24.6	23.8	23.1	22.4	21.7	21.0	20.3	19.7
79	26.0	25.2	24.4	23.7	22.9	22.2	21.5	20.8	20.1	19.5

AGES	60	61	62	63	64	65	66	67	68	69
80	25.9	25.1	24.3	23.6	22.8	22.1	21.3	20.6	20.0	19.3
81	25.8	25.0	24.2	23.4	22.7	21.9	21.2	20.5	19.8	19.1
82	25.8	24.9	24.1	23.4	22.6	21.8	21.1	20.4	19.7	19.0
83	25.7	24.9	24.1	23.3	22.5	21.7	21.0	20.2	19.5	18.8
84	25.6	24.8	24.0	23.2	22.4	21.6	20.9	20.1	19.4	18.7
85	25.6	24.8	23.9	23.1	22.3	21.6	20.8	20.1	19.3	18.6
86	25.5	24.7	23.9	23.1	22.3	21.5	20.7	20.0	19.2	18.5
87	25.5	24.7	23.8	23.0	22.2	21.4	20.7	19.9	19.2	18.4
88	25.5	24.6	23.8	23.0	22.2	21.4	20.6	19.8	19.1	18.3
89	25.4	24.6	23.8	22.9	22.1	21.3	20.5	19.8	19.0	18.3
90	25.4	24.6	23.7	22.9	22.1	21.3	20.5	19.7	19.0	18.2
91	25.4	24.5	23.7	22.9	22.1	21.3	20.5	19.7	18.9	18.2
92	25.4	24.5	23.7	22.9	22.0	21.2	20.4	19.6	18.9	18.1
93	25.4	24.5	23.7	22.8	22.0	21.2	20.4	19.6	18.8	18.1
94	25.3	24.5	23.6	22.8	22.0	21.2	20.4	19.6	18.8	18.0
95	25.3	24.5	23.6	22.8	22.0	21.1	20.3	19.6	18.8	18.0
96	25.3	24.5	23.6	22.8	21.9	21.1	20.3	19.5	18.8	18.0
97	25.3	24.5	23.6	22.8	21.9	21.1	20.3	19.5	18.7	18.0
98	25.3	24.4	23.6	22.8	21.9	21.1	20.3	19.5	18.7	17.9
99	25.3	24.4	23.6	22.7	21.9	21.1	20.3	19.5	18.7	17.9
100	25.3	24.4	23.6	22.7	21.9	21.1	20.3	19.5	18.7	17.9
101	25.3	24.4	23.6	22.7	21.9	21.1	20.2	19.4	18.7	17.9
102	25.3	24.4	23.6	22.7	21.9	21.1	20.2	19.4	18.6	17.9
103	25.3	24.4	23.6	22.7	21.9	21.0	20.2	19.4	18.6	17.9
104	25.3	24.4	23.5	22.7	21.9	21.0	20.2	19.4	18.6	17.8
105	25.3	24.4	23.5	22.7	21.9	21.0	20.2	19.4	18.6	17.8
106	25.3	24.4	23.5	22.7	21.9	21.0	20.2	19.4	18.6	17.8
107	25.2	24.4	23.5	22.7	21.8	21.0	20.2	19.4	18.6	17.8
108	25.2	24.4	23.5	22.7	21.8	21.0	20.2	19.4	18.6	17.8
109	25.2	24.4	23.5	22.7	21.8	21.0	20.2	19.4	18.6	17.8
110	25.2	24.4	23.5	22.7	21.8	21.0	20.2	19.4	18.6	17.8
111	25.2	24.4	23.5	22.7	21.8	21.0	20.2	19.4	18.6	17.8
112	25.2	24.4	23.5	22.7	21.8	21.0	20.2	19.4	18.6	17.8
113	25.2	24.4	23.5	22.7	21.8	21.0	20.2	19.4	18.6	17.8
114	25.2	24.4	23.5	22.7	21.8	21.0	20.2	19.4	18.6	17.8
115+	25.2	24.4	23.5	22.7	21.8	21.0	20.2	19.4	18.6	17.8

AGES	70	71	72	73	74	75	76	77	78	79
70	21.8	21.3	20.9	20.6	20.2	19.9	19.6	19.4	19.1	18.9
71	21.3	20.9	20.5	20.1	19.7	19.4	19.1	18.8	18.5	18.3
72	20.9	20.5	20.0	19.6	19.3	18.9	18.6	18.3	18.0	17.7
73	20.6	20.1	19.6	19.2	18.8	18.4	18.1	17.8	17.5	17.2
74	20.2	19.7	19.3	18.8	18.4	18.0	17.6	17.3	17.0	16.7

AGES	70	71	72	73	74	75	76	77	78	79
75	19.9	19.4	18.9	18.4	18.0	17.6	17.2	16.8	16.5	16.2
76	19.6	19.1	18.6	18.1	17.6	17.2	16.8	16.4	16.0	15.7
77	19.4	18.8	18.3	17.8	17.3	16.8	16.4	16.0	15.6	15.3
78	19.1	18.5	18.0	17.5	17.0	16.5	16.0	15.6	15.2	14.9
79	18.9	18.3	17.7	17.2	16.7	16.2	15.7	15.3	14.9	14.5
80	18.7	18.1	17.5	16.9	16.4	15.9	15.4	15.0	14.5	14.1
81	18.5	17.9	17.3	16.7	16.2	15.6	15.1	14.7	14.2	13.8
82	18.3	17.7	17.1	16.5	15.9	15.4	14.9	14.4	13.9	13.5
83	18.2	17.5	16.9	16.3	15.7	15.2	14.7	14.2	13.7	13.2
84	18.0	17.4	16.7	16.1	15.5	15.0	14.4	13.9	13.4	13.0
85	17.9	17.3	16.6	16.0	15.4	14.8	14.3	13.7	13.2	12.8
86	17.8	17.1	16.5	15.8	15.2	14.6	14.1	13.5	13.0	12.5
87	17.7	17.0	16.4	15.7	15.1	14.5	13.9	13.4	12.9	12.4
88	17.6	16.9	16.3	15.6	15.0	14.4	13.8	13.2	12.7	12.2
89	17.6	16.9	16.2	15.5	14.9	14.3	13.7	13.1	12.6	12.0
90	17.5	16.8	16.1	15.4	14.8	14.2	13.6	13.0	12.4	11.9
91	17.4	16.7	16.0	15.4	14.7	14.1	13.5	12.9	12.3	11.8
92	17.4	16.7	16.0	15.3	14.6	14.0	13.4	12.8	12.2	11.7
93	17.3	16.6	15.9	15.2	14.6	13.9	13.3	12.7	12.1	11.6
94	17.3	16.6	15.9	15.2	14.5	13.9	13.2	12.6	12.0	11.5
95	17.3	16.5	15.8	15.1	14.5	13.8	13.2	12.6	12.0	11.4
96	17.2	16.5	15.8	15.1	14.4	13.8	13.1	12.5	11.9	11.3
97	17.2	16.5	15.8	15.1	14.4	13.7	13.1	12.5	11.9	11.3
98	17.2	16.4	15.7	15.0	14.3	13.7	13.0	12.4	11.8	11.2
99	17.2	16.4	15.7	15.0	14.3	13.6	13.0	12.4	11.8	11.2
100	17.1	16.4	15.7	15.0	14.3	13.6	12.9	12.3	11.7	11.1
101	17.1	16.4	15.6	14.9	14.2	13.6	12.9	12.3	11.7	11.1
102	17.1	16.4	15.6	14.9	14.2	13.5	12.9	12.2	11.6	11.0
103	17.1	16.3	15.6	14.9	14.2	13.5	12.9	12.2	11.6	11.0
104	17.1	16.3	15.6	14.9	14.2	13.5	12.8	12.2	11.6	11.0
105	17.1	16.3	15.6	14.9	14.2	13.5	12.8	12.2	11.5	10.9
106	17.1	16.3	15.6	14.8	14.1	13.5	12.8	12.2	11.5	10.9
107	17.0	16.3	15.6	14.8	14.1	13.4	12.8	12.1	11.5	10.9
108	17.0	16.3	15.5	14.8	14.1	13.4	12.8	12.1	11.5	10.9
109	17.0	16.3	15.5	14.8	14.1	13.4	12.8	12.1	11.5	10.9
110	17.0	16.3	15.5	14.8	14.1	13.4	12.7	12.1	11.5	10.9
111	17.0	16.3	15.5	14.8	14.1	13.4	12.7	12.1	11.5	10.8
112	17.0	16.3	15.5	14.8	14.1	13.4	12.7	12.1	11.5	10.8
113	17.0	16.3	15.5	14.8	14.1	13.4	12.7	12.1	11.4	10.8
114	17.0	16.3	15.5	14.8	14.1	13.4	12.7	12.1	11.4	10.8
115+	17.0	16.3	15.5	14.8	14.1	13.4	12.7	12.1	11.4	10.8

AGES	80	81	82	83	84	85	86	87	88	89
80	13.8	13.4	13.1	12.8	12.6	12.3	12.1	11.9	11.7	11.5
81	13.4	13.1	12.7	12.4	12.2	11.9	11.7	11.4	11.3	11.1
82	13.1	12.7	12.4	12.1	11.8	11.5	11.3	11.0	10.8	10.6
83	12.8	12.4	12.1	11.7	11.4	11.1	10.9	10.6	10.4	10.2
84	12.6	12.2	11.8	11.4	11.1	10.8	10.5	10.3	10.1	9.9
85	12.3	11.9	11.5	11.1	10.8	10.5	10.2	9.9	9.7	9.5
86	12.1	11.7	11.3	10.9	10.5	10.2	9.9	9.6	9.4	9.2
87	11.9	11.4	11.0	10.6	10.3	9.9	9.6	9.4	9.1	8.9
88	11.7	11.3	10.8	10.4	10.1	9.7	9.4	9.1	8.8	8.6
89	11.5	11.1	10.6	10.2	9.9	9.5	9.2	8.9	8.6	8.3
90	11.4	10.9	10.5	10.1	9.7	9.3	9.0	8.6	8.3	8.1
91	11.3	10.8	10.3	9.9	9.5	9.1	8.8	8.4	8.1	7.9
92	11.2	10.7	10.2	9.8	9.3	9.0	8.6	8.3	8.0	7.7
93	11.1	10.6	10.1	9.6	9.2	8.8	8.5	8.1	7.8	7.5
94	11.0	10.5	10.0	9.5	9.1	8.7	8.3	8.0	7.6	7.3
95	10.9	10.4	9.9	9.4	9.0	8.6	8.2	7.8	7.5	7.2
96	10.8	10.3	9.8	9.3	8.9	8.5	8.1	7.7	7.4	7.1
97	10.7	10.2	9.7	9.2	8.8	8.4	8.0	7.6	7.3	6.9
98	10.7	10.1	9.6	9.2	8.7	8.3	7.9	7.5	7.1	6.8
99	10.6	10.1	9.6	9.1	8.6	8.2	7.8	7.4	7.0	6.7
100	10.6	10.0	9.5	9.0	8.5	8.1	7.7	7.3	6.9	6.6
101	10.5	10.0	9.4	9.0	8.5	8.0	7.6	7.2	6.9	6.5
102	10.5	9.9	9.4	8.9	8.4	8.0	7.5	7.1	6.8	6.4
103	10.4	9.9	9.4	8.8	8.4	7.9	7.5	7.1	6.7	6.3
104	10.4	9.8	9.3	8.8	8.3	7.9	7.4	7.0	6.6	6.3
105	10.4	9.8	9.3	8.8	8.3	7.8	7.4	7.0	6.6	6.2
106	10.3	9.8	9.2	8.7	8.2	7.8	7.3	6.9	6.5	6.2
107	10.3	9.8	9.2	8.7	8.2	7.7	7.3	6.9	6.5	6.1
108	10.3	9.7	9.2	8.7	8.2	7.7	7.3	6.8	6.4	6.1
109	10.3	9.7	9.2	8.7	8.2	7.7	7.2	6.8	6.4	6.0
110	10.3	9.7	9.2	8.6	8.1	7.7	7.2	6.8	6.4	6.0
111	10.3	9.7	9.1	8.6	8.1	7.6	7.2	6.8	6.3	6.0
112	10.2	9.7	9.1	8.6	8.1	7.6	7.2	6.7	6.3	5.9
113	10.2	9.7	9.1	8.6	8.1	7.6	7.2	6.7	6.3	5.9
114	10.2	9.7	9.1	8.6	8.1	7.6	7.1	6.7	6.3	5.9
115+	10.2	9.7	9.1	8.6	8.1	7.6	7.1	6.7	6.3	5.9
AGES	**90**	**91**	**92**	**93**	**94**	**95**	**96**	**97**	**98**	**99**
90	7.8	7.6	7.4	7.2	7.1	6.9	6.8	6.6	6.5	6.4
91	7.6	7.4	7.2	7.0	6.8	6.7	6.5	6.4	6.3	6.1
92	7.4	7.2	7.0	6.8	6.6	6.4	6.3	6.1	6.0	5.9
93	7.2	7.0	6.8	6.6	6.4	6.2	6.1	5.9	5.8	5.6

AGES	90	91	92	93	94	95	96	97	98	99
94	7.1	6.8	6.6	6.4	6.2	6.0	5.9	5.7	5.6	5.4
95	6.9	6.7	6.4	6.2	6.0	5.8	5.7	5.5	5.4	5.2
96	6.8	6.5	6.3	6.1	5.9	5.7	5.5	5.3	5.2	5.0
97	6.6	6.4	6.1	5.9	5.7	5.5	5.3	5.2	5.0	4.9
98	6.5	6.3	6.0	5.8	5.6	5.4	5.2	5.0	4.8	4.7
99	6.4	6.1	5.9	5.6	5.4	5.2	5.0	4.9	4.7	4.5
100	6.3	6.0	5.8	5.5	5.3	5.1	4.9	4.7	4.5	4.4
101	6.2	5.9	5.6	5.4	5.2	5.0	4.8	4.6	4.4	4.2
102	6.1	5.8	5.5	5.3	5.1	4.8	4.6	4.4	4.3	4.1
103	6.0	5.7	5.4	5.2	5.0	4.7	4.5	4.3	4.1	4.0
104	5.9	5.6	5.4	5.1	4.9	4.6	4.4	4.2	4.0	3.8
105	5.9	5.6	5.3	5.0	4.8	4.5	4.3	4.1	3.9	3.7
106	5.8	5.5	5.2	4.9	4.7	4.5	4.2	4.0	3.8	3.6
107	5.8	5.4	5.1	4.9	4.6	4.4	4.2	3.9	3.7	3.5
108	5.7	5.4	5.1	4.8	4.6	4.3	4.1	3.9	3.7	3.5
109	5.7	5.3	5.0	4.8	4.5	4.3	4.0	3.8	3.6	3.4
110	5.6	5.3	5.0	4.7	4.5	4.2	4.0	3.8	3.5	3.3
111	5.6	5.3	5.0	4.7	4.4	4.2	3.9	3.7	3.5	3.3
112	5.6	5.3	4.9	4.7	4.4	4.1	3.9	3.7	3.5	3.2
113	5.6	5.2	4.9	4.6	4.4	4.1	3.9	3.6	3.4	3.2
114	5.6	5.2	4.9	4.6	4.3	4.1	3.9	3.6	3.4	3.2
115+	5.5	5.2	4.9	4.6	4.3	4.1	3.8	3.6	3.4	3.1
AGES	**100**	**101**	**102**	**103**	**104**	**105**	**106**	**107**	**108**	**109**
100	4.2	4.1	3.9	3.8	3.7	3.5	3.4	3.3	3.3	3.2
101	4.1	3.9	3.7	3.6	3.5	3.4	3.2	3.1	3.1	3.0
102	3.9	3.7	3.6	3.4	3.3	3.2	3.1	3.0	2.9	2.8
103	3.8	3.6	3.4	3.3	3.2	3.0	2.9	2.8	2.7	2.6
104	3.7	3.5	3.3	3.2	3.0	2.9	2.7	2.6	2.5	2.4
105	3.5	3.4	3.2	3.0	2.9	2.7	2.6	2.5	2.4	2.3
106	3.4	3.2	3.1	2.9	2.7	2.6	2.4	2.3	2.2	2.1
107	3.3	3.1	3.0	2.8	2.6	2.5	2.3	2.2	2.1	2.0
108	3.3	3.1	2.9	2.7	2.5	2.4	2.2	2.1	1.9	1.8
109	3.2	3.0	2.8	2.6	2.4	2.3	2.1	2.0	1.8	1.7
110	3.1	2.9	2.7	2.5	2.3	2.2	2.0	1.9	1.7	1.6
111	3.1	2.9	2.7	2.5	2.3	2.1	1.9	1.8	1.6	1.5
112	3.0	2.8	2.6	2.4	2.2	2.0	1.9	1.7	1.5	1.4
113	3.0	2.8	2.6	2.4	2.2	2.0	1.8	1.6	1.5	1.3
114	3.0	2.7	2.5	2.3	2.1	1.9	1.8	1.6	1.4	1.3
115+	2.9	2.7	2.5	2.3	2.1	1.9	1.7	1.5	1.4	1.2

AGES	110	111	112	113	114	115+				
110	1.5	1.4	1.3	1.2	1.1	1.1				
111	1.4	1.2	1.1	1.1	1.0	1.0				
112	1.3	1.1	1.0	1.0	1.0	1.0				
113	1.2	1.1	1.0	1.0	1.0	1.0				
114	1.1	1.0	1.0	1.0	1.0	1.0				
115+	1.1	1.0	1.0	1.0	1.0	1.0				

Appendix IV

RETIREMENT PLANNING RESOURCES FOR CONSUMERS AND FINANCIAL ADVISORS

WEBSITES:

www.irahelp.com

Here you will find a wealth of retirement planning and distribution information and breaking news. You will also be able to get on our mailing list and have the latest retirement and IRA tax law and ruling alerts e-mailed to you when they are released by Congress, the IRS, and other authorities. In addition, you can join our Discussion Forum, a free resource open to anyone with a question about retirement planning, distribution, and estate planning. There are thousands of questions and answers posted here for your reference, so chances are whatever questions you may have about how to handle your retirement savings will be answered here. The website also provides a complete listing of all my seminars, advisor training workshops, and education programs for consumers, company employees, credit unions, and professional advisors throughout the year.

www.leimbergservices.com

For more estate planning information, tax strategies, and almost daily briefings on how to make the most of the new estate planning opportunities, I highly recommend you sign up with Leimberg Information Services Inc. (LISI). You'll gain access to this incredible e-mail/database resource that contains a wealth of up-to-the-minute information and analysis on employee benefit planning, IRA, pension, and estate planning cases, rulings, and legislation. You'll receive fast, frank, incisive commentary by the nation's leading experts in each specific area and a virtual daily newsletter. Amazingly, all of these services are included in the $24.95 monthly fee. Take a free look and then sign up for LISI at www.leimbergservices.com.

www.pensco.com

PENSCO Trust Company is a leading financial institution in the area of self-directed IRAs for those making nontraditional types of investments, such as real estate, mortgages, private placements, and other property, with their IRAs and other retirement funds.

NEWSLETTERS:

Ed Slott's IRA Advisor

My monthly newsletter (twelve issues per year)—$125 a year. Each issue contains clear and accurate explanations of the latest IRA- and retirement-related tax rulings, cases, and tax law changes and also shows you how to use this information to benefit your clients and build your practice, including easy to view summaries of key points and advisor action plans. Order the online version (at www.irahelp.com or call 800-663-1340) at the same $125, and get much more. With the online version you gain access to our complete online research library of back issues, back to 2001 when the IRS overhauled the retirement distribution rules. For financial advisors especially, this can be invaluable if a client, prospect, CPA, or attorney has an issue and you need to look up a ruling, court case, or a tax law change quickly and know you have the right answer. Whatever you are looking for, chances are that it has been covered in a past issue. To make your search easier, you can also use the December issue, which includes a cumulative index of all the items we covered for that year. They will all wonder how you know so much and found the correct answer so quickly!

BOOKS:

Parlay Your IRA Into a Family Fortune (Viking, 2005) by Ed Slott, a three-step strategy for creating a lifetime supply of tax-deferred, even tax-free, wealth for you and your family.

The Retirement Savings Time Bomb . . . and How to Defuse It (Viking, 2003) by Ed Slott, a five-step action plan for protecting your IRAs, 401(k)s, and other retirement plans from near annihilation by the Taxman.

Life and Death Planning for Retirement Benefits by Natalie B. Choate (Ataxplan Publications, 2006, $89.95 plus $7 shipping. Call 800-247-6553, or visit www.ataxplan.com). Now in its sixth edition, this is the industry bible on retirement distribution and estate planning, the essential reference resource for every financial advisor, attorney, CPA, and estate planner who advises their clients on these issues. You cannot seriously be in this business without it.

The Advisor's Guide to the Retirement Distribution Rules by Seymour Goldberg, published by the American Bar Association. Order online at: www.abanet.org/abastore. (Type Product Code 1610053 into "search" box.) Format: Download. ABA Member Price: $79.95 / Non-Member: $89.95. Seymour Goldberg is a senior partner in the law firm of Goldberg & Goldberg, P.C., Jericho, New York. He is Professor Emeritus of Law and Taxation at Long Island University. Goldberg is the recipient of the American Jurisprudence Award in Federal Estate and Gift Taxation from St. John's University School of Law. He is also a member of the IRS Northeast Pension Liaison Group. He can be reached at (516) 222-0422, extension 15.

ESTATE, TAX, AND FINANCIAL PLANNING SOFTWARE:

NumberCruncher. An estate and financial planning program created by Stephan R. Leimberg and Robert T. LeClair that is essential for every financial advisor. I use this program for all the estate, income tax, and compound interest computations in my books, newsletters, and advisor course manuals, but most of all we use it to do planning for our clients and you should too. "NumberCruncher" includes a financial planning module in addition to the estate-planning module. It's the only program professional advisors need to instantly put real numbers on any type of planning situation. It includes every imaginable tax and financial planning calculation. It sells for $395 (plus shipping and handling) and can be ordered at www.leimberg.com.

Pension & Roth IRA Analyzer. This program from Brentmark Software may be used to evaluate various strategies of taking distributions from traditional IRAs, Roth IRAs, and qualified pension plans. Calculates up to four alternatives simultaneously for varying types of distributions; handles issues such as new tax law changes; additional contributions to pension fund; distributions to fund living expenses (subject to minimum distribution rules); insurance premiums and proceeds, and pre-59½ distributions that avoid the 10 percent penalty; and Roth conversion analysis. Estate tax may be handled by the entry of taxable estate values or by having the program calculate the taxable estate if you enter the value of other assets. Income tax rates may be entered on a yearly basis. Growth of other assets may even be modeled as realized or unrealized capital gains, if desired. Multiple beneficiaries (up to five) are handled by the program also. Order online at www.brentmark.com, or by phone at 800-879-6665. It is priced at $395.

Index

Acknowledgments

Beverly DeVeny deserves much of the credit for this book since it could not possibly have been completed without her hard work and input. Beverly is an IRA expert and I am lucky to have her on staff as an IRA technical consultant. She has checked and rechecked every word of this manuscript for accuracy, but as always, I take responsibility for any errors. She did an amazing job here on a very tight schedule that involved working late at night and on weekends, all the while traveling to seminars, preparing course manuals, answering countless e-mails from financial advisors, consulting with advisors and consumers who call our office with their IRA issues, and helping with our newsletter, "Ed Slott's IRA Advisor." Thank you, Beverly, for the fantastic job you do year-round.

Thank you to all of the financial, insurance, and tax advisors who attend my seminars and support my work on behalf of America's retirees and retirees-to-be. If not for you, my message would not get out to the very people who can benefit from it most. I applaud you for investing in your continuing IRA education so you can help your clients make the best moves with their retirement savings.

I also must thank the numerous financial institutions that support my retirement planning training programs, seminars, and workshops. These include insurance companies, broker-dealers, mutual fund companies, banks, brokerage firms, financial planning firms, and other sponsoring organizations who bring me in to train and educate their staff and clients. Without your funding of these educational programs, consumers would not be as well served. Thank you for your vision in helping to improve the financial lives of your advisors and their clients and families. Here is just a partial list of many of these companies I work with: Principal Financial Group, ING, WM Funds, Fidelity Investments, Oppenheimer Funds, MFS, Merrill Lynch, UBS, Smith Barney, RBC Dain Rauscher, A.G. Edwards, AXA Distributors, Jackson National Life, Prudential Financial, Genworth Financial, CUSO Financial Services, John Hancock Funds, New York Life, Met Life, Nationwide Financial, Ameriprise, Wachovia Securities, LPL Financial Advisors, AIG Sun America, Securities America, Asset Protectors, and many others. Again, thank you all.

Thanks also to the people at Random House who helped me bring this book to you, especially Jane von Mehren (Publisher, Random House Publishing Group Trade Paperbacks) who I have worked with before. Jane shares my vision and was a key player in getting this book to market. Thanks also to my editors, Ben Loehnen and Christina Duffy, for guiding me through the process, and to the others at Random House who assisted in making this book possible:

Gina Centrello (Publisher, Random House Publishing Group)
Libby McGuire (Publisher, Ballantine)
Subrights: Rachel Bernstein
Production: Lisa Feuer, Crystal Velasquez, Alexandra Krijgsman, and Grant Neumann
Marketing: Kim Hovey, Stacey Witcraft, and Katie O'Callaghan
Sales: Jack Perry and Kelle Ruden
Publicity: Patty Park and Brian McLendon
Art: Derek Walls and Gene Mydlowski

Thanks to Joy Tutela, my literary agent at the David Black Agency Inc. for putting up with me and taking care of everything from contract negotiations to getting my books on the shelves. Thanks for your support day in and day out.

John McCarty collaborated with me on my previous books, *The Retirement Savings Time Bomb . . . and How to Defuse It* and *Parlay Your IRA Into a Family Fortune*, and did so again on this one, the third installment in my retirement distribution planning series and the last piece of the puzzle to protecting your nest egg from the Taxman. John and I share the same sense of humor. He is a workhorse and we function together like a watch, especially on tight schedules. Everything I write reads much better because of John's writing and editing skills. Publishers love his work and ability to meet deadlines too! Thanks, John.

I also must thank the New York State Society of CPAs, The American Institute of Certified Public Accountants (AICPA), The Estate Planning Council of New York City Inc., and the National Conference of CPA Practitioners. These are the professional organizations that gave me an opportunity to hone my professional and technical skills by providing me with a forum at their conferences and meetings. This is where it all began for me, so I encourage anyone in any profession to get involved with your own professional organizations. You will develop lifelong relationships that will help you succeed at your chosen field. This has been especially true for me and I thank all of my colleagues at these groups who have helped me along the way and still provide incredible support.

Tax legend Sidney Kess is an example of the kind of people you meet along the way in life who love to help. He has mentored me and many others. Sid is always helping someone become more successful and everyone has the same wonderful things to say about him. Thank you, Sid, for giving me the chance to speak at your programs and get my feet wet.

Sanford M. Fisch is the Founder and Chief Executive Officer of the American Academy of Estate Planning Attorneys, an exclusive group of highly trained attorneys who have expertise in creating estate plans for clients with retirement assets. I acknowledge Sanford here for his vision and commitment to the continuing education of the Academy members. He saw that more and more consumers had retirement savings plans and needed to find attorneys who were trained in distribution planning as well as estate planning. Sanford made sure that this specialized training was made available to all Academy members. The Academy became the first attorney group in the country to take our specialized retirement distribution training so that the attorneys could competently integrate their clients' retirement plans with their overall estate plans. Many of the Academy members have taken this training and continue to do so. I encourage both consumers and professional advisors to work with them. I have also posted the names of the trained attorneys on our website (www.irahelp.com) so that you can more easily find them. I applaud Sanford Fisch and the American Academy of Estate Planning Attorneys for their efforts to continually enhance their education and for their commitment to their clients.

Million Dollar Round Table is a first-class organization whose members include the world's finest insurance professionals. I am so thankful to Million Dollar Round Table and Top of the Table for their consistent support of my books and programs and for inviting me to speak at their functions. It is always a high honor to be able to present to their members and I deeply appreciate the many opportunities MDRT has provided me to do so. I am always looking forward to the next meeting so I can reconnect with my many MDRT friends. Thank you for including me in your prestigious programs.

Thanks to AALU (Association for Advanced Life Underwriting) for inviting me to present at your exclusive annual meetings. This is a great honor and I love being a part of your program.

Thanks to my friends at *Financial Planning* magazine including Jennifer

Liptow, Dan Goldeman, Marion Asnes, Pamela Black, and Pat Durner, a first-class team if ever there was one. I am proud to be associated with you as a contributor to this fine publication for the past fifteen years.

Thanks to the editors and publishers of the Bottom Line Publications, including *Tax Hotline* and *Bottom Line Personal,* for including me on their editorial boards and featuring me in many articles. The exposure through the Bottom Line networks is really amazing and I thank you for that opportunity. Thanks also for the wonderful job your staff of excellent writers and editors do to make your publications so accurate and informative.

Sandeep Varma is one of the best and most successful financial advisors in the country, but the reason I acknowledge him here is because he is also a great friend, and a generous and honorable person. He has a well-earned reputation for giving of himself to many national charities and organizations where he solves clients' problems with creative solutions that many times benefit the charities as well. Sandeep and his wife, Nisha, run Advanced Trustee Strategies Inc. in San Diego, California. Sandeep, Nisha, and their entire staff are great people to work with. I am glad to know you, Sandeep, and I value our friendship.

Mark Rozell is my own estate-planning attorney and I thank him for helping me implement a plan that protects my family, my employees, and my business.

Alan Kahn is my financial advisor and insurance professional. As you know from my books, even though I do not sell life insurance, I believe in the concept as a means to leverage current assets and protect my family. Since I practice what I preach, I want to thank to Alan for making sure this was taken care of for me and my family.

Seymour "Sy" Goldberg is my friend and the person I must always credit for showing me the light of retirement distribution planning and the impact it has on so many people and advisors. Sy is a true visionary. He saw this market emerging years before anyone else and I was lucky to meet him early on in my career. Thanks for sharing your IRA brilliance with me, Sy.

Thanks also to my IRA colleague, Natalie B. Choate, Esq. for her support of my IRA newsletter and advisor training programs. Natalie is a true IRA guru and we spend much of our time spreading the IRA gospel throughout the country with our numerous seminars. Thanks, Natalie, for all your help. The work you do benefits so many financial advisors and their clients. See you on the road!

Denise Appleby is an all-around retirement expert with her own financial planning firm, Appleby Retirement Consulting, and is a technical advisor to me. In addition to being a distinguished member of Ed Slott's Elite IRA Advisor Group (Master Elite), Denise has every designation you could possibly think of including the Accredited Pension Administrator (APA) from the

National Institute of Pension Administrators; the Certified IRA Services Professional (CISP) designation from the Institute of Certified Bankers; the Chartered Retirement Plans Specialist (CRPS) designation from the College for Financial Planning; Certified Retirement Services Professional (CRSP) designation from the Institute of Certified Bankers; and the Certified Retirement Counselor (CRC) designation from the International Foundation for Retirement Education (InFRE), just to name a few. Thanks, Denise, for all your technical assistance and support.

Retirement planning tax law is not easy stuff and I could not possibly do it all alone. In addition to Sy Goldberg and Natalie Choate, and our own Beverly DeVeny and Denise Appleby, I would also like to thank and recognize several other IRA experts. Bob Keebler, Mike Jones, Stephen Krass, David Foster, Gordon Weis, Steven Lockwood, Martin Shenkman, Guerdon Ely, Jeremiah Doyle, Steven Trytten, Tom Gau, Mary Kay Foss, Sally Mulhern, Joel Bruckenstein, Gary Lesser, John Bledsoe, James Lange, Barry Picker, Bruce Steiner, and Victor Finmann.

Thanks to Stephan R. Leimberg, a great friend and an amazing person, who believes in sharing and giving. Steve, along with his partner, Robert T. LeClair, runs Leimberg Information Services Inc. (LISI), the best estate, tax, and retirement planning information service available. I appreciate your support, Steve, and thank you for the meaningful work you do. I love telling advisors about you.

Thanks to Marvin R. Rotenberg, the Director of Individual Retirement Services, Retirement Solutions Group at Bank of America. Marvin is responsible for creating distribution strategies from qualified plans and IRAs for clients with substantial net worth. Marvin is one of the nicest people I know and so generous with his time and resources, along with Mark LaVangie and Richard B. James, who work with Marvin. They all help with the editing of my newsletters and books and are always there for those tough IRA questions. They have been a valuable resource for me for many years and I appreciate our friendship. Thanks, guys.

A big part of retirement distribution planning involves the software tools that make life easier, and for that I thank Gregory Kolojeski, president of Brentmark Software, for the products he produces that I use in my books and advisor training seminars. Jane Schuck is Brentmark's field representative and brings real value to Brentmark's software products because she is always willing to spend time with advisors, showing them how to make the most of these important tools. Thanks, Greg and Jane.

Bill Nelson of the Nelson Financial Group in Dayton, Ohio, is a super financial advisor and trainer. He is in the stratosphere when it comes to selling and is literally one of the top producers in the world. Bill is also the founder of the Learning Institute for Financial Executives (LIFE School). This is a comprehensive program that helps financial advisors aid their clients in growing, distributing, and leaving their money in a tax-efficient manner. He shows other financial and insurance advisors how to create the success that Bill has had. Bill is making a big difference in the lives of millions, including mine, through his genius and his generosity in sharing that genius with others. If you are an insurance or financial advisor you should look into Bill Nelson's LIFE School to jumpstart your business now and serve your clients better. You can call Bill at (937) 426-7032, and mention my name! Bill is a credit to his profession and I admire his work and his message.

Special thanks to Paul Peterson, president of Emerald Publications, the nation's leading provider of innovative marketing and technology tools that help financial professionals succeed. Also, special thanks to financial-planning wizard Bill Nelson, the mastermind behind *Retirement Unlimited,* a hands-on personal finance workshop that shows individuals how to get the most out of my IRA strategies. To find out more about *Retirement Unlimited* or to order it, call (800) 233-2834.

Donald Jay Korn is one of the truly great tax and financial writers and I am lucky to have him as an interviewer and writer for my newsletter. Don has a long list of other professional credentials including *The New York Times, Investor's Business Daily, Financial Planning* magazine, *Bottom Line* Publications, and many others. Thanks, Don, for your great work taking very technical tax topics and making them easier for us all to read and learn from.

Thanks to Dan Sullivan and Dan Taylor at The Strategic Coach. This is one of the great programs available for helping people reach professional goals that once seemed only distant dreams. They do fantastic work and I encourage others to get to know the "Coach" program. Thanks for a lifetime of success.

Doug Davidoff of Imagine Consulting has helped my company find its way and helped it grow by creating business plans and strategies. We consult with Doug year-round. His ideas make sense and have helped us move the company to the next level. Thanks, Doug.

Publicity is a part of getting our message out and I thank Brian Feinblum at PTA (Planned Television Artists) for the job he has done for me with my national radio tours. I have found him and his staff to be highly professional, honest, and reliable. They do what they say they will do and that, as they say, is saying something these days. Thanks, Brian.

Thanks to my long-time media friends Ken and Daria Dolan. They not only provide reliable financial information to millions of people, but they are really nice folks, and I enjoy being part of their radio and television programs.

This book and my others have all shared the goal of educating readers so they can take the steps necessary to protect and preserve their life savings. But I also make it clear that they need competent advisors to help them properly execute their planning decisions. This goal is now even more attainable for every reader thanks to all the financial advisors who are members of *Ed Slott's Elite IRA Advisor Group™* and *Master Elite IRA Advisors*. These are some of the best and most qualified and educated advisors in the country. These groups are my pride and joy. I love to see the difference they are making in their clients' lives. Thanks to these advisors for helping get my message out to the public to accept "only the best advice" when it comes to your retirement savings. These Elite IRA Advisors are making people's lives more financially secure.

Laurin Levine is the managing partner of our company and a true friend to me. Laurin runs all aspects of our various businesses and has helped build the company from the minute she came aboard many years ago. Anyone who knows me probably also knows Laurin and knows why I think so highly of her. Thank you, Laurin, for our success, which would not have been possible without you.

Laurin has two secret weapons in our office: Pat Pakus and Glenda Zolezzi. They are the ones who make sure all the details are taken care of, whether it is making and fixing travel plans for me, sending out seminar packages and promotional materials, or taking calls from newsletter subscribers, clients, and financial advisors. They do it all. Thank you too, Pat and Glenda, for being such a big part of our team.

Margot Reilly and Mike Lichter, CPA run our tax practice year-round and have been with me for many years. Thanks to Margot and Mike I can be out on the road doing my seminars knowing that they are taking good care of our clients, which is our number one concern.

Chris Paliani is our director of operations and is a truly good person who cares about others. Chris is one of the most dedicated people I know and he shares our goals and dreams. Chris also has great people helping him, including Ryan Fortese, Pat Hawk, and Janet Flood. They work with Chris extensively on our advisor training programs and our Elite IRA Advisor Groups and do all of our strategic marketing. You are all very much appreciated for the job you do. Thank you very much for your dedication to our vision and helping us grow. The future is brighter with all of you on board.

I thank my family for being supportive of my work and rigorous travel schedule, which keep me away from home and from them too much of the time. But when I am home my wife Linda, and my children Ilana and Rachel are great to be with and I look forward to every minute I get to spend with them. Thank you for your love and understanding of my work.

My dad won't see this but I wish he could have. I still thank him every day for what I am and what I have and the family and business values he instilled in me. Thanks go equally to my mom, the youngest 80-year-old I have ever known, who, with my dad, has always supported my goals and dreams. I credit every accomplishment to my wonderful parents and I hope I can do the same for my children.

PHOTO: © BRAD WILSON

ED SLOTT is a nationally recognized IRA distribution expert, a professional speaker, and hosts the website www.irahelp.com. He regularly presents continuing professional education seminars on IRA distribution planning and estate planning at major conferences for financial advisor firms, mutual fund companies, brokerage firms, insurance professionals, financial planners, trust companies, banks, CPAs, and attorneys. He has established Ed Slott's Elite IRA Advisor Group™, whose members attend advanced continuing education programs for financial advisors, who, as part of their practice, specialize in retirement distribution planning. In addition, Mr. Slott has created The IRA Leadership Program™ (www.iraleadership.com), developed specifically to help financial institutions, financial advisor firms, and insurance companies become recognized leaders in the IRA marketplace.

Mr. Slott is the author of the top-selling *Parlay Your IRA into a Family Fortune* (Viking, 2005) and *The Retirement Savings Time Bomb . . . and How to Defuse It* (Viking, 2003)—both have hit Amazon.com's "Hot 100" list. He is also the writer and publisher of *Ed Slott's IRA Advisor Newsletter* and a personal finance columnist for numerous financial publications.

Additionally, Mr. Slott is a past chairman of the New York State Society of CPAs Estate Planning Committee and editor of the IRA Planning section of *The CPA Journal.* He is the recipient of the prestigious "Excellence in Estate Planning" and "Outstanding Service" awards presented by the Foundation for Accounting Education.

A frequent contributor to *The CPA Journal, The Practical Accountant,* and *Trusts and Estates,* and a past editor of the estates and trusts section of *The CPA Journal,* Mr. Slott is a member of the National Conference of CPA Practitioners and a former board member of The Estate Planning Council of New York City. He is often quoted in *The New York Times, Newsday, The Wall Street Journal, The Washington Post,* the *Los Angeles Times, The Boston Globe, Time, Newsweek, Fortune* magazine, *Forbes* magazine, *Money* magazine, *Kiplinger's Personal Finance* magazine, *USA Today, Bloomberg Personal, Medical Economics, Investor's Business Daily, Smart Money,* and a host of additional national magazines and financial publications. He has appeared on NBC, ABC, CBS, CNBC, CNN, FOX, PBS, National Public Radio, and Bloomberg TV and radio.

Mr. Slott is also an Internet consultant to numerous financial information websites.

For information on booking Ed Slott as a keynote speaker for your next conference, meeting, or company event, or to learn more about Ed Slott's IRA Leadership Program™, a customized full-day advisor training and marketing program for companies that want to be recognized as leaders in the IRA market and increase their retirement-related business, contact:

Laurin Levine
Ed Slott and Company
telephone: (800) 663-1340
fax: (516) 536-8852
e-mail: *laurin@irahelp.com*
address: 100 Merrick Road
Suite 200 East
Rockville Centre, NY 11570
website: www.irahelp.com

About the Type

ITC Berkeley designed in 1983 by Tony Stan, is a variation of the University of California Old Style, which was created by Frederick Goudy. While capturing the feel and traits of its predecessor, ITC Berkeley Old Style shows influences from Kennerly, Goudy Old Style, Deepdene, and Booklet Oldstyle, all of which were also designed by Goudy. It is characterized by its calligraphic weight stress, and its x-height, now described as classic, is smaller than most other ITC designs of the day. The generous ascenders and descenders provide variations in text color, easy legibility, and an overall inviting appearance.